Real-Resumes for Sales

Anne McKinney, Editor

PREP PUBLISHING

FAYETTEVILLE, NC

PREP Publishing
1110½ Hay Street
Fayetteville, NC 28305
(910) 483-6611

Cover design by Chris Pearl

Library of Congress Cataloging-in-Publication Data

Real-resumes for sales : actual resumes, easy to personalize, creating your own powerful door-opening resume! / Anne McKinney (editor).
    p. cm. -- (Real-resumes series)
    ISBN 1-885288-16-6
    1. Résumés (Employment) 2. Sales personnel. I. McKinney, Anne, 1948- II. Series.

  HF5383.R396 2000
  808' .06665–dc21
                                            00-025629
                                                CIP

Printed in the United States of America

By PREP Publishing

Business and Career Series:

RESUMES AND COVER LETTERS THAT HAVE WORKED

RESUMES AND COVER LETTERS THAT HAVE WORKED FOR MILITARY PROFESSIONALS

GOVERNMENT JOB APPLICATIONS AND FEDERAL RESUMES

COVER LETTERS THAT BLOW DOORS OPEN

LETTERS FOR SPECIAL SITUATIONS

RESUMES AND COVER LETTERS FOR MANAGERS

REAL-RESUMES FOR TEACHERS

REAL-RESUMES FOR STUDENTS

REAL-RESUMES FOR CAREER CHANGERS

REAL-RESUMES FOR SALES

REAL ESSAYS FOR COLLEGE & GRADUATE SCHOOL

Judeo-Christian Ethics Series:

SECOND TIME AROUND

BACK IN TIME

WHAT THE BIBLE SAYS ABOUT...Words that can lead to success and happiness

A GENTLE BREEZE FROM GOSSAMER WINGS

BIBLE STORIES FROM THE OLD TESTAMENT

Fiction:

KIJABE...An African Historical Saga

Table of Contents

A WORD FROM THE EDITOR:
ABOUT THE REAL-RESUMES SERIES

Welcome to the Real-Resumes Series. The Real-Resumes Series is a series of books which have been developed based on the experiences of real job hunters and which target specialized fields or types of resumes. As the editor of the series, I have carefully selected resumes and cover letters (with names and other key data disguised, of course) which have been used successfully in real job hunts. That's what we mean by "Real-Resumes." What you see in this book are *real* resumes and cover letters which helped real people get ahead in their careers.

The Real-Resumes Series is based on the work of the country's oldest resume-preparation company known as PREP Resumes. If you would like a free information packet describing the company's resume preparation services, call 910-483-6611 or write to PREP at 1110½ Hay Street, Fayetteville, NC 28305. If you have a job hunting experience you would like to share with our staff at the Real-Resumes Series, please contact us at preppub@aol.com or visit our website at http://www.prep-pub.com.

The resumes and cover letters in this book are designed to be of most value to people already in sales or to people who want to be in a sales career. If we could give you one word of advice about your career, here's what we would say: Manage your career and don't stumble from job to job in an incoherent pattern. Try to find work that interests you, and then identify prosperous industries which need work performed of the type you want to do. Learn early in your working life that a great resume and cover letter can blow doors open for you and help you maximize your salary.

This book is dedicated to the sales professionals who are on the "front line" of our economy. Without sales professionals, no profit-making company and few organizations of any type would exist because every product and every service needs to be sold. Thanks to the sales professionals who make it happen!

As the editor of this book, I would like to give you some tips on how to make the best use of the information you will find here. Because you are in sales or want to be in sales, you already understand the concept of managing your career for maximum enjoyment and self-fulfillment. The purpose of this book is to help you manage your career and show you resumes and cover letters that will be essential career tools.

Overview of the Book
Every resume and cover letter in this book actually worked. And most of the resumes and cover letters have common features: all are one-page, all are in the chronological format, and all resumes are accompanied by a companion cover letter. The book is divided into two parts. Part One provides some advice about job hunting. Step One begins with a discussion of why employers prefer the one-page, chronological resume. In Step Two you are introduced to the direct approach and to the proper format for a cover letter. In Step Three you learn the 14 main reasons why job hunters are not offered the jobs they want, and you learn the six key areas employers focus on when they interview you. Step Four gives nuts-and-bolts advice on how to handle the interview, send a follow-up letter after an interview, and negotiate your salary. At the end of Part One, you'll find advice about how to research and locate the companies and organizations to which you want to send your resume.

Part Two of the book shows you resumes and cover letters that have worked for sales professionals from all types of industries. You'll find the resumes and cover letters of professionals involved in sales related to financial services, retail, bookselling, cosmetics, credit card services, food products, furniture and home comfort products, industrial products, insurance, medical and pharmaceutical products, mortgage services, nutrition products, automotive parts, automobiles, personnel recruiting services, printing products and services, property rentals, real estate, software products, telephone services, television advertising, wholesale food and beverages, travel industry services, and many more. You will see people seeking both inside sales and outside sales positions, and you will see examples of people who want to manage sales in a store, area, territory, district, and many other settings.

But before you proceed further, think about why you picked up this book.
- Are you dissatisfied with the type of work you are now doing?
- Would you like to change careers or change companies?
- Are you satisfied with your career field but not with your opportunities for advancement?
- Do you like the product or service you sell but desire a different compensation package?
- Do you enjoy sales but want to transfer your skills to a new product or service?
- Are you in sales seeking promotion to sales management?
- Has a competitor requested that you send a resume?
- Do executive recruiters call you frequently to ask for your resume?
- Are you aware of the importance of a great cover letter but unsure of how to write one?
- Are you preparing to launch a second career after early retirement?
- Have you been downsized, or do you anticipate becoming a victim of downsizing?
- Do you need expert advice on how to plan and implement a job campaign that will open the maximum number of doors?
- Do you want to make sure you handle an interview to your maximum advantage?
- Would you like to master the techniques of negotiating salary and benefits?
- Do you want to learn the secrets and shortcuts of professional resume writers and employment placement specialists?

Using the Direct Approach

Even if you are not now in a job hunt or career change, you need to be aware that most people end up having at least three distinctly different careers in their working lifetimes, and often those careers are different from each other. Yet people usually stumble through each job campaign, unsure of what they should be doing. Whether you find yourself voluntarily or unexpectedly in a job hunt, the direct approach is the job hunting strategy most likely to yield a full-time permanent job. The direct approach is an active, take-the-initiative style of job hunting in which you choose your next employer rather than relying on responding to ads, using employment agencies, or depending on other methods of finding jobs. You will learn how to use the direct approach in this book, and you will see that an effective cover letter is a critical ingredient in using the direct approach.

The "direct approach" is the style of job hunting most likely to yield the maximum number of job interviews.

Lack of Experience In an Industry Not a Major Barrier to Entering New Field

"Lack of experience" is often the last reason people are not offered jobs, according to the companies who do the hiring. If you are an experienced sales professional changing industries so that you can apply your sales skills on a new service or product, you will be glad to learn that even experienced professionals often are selling "potential" rather than experience in a job hunt. Companies often seek proven sales performers and look for personal qualities that they know tend to be present in their most effective professionals, such as communication skills, initiative, persistence, organizational and time management skills, and creativity. Frequently companies are trying to discover "personality type," "talent," "ability," "aptitude," and "potential" rather than seeking actual hands-on experience, so your resume should be designed to aggressively present your sales accomplishments. Attitude, enthusiasm, personality, and a track record of achievements in any type of sales are the primary "indicators of success" which employers are seeking, and you will see numerous examples in this book of resumes written in an all-purpose fashion so that the sales professional can approach various industries and types of companies.

Using references in a skillful fashion in your job hunt will inspire confidence in prospective employers and help you "close the sale" after interviews.

The Art of Using References in a Job Hunt

You probably already know that you need to provide references during a job hunt, but you may not be sure of how and when to use references for maximum advantage. You can use references very creatively during a job hunt to call attention to your strengths and make yourself "stand out." Your references will rarely get you a job, no matter how impressive the names, but the way you use references can boost the employer's confidence in you and lead to a job offer in the least time. You should ask from three to five people, including people who have supervised you, if you can use them as a reference during your job hunt. You may not be able to ask your current boss since your job hunt is probably confidential. A common question in resume preparation is: "Do I need to put my references on my resume?" No, you don't. And even if you create a page of references at the same time that you prepare your resume, you don't need to mail your references page with the resume and cover letter. The potential employer is not interested in your references until he meets and gets interested in you, so the earliest you need to have references ready is at the first interview. An excellent attention-getting technique is to take to the first interview not just a page of references (giving names, addresses, and telephone numbers) but an actual letter of reference written by someone who knows you well and who preferably has supervised or employed you. A professional way to close the first interview is to thank the interviewer, shake his or her hand, and then say you'd like to give him or her a copy of a letter of reference from a previous employer. Hopefully you already made a good impression during the interview, but you'll "close the sale" in a dynamic fashion if you leave a letter praising you and your accomplishments. For that reason, it's a good idea to ask employers during your final weeks in a job if they will provide you with a written letter of recommendation which you can use in future job hunts. Most employers will oblige, and you will have a letter that has a useful "shelf life" of many years. Such a letter often gives the prospective employer enough confidence in his opinion of you that he may forego checking out other references and decide to offer you the job in the next few days. Whom should you ask to serve as references? References should be people who have known or supervised you in a professional, academic, or work situation. Most employers know that your pastor will almost certainly be your ally, so avoid asking your minister. References with big titles, like school superintendent or congressman, are fine, but remind busy people when you get to the interview stage that they may be contacted soon. Make sure the busy official recognizes your name and has instant positive recall of you! If you're asked to provide references on a formal company application, you can simply transcribe names from your references list. In summary, follow this rule in using references: If you've got them, flaunt them! If you've obtained well-written letters of reference, make sure you find a polite way to push those references under the nose of the interviewer so he or she can hear someone other than you describing your strengths. Your references probably won't ever get you a job, but glowing letters of reference can give you credibility and visibility that can make you stand out among candidates with similar credentials and potential!

With regard to references, it's best to provide the names and addresses of people who have supervised you or observed you in a work situation.

In general, you will find that the approach taken by this book is to (1) help you master the proven best techniques of conducting a job hunt and (2) show you how to stand out in a job hunt through your resume, cover letter, interviewing skills, as well as the way in which you present your references and follow up on interviews.

The best way to "get in the mood" for writing your own resume and cover letter is to select samples from the Table of Contents that interest you and then read them. A great resume is a "photograph," usually on one page, of an individual, and you will meet some talented people between the covers of this book. If you wish to seek professional advice in preparing your resume, you may contact one of the professional writers at Professional Resume & Employment Placement (PREP) for a brief free consultation by calling 1-910-483-6611.

Part One: Some Advice About Your Job Hunt

What if you don't know what you want to do?

Your job hunt will be more comfortable if you can figure out what type of sales you want to do. But you are not alone if you have no idea what you want to do next! You may have knowledge and skills in certain areas but want to get into another type of work. What *The Wall Street Journal* has discovered in its research on careers is that most of us end up having at least three distinctly different careers in our working lives; it seems that, even if we really like a particular kind of activity, twenty years of doing it is enough for most of us and we want to move on to something else!

That's why at PREP we strongly believe that you need to spend some time figuring out **what interests you** rather than taking an inventory of the skills you have. You may have skills that you simply don't want to use, but if you can build your career on the things that interest you, you will be more likely to be happy and satisfied in your job. Realize, too, that interests can change over time; the activities that interest you now may not be the ones that interested you years ago. For example, some professionals may decide that they've had enough of retail sales and want a job selling another product or service, even though they have earned a reputation for being an excellent retail manager. We strongly believe that interests rather than skills should be the determining factor in deciding what types of jobs you want to apply for and what directions you explore in your job hunt. Obviously one cannot be a lawyer without a law degree or a secretary without secretarial skills; but a professional can embark on a next career as a financial consultant, property manager, plant manager, production supervisor, retail manager, or other occupation if he/she has a strong interest in that type of work and can provide a resume that clearly demonstrates past excellent performance in *any* field and *potential* to excel in another field. As you will see later in this book, "lack of exact experience" is the last reason why people are turned down for the jobs they apply for.

> Figure out what interests you and you will hold the key to a successful job hunt and working career. (And be prepared for your interests to change over time!)

How can you have a resume prepared if you don't know what you want to do?

You may be wondering how you can have a resume prepared if you don't know what you want to do next. The approach to resume writing which PREP has used successfully for many years is to develop an "all-purpose" resume that translates your skills, experience, and accomplishments into language employers can understand. What most people need in a job hunt is a versatile resume that will allow them to apply for numerous types of jobs. For example, you may want to apply for a job in pharmaceutical sales but you may also want to have a resume that will be versatile enough for you to apply for jobs in the construction, financial services, or automotive industries.

> "Lack of exact experience" is the last reason people are turned down for the jobs for which they apply.

Based on 20 years of serving job hunters, we at PREP have found that **an all-purpose resume** and **specific cover letters tailored to specific fields** is often your best approach to job hunting rather than trying to create different resumes for different occupational areas. Usually, you will not even need more than one "all-purpose" cover letter, although the cover letter rather than the resume is the place to communicate your interest in a narrow or specific field. An all-purpose resume and cover letter that translate your experience and accomplishments into plain English are the tools that will maximize the number of doors which open for you while permitting you to "fish" in the widest range of job areas.

Your resume will provide the script for your job interview.
When you get down to it, your resume has a simple job to do: Its purpose is to blow as many doors open as possible and to make as many people as possible want to meet you. So a well-written resume that really "sells" you is a key that will create opportunities for you in a job hunt.

This statistic explains why: The typical newspaper advertisement for a job opening receives more than 245 replies. And normally only 10 or 12 will be invited to an interview.

But here's another purpose of the resume: it provides the "script" the employer uses when he interviews you. If your resume has been written in such a way that your strengths and achievements are revealed, that's what you'll end up talking about at the job interview. Since the resume will govern what you get asked about at your interviews, you can't overestimate the importance of making sure your resume makes you look and sound as good as you are.

Your resume is the "script" for your job interviews. Make sure you put on your resume what you want to talk about or be asked about at the job interview.

So what is a "good" resume?
Very literally, your resume should motivate the person reading it to dial the phone number you have put on the resume. (If you are relocating, that's one reason you should think about putting a local phone contact number on your resume, if possible, when your contact address is several states away; employers are much more likely to dial a local telephone number than a long-distance number when they're looking for potential employees.)

If you have a resume already, look at it objectively. Is it a limp, colorless "laundry list" of your job titles and duties? Or does it "paint a picture" of your skills, abilities, and accomplishments in a way that would make someone want to meet you? Can people understand what you're saying?

How long should your resume be?
One page, maybe two. Usually only people in the academic community have a resume (which they usually call a *curriculum vitae*) longer than one or two pages. Remember that your resume is almost always accompanied by a cover letter, and a potential employer does not want to read more than two or three pages about a total stranger in order to decide if he wants to meet that person! Besides, don't forget that the more you tell someone about yourself, the more opportunity you are providing for the employer to screen you out at the "first-cut" stage. A resume should be concise and exciting and designed to make the reader want to meet you in person!

The one-page resume in chronological format is the format preferred by most employers.

Should resumes be functional or chronological?
Employers almost always prefer a chronological resume; in other words, an employer will find a resume easier to read if it is immediately apparent what your current or most recent job is, what you did before that, and so forth, in reverse chronological order. A resume that goes back in detail for the last ten years of employment will generally satisfy the employer's curiosity about your background. Employment more than ten years old can be shown even more briefly in an "Other Experience" section at the end of your "Experience" section. Remember that your intention is not to tell everything you've done but to "hit the high points" and especially hit the employer with what you learned, contributed, or accomplished in each job you describe.

Once you get your resume, what do you do with it?
You will be using your resume to answer ads, as a tool to use in talking with friends and relatives about your job search, and, most importantly, in using the "direct approach" described in this book.

When you mail your resume, always send a "cover letter."
A "cover letter," sometimes called a "resume letter" or "letter of interest," is a letter that accompanies and introduces your resume. Your cover letter is a way of personalizing the resume by sending it to the specific person you think you might want to work for at each company. Your cover letter should contain a few highlights from your resume—just enough to make someone want to meet you. Cover letters should always be typed or word processed on a computer—never handwritten.

Never mail or fax your resume without a cover letter.

1. Learn the art of answering ads.
There is an "art," part of which can be learned, in using your "bestselling" resume to reply to advertisements.

Sometimes an exciting job lurks behind a boring ad that someone dictated in a hurry, so reply to any ad that interests you. Don't worry that you aren't "25 years old with an MBA" like the ad asks for. Employers will always make compromises in their requirements if they think you're the "best fit" overall.

What about ads that ask for "salary requirements?"
What if the ad you're answering asks for "salary requirements?" The first rule is to avoid committing yourself in writing at that point to a specific salary. You don't want to "lock yourself in."

What if the ad asks for your "salary requirements?"

There are two ways to handle the ad that asks for "salary requirements."
First, you can ignore that part of the ad and accompany your resume with a cover letter that focuses on "selling" you, your abilities, and even some of your philosophies about work or your field. You may include a sentence in your cover letter like this: "I can provide excellent personal and professional references at your request, and I would be delighted to share the private details of my salary history with you in person."

Second, if you feel you must give some kind of number, just state a range in your cover letter that includes your medical, dental, other benefits, and expected bonuses. You might state, for example, "my current compensation, including benefits and bonuses, is in the range of $30,000-$40,000."

Analyze the ad and "tailor" yourself to it.
When you're replying to ads, a finely-tailored cover letter is an important tool in getting your resume noticed and read. On the next page is a cover letter which has been "tailored to fit" a specific ad. Notice the "art" used by PREP writers of analyzing the ad's main requirements and then writing the letter so that the person's background, work habits, and interests seem "tailor-made" to the company's needs. Use this cover letter as a model when you prepare your own reply to ads.

Date

Mr. Arthur Wise
Chamber of Commerce of the U.S.
9439 Goshen Lane
Dallas, TX 22105

Dear Mr. Wise:

I would appreciate an opportunity to show you in person, soon, that I am the energetic, dynamic salesperson you are looking for as a Membership Sales Representative of the Chamber of Commerce.

Here are just three reasons why I believe I am the effective young professional you seek:

- *I myself am "sold" on the Chamber of Commerce* and have long been an admirer of its goal of forming a cohesive business organization to promote the well-being of communities and promote business vigor. As someone better known than I put it long ago, "the business of America is business." I wholeheartedly believe that the Chamber's efforts to unite, solidify, and mobilize American business can be an important key in unlocking the international competitiveness and domestic vitality of our economy. I am eager to contribute to that effort.

- *I am a proven salesperson* with a demonstrated ability to "prospect" and produce sales. In my current job as a sales representative, I contact more than 150 business professionals per week and won my company's annual award for outstanding sales performance.

- *I enjoy traveling and am eager to assist in the growth of Texas and vicinity.* I am fortunate to have the natural energy, industry, and enthusiasm required to put in the long hours necessary for effective sales performance.

You will find me, I am certain, a friendly, good-natured person whom you would be proud to call part of the Chamber's "team."

I hope you will call or write me soon to suggest a convenient time when we might meet to discuss your needs further and how I might serve them.

Yours sincerely,

Your Name

Employers are trying to identify the individual who wants the job they are filling. Don't be afraid to express your enthusiasm in the cover letter!

2. Talk to friends and relatives.

Don't be shy about telling your friends and relatives the kind of job you're looking for. Looking for the job you want involves using your network of contacts, so tell people what you're looking for. They may be able to make introductions and help set up interviews.

About 25% of all interviews are set up through "who you know," so don't ignore this approach.

The "direct approach" is a strategy in which you choose your next employer.

3. Finally, and most importantly, use the "direct approach."

More than 50% of all job interviews are set up by the "direct approach." That means you actually send a resume and a cover letter to a company you think might be interested in employing your skills.

To whom do you write?

In general, you should write directly to the <u>exact</u> <u>name</u> of the person who would be hiring you: say, the vice-president of marketing or data processing. If you're in doubt about to whom to address the letter, address it to the president by name and he or she will make sure it gets forwarded to the right person within the company who has hiring authority in your area.

How do you find the names of potential employers?

You're not alone if you feel that the biggest problem in your job search is finding the right names at the companies you want to contact. But you can usually figure out the names of companies you want to approach by deciding first if your job hunt is primarily geography-driven or industry-driven.

In a geography-driven job hunt, you could select a list of, say, 50 companies you want to contact **by location** from the lists that the U.S. Chambers of Commerce publish yearly of their "major area employers." There are hundreds of local Chambers of Commerce across America, and most of them will have an 800 number which you can find through 1-800-555-1212. If you and your family think Atlanta, Dallas, Ft. Lauderdale, and Virginia Beach might be nice places to live, for example, you could contact the Chamber of Commerce in those cities and ask how you can obtain a copy of their list of major employers. Your nearest library will have the book which lists the addresses of all chambers.

In an industry-driven job hunt, and if you are willing to relocate, you will be identifying the companies which you find most attractive in the industry in which you want to work. When you select a list of companies to contact **by industry,** you can find the right person to write and the address of firms by industrial category in *Standard and Poor's, Moody's,* and other excellent books in public libraries. Many web sites also provide contact information.

Many people feel it's a good investment to actually call the company to either find out or double-check the name of the person to whom they want to send a resume and cover letter. It's important to do as much as you feasibly can to assure that the letter gets to the right person in the company.

At the end of Part One, you will find some advice about how to conduct library research and how to locate organizations to which you could send your resume.

What's the correct way to follow up on a resume you send?

There is a polite way to be aggressively interested in a company during your job hunt. It is ideal to end the cover letter accompanying your resume by saying "I hope you'll welcome my call next week when I try to arrange a brief meeting at your convenience to discuss your current and future needs and how I might serve them." Keep it low key, and just ask for a "brief meeting," not an interview. Employers want people who show a determined interest in working with them, so don't be shy about following up on the resume and cover letter you've mailed.

STEP THREE: Preparing for Interviews

A resume and cover letter by themselves can't get you the job you want. You need to "prep" yourself before the interview. Step Three in your job campaign is "Preparing for Interviews." First, let's look at interviewing from the company's point of view.

What are the biggest "turnoffs" for companies?

One of the ways to help yourself perform well at an interview is to look at the main reasons why companies *don't* hire the people they interview, according to companies that do the interviewing.

Notice that "lack of appropriate background" (or lack of experience) is the *last* reason for not being offered the job.

The 14 Most Common Reasons Job Hunters Are Not Offered Jobs (according to the companies who do the interviewing and hiring):

1. Low level of accomplishment
2. Poor attitude, lack of self-confidence
3. Lack of goals/objectives
4. Lack of enthusiasm
5. Lack of interest in the company's business
6. Inability to sell or express yourself
7. Unrealistic salary demands
8. Poor appearance
9. Lack of maturity, no leadership potential
10. Lack of extracurricular activities
11. Lack of preparation for the interview, no knowledge about company
12. Objecting to travel
13. Excessive interest in security and benefits
14. Inappropriate background

Department of Labor studies since the 1950s have proven that smart, "prepared" job hunters can increase their beginning salary while getting a job in *half* the time it normally takes. (4½ months is the average national length of a job search.) Here, from PREP, are some questions that can prepare you to find a job faster.

Are you in the "right" frame of mind?

It seems unfair that we have to look for a job just when we're lowest in morale. Don't worry *too* much if you're nervous before interviews (Johnny Carson said he usually was, too!). You're supposed to be a little nervous, especially if the job means a lot to you. But

It pays to be aware of the 14 most common pitfalls for job hunters.

the best way to kill unnecessary fears about job hunting is through 1) making sure you have a great resume and 2) preparing yourself for the interview. Here are three main areas you need to think about before each interview.

Do you know what the company does?
Don't walk into an interview giving the impression that, "If this is Tuesday, this must be General Motors."

Find out before the interview what the company's main product or service is. Where is the company heading? Is it in a "growth" or declining industry? (Answers to these questions may influence whether or not you want to work there!)

Information about what the company does is in annual reports as well as newspaper and magazine articles. Just visit your nearest library and ask the reference librarian to guide you to materials on the company. Internet searches may also yield valuable information. At the end of Part One you will find many suggestions about how to research companies.

Do you know what you want to do for the company?
Before the interview, try to decide how you see yourself fitting into the company. Remember, "lack of exact background" the company wants is usually the *last* reason people are not offered jobs.

Understand before you go to each interview that the burden will be on you to "sell" the interviewer on why you're the best person for the job and the company.

How will you answer the critical interview questions?
Put yourself in the interviewer's position and think about the questions you're most likely to be asked. Here are some of the most commonly asked interview questions:

Q: "What are your greatest strengths?"

A: Don't say you've never thought about it! Go into an interview knowing the three main impressions you want to leave about yourself, such as "I'm hard-working, loyal, and an imaginative cost-cutter."

Q: "What are your greatest weaknesses?"

A: Don't confess that you're lazy or have trouble meeting deadlines! Confessing that you tend to be a "workaholic" or "tend to be a perfectionist and sometimes get frustrated when others don't share my high standards" will make your prospective employer see a "weakness" that he likes. Name a weakness that your interviewer will perceive as a strength.

Q: "What are your long-range goals?"

A: If you're interviewing with Microsoft, don't say you want to work for IBM in five years! Say your long-range goal is to be *with* the company, contributing to its goals and success.

Q: "What motivates you to do your best work?"

A: Don't get dollar signs in your eyes here! "A challenge" is not a bad answer, but it's a little cliched. Saying something like "troubleshooting" or "solving a tough problem" is more interesting and specific. Give an example if you can.

Research the company before you go to interviews.

Anticipate the questions you will be asked at the interview, and prepare your responses in advance.

Q: "What do you know about this company?"

A: Don't say you never heard of it until they asked you to the interview! Name an interesting, positive thing you learned about the company recently from your research. Remember, company executives can sometimes feel rather "maternal" about the company they serve. Don't get onto a negative area of the company if you can think of positive facts you can bring up. Of course, if you learned in your research that the company's sales seem to be taking a nose-dive, or that the company president is being prosecuted for taking bribes, you might politely ask your interviewer to tell you something that could help you better understand what you've been reading. Those are the kinds of company facts that can help you determine whether you want to work there or not.

Q: "Why should I hire you?"

A: "I'm unemployed and available" is the wrong answer here! Get back to your strengths and say that you believe the organization could benefit by a loyal, hard-working cost-cutter like yourself.

In conclusion, you should decide in advance, before you go to the interview, how you will answer each of these commonly asked questions.

Have some practice interviews with a friend to role-play and build your confidence.

STEP FOUR: Handling the Interview and Negotiating Salary

> Go to an interview prepared to tell the company why it should hire you.

> A smile at an interview makes the employer perceive you as intelligent!

Now you're ready for Step Four: actually handling the interview successfully and effectively. Remember, the purpose of an interview is to get a job offer.

Eight "do's" for the interview

According to leading U.S. companies, there are eight key areas in interviewing success. You can fail at an interview if you mishandle just one area.

1. *DO Wear Appropriate Clothes.*
    You can never go wrong by wearing a suit to an interview.

2. *DO Be Well Groomed.*
    Don't overlook the obvious things like having clean hair, clothes, and fingernails for the interview.

3. *DO Give a Firm Handshake.*
    You'll have to shake hands twice in most interviews: first, before you sit down, and second, when you leave the interview. Limp handshakes turn most people off.

4. *DO Smile and Show a Sense of Humor.*
    Interviewers are looking for people who would be nice to work with, so don't be so somber that you don't smile. In fact, research shows that people who smile at interviews are perceived as more intelligent. So, smile!

5. *DO Be Enthusiastic.*
    Employers tell PREP they are "turned off" by lifeless, unenthusiastic job hunters who show no special interest in that company. The best way to show some enthusiasm for the employer's operation is to find out about the business beforehand.

6. *DO Show You Are Flexible and Adaptable.*
An employer is looking for someone who can contribute to his organization in a flexible, adaptable way. No matter what skills and training you have, employers know every new employee must go through initiation and training on the company's turf. Certainly show pride in your past accomplishments in a specific, factual way ("I saved my last employer $50 a week by a new cost-cutting measure I developed"). But don't come across as though there's nothing about the job you couldn't easily handle.

7. *DO Ask Intelligent Questions about the Employer's Business.*
An employer is hiring someone because of certain business needs. Show interest in those needs. Asking questions to get a better idea of the employer's needs will help you "stand out" from other candidates interviewing for the job.

8. *DO "Take Charge" when the Interviewer "Falls Down" on the Job.*
Go into every interview knowing the three or four points about yourself you want the interviewer to remember. And be prepared to take an active part in leading the discussion if the interviewer's "canned approach" does not permit you to display your "strong suit." You can't always depend on the interviewer's asking you the "right" questions so you can stress your strengths and accomplishments.

Employers are seeking people with good attitudes whom they can train and coach to do things their way.

An important "don't"
Don't ask questions about salary or benefits at the first interview.

Employers don't take warmly to people who look at their organization as just a place to satisfy salary and benefit needs. Don't risk making a negative impression by appearing greedy or self-serving.

The place to discuss salary and benefits is normally at the second interview, and the employer will bring it up. Then you can ask any questions you like without appearing excessively interested in what the organization can do for you.

"Sell yourself" before talking salary
Make sure you've "sold" yourself before talking salary. First show you're the "best fit" for the employer and then you'll be in a stronger position from which to negotiate salary.

Interviewers sometimes throw out a salary figure at the first interview to see if you'll accept it. Don't commit yourself. You may be able to negotiate a better deal later on. Get back to finding out more about the job. This lets the interviewer know you're interested primarily in the job and not the salary.

Now...negotiating your salary
Don't appear excessively interested in salary and benefits at the interview.

You must avoid stating a "salary requirement" in your initial cover letter, and you must avoid even appearing **interested** in salary before you are offered the job.

Never bring up the subject of salary yourself. Employers say there's no way you can avoid looking greedy if you bring up the issue of salary and benefits before the company has identified you as its "best fit."

When the company brings up salary, it may say something like this: "Well, Mary, we think you'd make a good candidate for this job. What kind of salary are we talking about?"

Never name a number here, either. Give the ball back to the interviewer. Act as though you hadn't given the subject of salary much thought and respond something like this: "Ah, Mr. Jones, salary. . .well, I wonder if you'd be kind enough to tell me what salary you had in mind when you advertised the job?" Or ... "What is the range you have in mind?"

Don't worry, if the interviewer names a figure that you think is too low, you can say so without turning down the job or locking yourself into a rigid position. The point here is to negotiate for yourself as well as you can. You might reply to a number named by the interviewer that you think is low by saying something like this: "Well, Mr. Lee, the job interests me very much, and I think I'd certainly enjoy working with you. But, frankly, I was thinking of something a little higher than that." That leaves the ball in your interviewer's court again, and you haven't turned down the job, either, in case it turns out that the interviewer can't increase the offer and you still want the job.

Salary negotiation can be tricky.

Last, send a follow-up letter
Finally, send a letter right after the interview telling your interviewer you enjoyed the meeting and are certain (if you are) you are the "best fit" for the job.

Again, employers have a certain maternal attitude toward their companies, and they are looking for people who want to work for *that* company in particular.

The follow-up letter you send might be just the deciding factor in your favor if the employer is trying to choose between you and someone else.

A follow-up letter can help the employer choose between you and another qualified candidate.

A sample follow-up letter prepared for you by PREP is shown at the end of this section. Be sure to modify it according to your particular skills and interview situation.

And, finally, from all of us at PREP, best wishes in your job hunt and in all your future career endeavors. We hope we may have the pleasure of serving you as a customer in the future should you find yourself in a job hunt or in a career transition.

Company Information Available at Libraries
Figuring out the names of the organizations to which you want to mail your resume is part of any highly successful job campaign. Don't depend on just answering ads, waiting for the ideal job to appear in a newspaper or magazine. Aggressively seek out a job in the companies you want to work for. Here is some information which you can use in researching the names of organizations for which you might be interested in working.

Most libraries have a variety of information available on various organizations throughout the U.S. and worldwide. Most of these materials are only available for use in the reference room of the library, but some limited items may be checked out. Listed below are some of the major sources to look for, but be sure and check at the information desk to see if there are any books available on the specific types of companies you wish to investigate.

The Worldwide Chamber of Commerce Directory
Most chambers of commerce annually produce a "list of major employers" for their market area (or city). Usually the list includes the name, address, and telephone number of the employer along with information about the number of people employed,

kinds of products and services produced, and a person to contact about employment. You can obtain the "list of major employers" in the city where you want to work by writing to that chamber. There is usually a small charge.

The *Worldwide Chamber of Commerce Directory* is an alphabetical listing of American and foreign chambers of commerce. It includes:
  All U.S. Chambers of Commerce (with addresses and phone numbers)
  American Chambers of Commerce abroad
  Canadian Chambers of Commerce
  Foreign Chambers of Commerce in principal cities worldwide
  Foreign Embassies and Consulates in the U.S.
  U.S. Consulates and Embassies throughout the world

Standard and Poor's Register of Corporations, Directors, and Executives
Standard and Poor's produce three volumes annually with information concerning over 77,000 American corporations. They are:

Volume I—**Corporations.** Here is an alphabetical listing of a variety of information for each of over 77,000 companies, including:
* name of company, address, telephone number
* names, titles, and functions of several key officers
* name of accounting firm, primary bank, and law firm
* stock exchange, description of products or services
* annual sales, number of employees
* division names and functions, subsidiary listings

Volume 2—**Directors and Executives.** This volume lists alphabetically over 70,000 officers, directors, partners, etc. by name. Information on each executive includes:
* principal business affiliation
* business address, residence address, year of birth
* college and year of graduation, fraternal affiliation

Volume 3—**Index.**

Moody's Manuals
Moody's Manuals provide information about companies traded on the New York and American Stock Exchanges and over the counter. They include:

Moody's Industrial Manual
Here, Moody's discusses detailed information on companies traded on the New York, American, and regional stock exchanges. The companies are listed alphabetically. Basic information about company addresses, phone numbers, and the names of key officers is available for each company listed. In addition, detailed information about the financial and operating data for each company is available. There are three levels of detail provided:

Complete Coverage. Companies in this section have the following information:
* *financial information* for the past 7 years (income accounts, balance sheets, financial and operating data).
* *detailed description of the company's business* including a complete list of

subsidiaries and office and property sites.
- *capital structure information,* which includes details on capital stock and long-term debt, with bond and preferred stock ratings and 2 years of stock and bond price ranges.
- *extensive presentation of the company's last annual report.*

Full Measure Coverage. Information on companies in this section includes:
- *financial information for the past 7 years* (income accounts, balance sheets, financial and operating data).
- *detailed description of company's business,* with a complete list of subsidiaries and plant and property locations.
- *capital structure information,* with details on capital stock and long term debt, with bond and preferred stock ratings and 2 years of stock and bond price changes.

Comprehensive Coverage. Information on companies in this section includes:
- *5 years of financial information* on income accounts, balance sheets, and financial and operating ratios.
- *detailed description of company's business,* including subsidiaries.
- *concise capital structure information,* including capital stock and long term debts, bond and preferred stock ratings.

Moody's OTC Manual
Here is information on U.S. firms which are unlisted on national and regional stock exchanges. There are three levels of coverage: complete, full measure, and comprehensive (same as described above). Other Moody's manuals include: *Moody's Public Utility Manual, Moody's Municipal and Government Manual,* and *Moody's Bank and Finance Manual.*

Dun's Million Dollar Directory
Three separate listings (alphabetical, geographic, and by-products) of over 120,000 U.S. firms. There are three volumes:
Volume 1—The 45,000 largest companies, net worth over $500,000
Volume 2—The 37,000 next largest companies
Volume 3—The 37,000 next largest companies

U.S. industrial directories
Ask your librarian to guide you to your library's collection of industrial directories. Almost every state produces a manufacturing directory, for example, and many libraries maintain complete collections of these directories. You may find information on products and the addresses and telephone numbers of industrial companies.

Thomas' Register of Manufacturers
16 volumes of information about manufacturing companies.
Volumes 1-8—Alphabetical listing by product.
Volumes 9-10—Alphabetical listing of manufacturing company names, addresses, telephone numbers, and local offices.
Volumes 11-16—Alphabetical company catalog information.

Information About Foreign Companies

If you'd like your next job to be overseas or with an international company, you can find much helpful information in the library. You approach these companies in the same way as you would approach U.S.-based companies.

Directory of Foreign Manufacturers in the U.S.

Alphabetical listing of U.S. manufacturing companies which are owned and operated by parent foreign firms. The information provided includes the name and address of the U.S. firm, the name and address of the foreign parent firm, and the products produced.

Directory of American Firms Operating in Foreign Countries

Alphabetical listing of the names, addresses, chief officers, products, and country operated in of U.S. firms abroad.

International Firms Directory

This lists foreign corporations.

Hoover's Handbook of World Business

This lists corporations in Asia and Europe.

Principal International Businesses

This is a comprehensive directory of international businesses.

Information Available From The Internet

Information about companies is also available through the Internet. You can use all the search engines to help you in your search for company information and company website addresses.

Date

Exact Name of Person
Title or Position
Name of Company
Address (number and street)
Address (city, state, and zip)

Dear Exact Name:

I am writing to express my appreciation for the time you spent with me on December 9, and I want to let you know that I am sincerely interested in the Sales Manager position which we discussed.

I feel confident that I could skillfully manage your 12-person work force, and I would cheerfully travel as your needs require. I want you to know, too, that I would not consider relocating to Salt Lake City to be a hardship! It is certainly one of the most beautiful areas I have ever seen.

As you described to me what you are looking for in a sales manager, I had a sense of "déjà vu" because my current company was in a similar position when I went to work there. They needed someone to come in and "turn around" a demoralized sales force and restore profitability to the district. I have played a key role in the growth and profitability of the district, and both my district colleagues and the sales associates whom I manage have come to depend on my leadership and resourcefulness. I have transformed a "secondary market" which was unattractive to most sales associates into a vital and profitable region which is now appealing as a sales environment to some of the most talented sales professionals. As a sales manager, I have come to believe that a key to success is attracting ambitious, quality individuals.

Although I have spent much of my career in the copier industry, I am confident that my sales abilities and "natural" sales personality would transfer effectively to the computer field. I am skilled at developing effective working relationships with fellow workers and customers, and I truly enjoy the challenge of playing a key role in solving my customers' business problems. I like your company's motto that you "provide business solutions" and I want to be a part of your team.

Although I have become an award-winning sales professional and feel I have much to offer, I am humbly aware of how much I have to learn in a new industry. It would be a pleasure to work for a company on the fast track, and I feel I could contribute significantly to your profitability. I would welcome being trained to do things your way, and I can assure you that I would, on my own initiative, seek out opportunities to become a top sales producer as well as an effective sales manager and motivator. I will look forward to hearing from you soon, and thanks again for your time.

Yours sincerely,

Jacob Evangelisto

Follow-up Letter

A great follow-up letter can motivate the employer to make the job offer, and the salary offer may be influenced by the style and tone of your follow-up letter, too!

In this section, you will find resumes and cover letters of sales professionals. How does a sales professional differ from other types of job hunters? Sales professionals are the true backbone of any company. A company can have a great product, or an organization can have a great service, but if there aren't people who are effective at selling the product or service, the organization will not last long or be successful.

The resumes of sales people must really "sell!"
This is not just a slogan in a book. One of the main motivating beliefs behind this book is that the resumes and cover letters of sales professionals must be "a cut above" the resumes and cover letters of ordinary job hunters. If a sales professional can't generate excitement in his resume and cover letter, how good is he or she?

How to use this book...
By deliberate design, this book has been developed as a manageable size so that its owner will have time to look over all of the resumes and cover letters. Visit the Table of Contents and you will find the resumes and cover letters shown in alphabetical order by type of industry or service. But regardless of what you are selling now or want to sell, you can learn something from any resume in this book.

Sales professionals often have an advantage over other types of professionals when they come to prepare their resume and cover letter. Usually sales professionals can express their accomplishments in numbers, percentages, and dollar amounts which will show off their ability to boost profit, sales, market share, and so forth.

- Even if you are not in the furniture industry, Ken Soifer's resume on page 95 will show you an example of a resume and cover letter of someone in career transition. And George Louik's resume and cover letter on page 165 show a sales professional in technical industrial sales transitioning from the textile industry.
- Want to see an example of a sales representative seeking a sales management job? See Ellie Hatherly's resume on page 157.
- Wonder how to write a cover letter if you are relocating to a new area? There are numerous examples of cover letters which will show you what to say and how to say it, including Sun L. Kagawa's resume and cover letter on page 153.
- If you are wondering what a cover letter and resume would look like for someone trying to transition to outside sales in a new industry, see the resume and cover letter of Robert W. Doyle on pages 166 and 167.
- Are you trying to respond to an ad for a specific job? Frances Rothstein's resume and cover letter on page 174 and 175 will be helpful to you.
- If you are a hard-working sales professional with limited time to put into a job hunt, you may wonder what an "all-purpose" resume and cover letter would look like. Several examples in the book, especially those on pages 26-33, illustrate all-purpose presentations which could be used for a variety of industries.

Learn from other sales professionals...
In conclusion, what we are saying is this: keep this book and use it throughout your sales career. You have probably gotten to your current level of success by learning from others, and that is true of this book, too. Inside these exciting pages, you will see the stories and the careers of other sales professionals. You can learn something from every resume and cover letter in this book. And we sincerely hope you do.

Date

Exact Name of Person
Exact Title
Exact Name of Company
Address
City, State, Zip

Account Sales

In a gracious way, this professional is announcing his desire to become a part of an organization which will use him in sales or sales management roles. Here's a tip about employers: they like people who know what they want to do, because if you are in a job doing what you want to do, you are more likely to excel — and make money for the company.

Dear Exact Name of Person (or Dear Sir or Madam if answering a blind ad):

With the enclosed resume, I would like to make you aware of my desire to seek employment with your organization and to contribute to your success through my strong sales skills.

As you will see from my resume, I am currently servicing 75 accounts and prospecting for new ones for a company which provides direct mail services.

In my prior work experience, I excelled in a track record of accomplishment as a military professional working for the famed "Special Operations Command," which is headquartered at the nation's largest U.S. military base. I was entrusted with a Top Secret security clearance, and I was handpicked for jobs which required an outstanding communicator who could "sell" ideas and concepts. In one position, I worked as the "right arm" for a three-star general and I was constantly involved in coordinating with the media and high-ranking VIPs including the Secretary of State and the Vice President of the U.S.

In another job, I managed three people while managing a budget of up to $1 million used for engineering projects. I was authorized to purchase up to $5,000 on a government credit card without approval.

My computer skills are very strong, and I have prepared numerous slide show presentations using PowerPoint. I am proficient in utilizing Microsoft Office, Excel, PowerPoint, Windows 95, WordPerfect, Lotus, and Word, and I offer a proven ability to rapidly master any type of software application.

If you can use a disciplined hard worker with a proven ability to contribute to the bottom line while satisfying customers and assuring the delivery of quality services, I hope you will contact me to suggest a time when we might meet to discuss your needs. Thank you in advance for your time.

Sincerely,

Wes T. Sevier

WES T. SEVIER

1110½ Hay Street, Fayetteville, NC 28305 • preppub@aol.com • (910) 483-6611

OBJECTIVE   To benefit an organization that can use an articulate professional with exceptional communication and organizational skills who offers strong computer proficiency and a track record of excellence in executive-level liaison, operations management, and administration.

EDUCATION   **College:** Completed nearly two years of college course work towards a **Bachelor of Science** in **Business Administration**, Washington State University, Seattle, WA; will complete my degree in my spare time in the evenings while working full-time.
Professional Development: As a military professional, completed extensive technical and management training including the Mid-Level Manager's Course, Primary Leadership Development Course, and the Administrative Specialist Course.

COMPUTERS   Proficient with many of the most popular computer operating systems and software, including Windows 95 & 98; Microsoft Office, including Word, Excel, Access, and PowerPoint; Lotus 1-2-3; and Harvard Graphics, among others.

EXPERIENCE   **SALES MANAGER.** Mountain Money Mailer, Olympia, WA (1998-present). Service 75 existing accounts and prospect for new business; promote sales of advertising space in the direct mail "Money Mailer" marketing tool on behalf of a local radio station.
- Develop a strong rapport with clients from diverse backgrounds, calling on local businesses to encourage them to place advertising or coupons in the "Money Mailer."
- Am an Ambassador for the city's Chamber of Commerce and am extensively involved in public relations and business liaison.

While serving with the U.S. Army, was promoted ahead of my peers and individually selected for highly sensitive positions of responsibility:
1997-1998: SUPERVISOR. Ft. Lewis, WA. Supervised and trained up to 60 employees while overseeing all operational aspects of the Special Operations Command mail room; held accountable for three vehicles and numerous pieces of mail handling equipment.

1994-1996: OFFICE MANAGER. Ft. Lewis, WA. Managed the engineering office for Special Operations Command, monitoring budgetary compliance, inventory control, and records keeping as well as reviewing all correspondence and personnel actions.
- Effectively managed an annual budget of up to $1 million dollars for engineering projects, verifying engineering requirements for pending work orders.
- Supervised three personnel; maintained records and prepared reports accurately and under deadlines.

1992-1994: GENERAL'S AIDE & EXECUTIVE ASSISTANT. Ft. Lewis, WA. Was handpicked for this high-visibility job as the "right arm" to a 3-star general; was selected because of my outstanding previous work performance as well as my reputation for impeccable manners and poise when dealing with others.
- Assisted the General and his staff on all matters pertaining to protocol, diplomacy, and customs; coordinated hotel and travel arrangements for worldwide itineraries.
- Assisted in developing itineraries for all VIPs to the headquarters; constantly interacted with the media and VIPs, including the Vice President of the U.S., the Secretary of State, and Ambassadors who visited the General.

PERSONAL   Excellent references on request. Outstanding reputation. Held a Top Secret clearance.

Date

Exact Name of Person
Title or Position
Name of Company
Address (number and street)
Address (city, state, and zip)

Advertising Sales

This is a young professional
who has excelled in the
advertising sales business.
Her resume and cover
letter are designed to sell
her ability to perform any
type of inside or outside
sales job. Notice how her
cover letter focuses on the
topics employers care most
about: making a profit,
satisfying customers,
increasing market share,
and improving sales.

Dear Sir or Madam:

With the enclosed resume, I would like to make you aware of my background as a self-motivated and persistent sales professional with exceptional communication and time-management skills who offers the proven ability to find and develop new accounts while increasing sales of existing accounts.

In my most recent position with WMJV Rock 99.5, I served ably as an Account Executive in the advertising sales department. Within two years on the job, I had nearly quadrupled my monthly sales average, from $15,000 per month when I took the position to nearly $60,000 per month. Due to my exceptional salesmanship, I was able to acquire or was given the responsibility for 60 additional accounts. I quickly built a strong rapport with clients, determining their goals and expectations in order to develop marketing and promotional strategies that will satisfy the needs of each individual customer.

Earlier, with Lancome cosmetics/Hecht's stores, I was entrusted with the responsibility of making all purchasing and inventory control decisions for this exclusive product line; I also supervised three Beauty Advisors at the Savannah Mall location. By planning and implementing innovative and effective marketing strategies, promotions, and other events, I was able to grow sales and increase market share for all products in the line.

If you can use an articulate sales professional with highly-developed account management and prospecting skills as well as the proven ability to increase market share while providing exceptional customer service, then I look forward to hearing from you soon. I can assure in advance that I have an outstanding reputation and would quickly become a valuable asset to your organization.

Sincerely,

Julia Creese

JULIA CREESE

1110½ Hay Street, Fayetteville, NC 28305 • preppub@aol.com • (910) 483-6611

OBJECTIVE

To contribute to an organization that can use an experienced sales professional with exceptional communication, customer service, and time-management skills who offers a background in radio advertising sales and brand management for consumer products.

EXPERIENCE

ACCOUNT EXECUTIVE. WMJV Radio (Menley Communications), Savannah, GA (2000-present). Service existing accounts and develop new clients, presenting the benefits and services of radio advertising and promotional events to businesses in our listening area.

- In two years, increased monthly sales from an average of $15,000 per month to nearly $60,000 per month; acquired or was given responsibility for 60 additional accounts.
- Create and develop radio ads and promotional campaigns designed to present the client's products and services to local consumers.
- Quickly build a rapport with clients, determining their goals and expectations in order to develop marketing/promotional strategies.
- Determine reasons for customer resistance, then overcome objections by presenting solutions in a positive, client-focused manner.
- On my own initiative, took over a territory which was considered a "secondary market" and which previously had been unprofitable and, through aggressive prospecting and effective sales, transformed the area into a top producer which is now a sought-after assignment.
- Became known among my clients for my ability to listen to their ideas and then communicate them to the graphics professionals in such as way that great advertising campaigns and slogans were born.

BUSINESS MANAGER. Lancome-Hecht's, Savannah, GA (1995-2000). Managed all aspects of marketing and sales for this major cosmetics company's operations in Hecht's retail locations throughout Georgia.

- Supervised three Beauty Advisors at Savannah Mall and one at Westridge, providing customer service and sales activities for the Lancome line of cosmetics.
- Collaborated with the Account Coordinator; planned and implemented marketing strategies and promotional events to increase market share.
- Maintained thorough records and conducted regular inventories to optimize ordering and ensure strong in-stock position.
- Assisted customers in the selection, use, and purchase of cosmetics.

DEPUTY CLERK. Superior Court, Savannah, GA (1991-1995). Performed a variety of administrative and clerical duties in support of the Clerk of Court's office.

- Processed records for Juvenile Court cases.
- Planned case loads and scheduled court cases in direct cooperation with the Judge and District Attorney.

EDUCATION

Attended the Regional Supervisory Program training course, sponsored by Hecht's Store Services, 1996.
Graduated from Meadowdale High School, Columbus, OH, 1990.

Date

Exact Name of Person
Title or Position
Name of Company
Address (no., street)
Address (city, state, zip)

Agricultural Sales

Dear Exact Name of Person: (or Dear Sir or Madam if answering a blind ad.)

Sometimes the Objective on a resume emphasizes personal qualities, as this one does. Since his job titles are nearly identical in each of his three jobs, he has a chance to reveal something about his strong personal characteristics in his Objective. Remember that a great resume helps an employer "get to know you."

I would appreciate an opportunity to show you soon in person that I am the young, energetic, dynamic salesperson you are looking for.

As you can see from my resume, I am a proven professional with a demonstrated ability to "prospect" and produce sales. Under my direction, The Tobacco Warehouse was able to maintain a sales volume of $3.5 million despite a depressed agricultural economy. As a salesman and warehouse supervisor with Industrial Agricultural Cooperative, I increased sales from $500,000 to $1.5 million in two years. I have earned a reputation for my dedication and hard work in addition to a sincere concern for the customers I serve.

I feel certain you would find me to be a well-organized, reliable professional with a genuine customer service orientation. I pride myself on my ability to make "cold calls" and relate to people at all levels of any organization, from the mail clerk to the president. I can provide excellent personal and professional references.

I hope you will welcome my call soon to arrange a brief meeting at your convenience to discuss your current and future needs and how I might serve them. Thank you in advance for your time.

Sincerely yours,

Larry McPhail

Alternate last paragraph:
I hope you will call or write me soon to suggest a time convenient for us to meet and discuss your current and future needs and how I might best serve them. Thank you in advance for your time.

LARRY MCPHAIL

1110½ Hay Street, Fayetteville, NC 28305 • preppub@aol.com • (910) 483-6611

OBJECTIVE	To offer my leadership, problem-solving ability, and public relations skills to an organization that can use a hard-working young professional who is known for unquestioned integrity, unflagging enthusiasm, and tireless dedication to excellence.
EXPERIENCE	**SALES MANAGER.** The Agricultural Market, Inc., Marietta, GA (1995-present). Applied my financial expertise and excellent public relations/communication skills to contribute to the "bottom line" of this agricultural chemical and fertilizer manufacturer.

- Performed "cold calls" within a 30-mile sales territory; established and maintained approximately 175-200 accounts with dealers and individual customers.
- Ensured timely delivery of products and services.
- Billed customers and collected on delinquent accounts.
- Supervised three employees in administration/distribution.

SALES SUPERVISOR. The Tobacco Warehouse, Graceland, KY (1990-1995).
Built "from scratch" this successful tobacco sales and distribution center with sales totaling $3.5 million even though the agricultural economy was at a low point.

- As co-owner, managed all administrative and financial aspects of operations.
- Hired, supervised, and trained 12 employees, including floor workers, secretaries, and bookkeepers.
- Developed and maintained a loyal customer network of local farmers.
- Organized and conducted auctions to sell the product to tobacco companies.

SALESMAN and **WAREHOUSE SUPERVISOR.** Industrial Agricultural Cooperative, Lexington, KY (1986-90).
Excelled in a variety of roles because of my versatile management skills.

- Was accountable for warehouse inventory; determined product line and ordered fertilizers and agricultural chemicals.
- Performed collections and made bank deposits.
- Astutely managed finances and purchasing, meeting the company's budget goals each year.
- Through exceptional customer service to approximately 200 accounts, was able to increase sales from $500,000 to $1.5 million in two years.

SALESMAN. Best Seed Co., North Carolina (1990).
As a "sideline" to my other sales positions, applied my top-notch customer service skills to introduce this company's cottonseed line to 12 distributors throughout the state.

SPECIALIZED TRAINING	Attend more than 36 hours of instruction on pesticides each year at Georgia State University, Kentucky University, and North Carolina State University to maintain GA, NC, and KY Dealers Association licenses.
PERSONAL	Am a hard worker with a high energy level. Enjoy the challenge of motivating a team of employees while contributing to my organization's "bottom line" and serving customers.

Date

Exact Name of Person
Title or Position
Name of Company
Address (number and street)
Address (city, state, and zip)

Dear Sir or Madam:

This young manager is using her cover letter and resume to formally apply for a variety of sales positions. She has succeeded in (1) owning and managing her own company and in (2) working for a large corporation, and she has decided that she prefers specializing in marketing and sales in a large corporate environment rather than running a small business.

With the enclosed resume, I would like to make you aware of the considerable sales, management, and marketing skills I could offer your organization.

As you will see from my resume, I have excelled most recently in managing a women's clothing store which has closed its doors after 25 years due to intensive pressure from the name-brand retailers in the malls. As General Manager, I hired and trained employees, handled accounts payable and receivable, and coordinated with a variety of vendors while handling the buying function.

In my previous position as Marketing Director and Events Coordinator with Towertech Corporation, I was involved in a wide range of management and marketing activities and was credited with playing a key role in the rapid growth of this multimillion-dollar company. I managed up to 10 branch managers while developing and coordinating advertising, marketing, and special events.

In a prior job with WGJX Broadcasting as an Advertising Consultant, I created effective advertising and became skilled in cold-calling business owners to sell them on radio advertising. While working with Towertech Corporation and WGJX Broadcasting, I was active with community organizations including the Chamber of Commerce.

If you can use a vibrant and hard-working professional with versatile sales and marketing skills, I hope you will contact me to suggest a time when we could meet to discuss your needs and how I might meet them. I feel certain that I could make valuable contributions to your organization through my diversified marketing and management experience as well as through my creativity, aggressive sales skills, and highly positive personal attitude. I can provide excellent references at the appropriate time.

Sincerely yours,

Leslie R. Miller

LESLIE R. MILLER

1110½ Hay Street, Fayetteville, NC 28305   •   preppub@aol.com   •   (910) 483-6611

___

OBJECTIVE

To contribute to an organization that can use an experienced manager who offers a background in managing retail and marketing operations, buying and controlling inventory, supervising and managing personnel, as well as in handling public relations.

EXPERIENCE

GENERAL MANAGER. Belle's Boutique, Inc., Dunn, NC (1997-present). In charge of all areas of operation as the General Manager of this high-end women's fashion store.
- Interview, hire, and train all employees; manage three people.
- Prepare business plans four times a year and review goal accomplishments on a monthly basis.
- Handle accounts payable and accounts receivable; reconcile invoices.
- Reconcile daily, weekly, and monthly receipts with actual deposits; handle all liaison with the bank.
- Make buying decisions and order inventory; coordinate with vendors and perform extensive liaison with suppliers and manufacturers who act as vendors.
- Purchase and distribute the full line of beauty control makeup products; create innovative and effective sales and marketing strategies.

MARKETING DIRECTOR & EVENTS COORDINATOR. Towertech Corp., Dunn, NC (1991-96). Joined one of the state's fastest-growing companies with sales of $18 million annually; played a key role in its impressive growth to well over $22 million; utilized my previous advertising sales and copywriting experience to create effective advertising and marketing concepts.
- Developed a newsletter of current events which acquainted the business community and employees with Towertech's business strategy and successes.
- Assumed a variety of management roles within this fast-growing company; managed 10 branch managers located throughout southeast North Carolina.
- Created and managed special events which celebrated company milestones and which established excellent public relations.
- Designed and directed innovative marketing activities; handled the development of co-op advertising for all branches and assisted the branches in developing their budgets.
- Became skilled in identifying the strengths and talents of key personnel in order to effectively delegate appropriate activities to them.
- Traveled extensively to coordinate with branch managers and others.
- Became known for my enthusiastic and outgoing personality and learned that a positive attitude is essential in developing an attitude of teamwork.

ADVERTISING CONSULTANT. WGJX Broadcasting, Dunn, NC (1987-90). While working with this popular radio station, excelled in numerous roles including working as an on-air personality in the News/Talk format.
- Prepared proposals for advertising plans and established projected budgets and goals for local businesses; became skilled in cold-calling companies.
- Performed on live remotes to promote products.
- Wrote effective advertising copy including jingles which became memorable.

EDUCATION

Completed extensive training related to marketing, management, sales, and other areas sponsored by employers including Towertech and WGJX Broadcasting.

PERSONAL

Can provide excellent personal and professional references. Am highly creative and enjoy new challenges. Enjoy the challenge of representing a quality product or service.

Date

Exact Name
Exact Title
Company Name
Address
City, state zip

All-Purpose Sales

Dear Sir or Madam:

Employers are *very*
inquisitive about why an
entrepreneur wants to
make a change. This
accomplished individual
uses his cover letter to
emphasize that he has
worked in a big company as
well as in the small
company which he founded,
and he makes it clear that
he now wishes to be
involved in sales.
(Employers are looking for
people who know what they
want to do; entrepreneurs
are usually definite in their
preferences about what
they want to do next.)

With the enclosed resume, I would like to introduce you to the sales expertise, leadership ability, and management skills which I could put to work for your organization.

I am in the process of selling a company which I built "from scratch" and which, through my strong sales and management skills, I have grown into a profitable and respected small company in only two years. Although I have been successful in this entrepreneurial venture, I have decided that I wish to devote most of my energies to sales rather than to the day-to-day management details of a small business.

As you will see from my resume, I also offer a track record of proven results in managing a large company. In my first job after leaving the University of North Carolina at Chapel Hill, I went to work for a company in the oil industry and I advanced into the General Manager position. During the 20 years which I spent managing this large, diversified business with wholesale and retail operations, I took the initiative in building the first 10-minute oil change unit in VA. After acting as sales manager and developing the commercial fleet business, I sold the business to the Fast Lube franchise for a profit.

I can assure you that I am a tireless hard worker who thoroughly enjoys selling and developing a new marketing program as well as a great product/service. Although much of my experience has been in petroleum operations/sales and in automotive parts/sales with specialized knowledge of lubricants sales, I have proven my ability to sell products in other industries. As a Sales Representative of insurance products, I exceeded all quotas and was named a National Quick Start winner.

A naturally outgoing individual with a proven ability to lead and motivate others, I have been active in numerous leadership capacities in my community. I am a past president of the Rotary Club and former director of the Chamber of Commerce. If you can use my considerable sales and management abilities, I hope you will write or call me to suggest a time when we could meet in person.

Sincerely,

Wallace Jackson

WALLACE JACKSON

1110½ Hay Street, Fayetteville, NC 28305 • preppub@aol.com • (910) 483-6611

OBJECTIVE
To benefit an organization which can use a dynamic communicator and creative sales professional with outstanding negotiating and management skills along with a proven ability to transform ideas into operating realties while maximizing profit and market share.

EXPERIENCE
PRESIDENT & SALES MANAGER. Tidewater Sales & Rentals, Richmond, VA (1995-present). Utilized my entrepreneurial ability, aggressive sales orientation, strategic planning capabilities, and management skills to start a pre-owned car business "from scratch."
- Although I have been successful in starting up and managing a profitable business, I have decided to sell the company and seek a full-time sales situation.

SALES REPRESENTATIVE. State Farm Insurance, Richmond, VA (1993-1995). As a Property and Casualty Insurance Sales Professional for State Farm, handled "Family Insurance Checkups" and personal lines.
- Excelled in my first sales experience outside the automotive and petroleum industry; was selected as a National Quick Start winner in 1993; received a company-paid excursion to Los Angeles, CA, for advanced training.
- Exceeded quotas and boosted insurance sales by introducing a unique insurance concept: a membership benefits package for independent business owners which provided clients with maximum insurance coverage through membership in the National Association for the Self-Employed (NASE) or other association programs.

GENERAL MANAGER. Jackson Oil Company Inc., Tidewater, VA (1973-1993). In my first job out of college, began with Mayfield Oil Company and advanced into the General Manager position; provided leadership in turning around a marginally profitable company and then helped it to achieve higher levels of sales and profitability each year; negotiated the buyout of key assets of Mayfield Oil Company by Jackson Oil Company in 1989 and continued as the corporation's chief executive officer.
- At the head of a diversified multiplex consisting of an oil company and a chain of convenience stores, worked at the wholesale buying level of the petroleum industry while gaining experience in managing a chain of retail convenience stores.
- Oversaw staffing, sales, purchasing, bookkeeping, financial management including accounts receivable/payable, vendor relations, and inventory control.
- Transformed a business with only 5 employees into a leading competitor in the region with a 40+ work force and profits which multiplied sevenfold.
- Took the initiative in building the first 10-minute oil change unit in VA and developed the operation from start-up to 35 cars a day; developed the commercial fleet accounts and then sold the business to the Fast Lube franchise for a profit in 1985!
- Established and managed a profitable automatic car wash business.

EDUCATION
Completed two years of college coursework, University of North Carolina at Chapel Hill, 1971-73.
Sales Training: Completed extensive sales and management seminars since 1973 including Dale Carnegie and A.L. Williams Management Seminars.
Technical Training: Completed numerous petroleum industry seminars and training programs sponsored by automotive and oil industry giants.

AFFILIATIONS
Former President, Rotary Club of the Tidewater Region. Membership Chairman, Social Chairman, and Chairman of the Board.
Other: Chairman of Miss Tidewater Pageant; Chairman of Tidewater Christmas Parade for five years; Chairman, Tidewater Centennial Parade; Co-Chairman of the Tidewater Heart Fund Drive; Member Tidewater ABC Advisory Board for five years.

PERSONAL
Enjoy hunting, saltwater fishing, golf, and UVA athletic events. Outstanding references.

Exact Name of Person
Title or Position
Name of Company
Address (no., street)
Address (city, state, zip)

All-Purpose Sales

Dear Exact Name of Person: (or Dear Sir or Madam if answering a blind ad.)

This businessman offers experience in establishing a successful company and then selling it to a chain. He may attract the attention of a small or medium-size company that would like to be turned into a viable acquisition candidate. On the other hand, a large company may be attracted to his creativity, sales skills, and proven ability to "make it happen."

I would appreciate an opportunity to talk with you soon about how I could contribute to your organization through my business management, sales, and communication skills.

As you will see from my resume, I have founded successful businesses, tripled the sales volume of an existing company, and directed projects which required someone who could take a concept and turn it into an operating reality. While excelling as a retailer and importer of products that included Oriental rugs and English antiques, I have become accustomed to working with a discriminating customer base of people regionally who trust my taste and character. In addition to a proven "track record" of producing a profit, I have earned a reputation for honesty and reliability. I believe there is no substitute in business for a good reputation.

I am ready for a new challenge, and that is why I have, in the last several months, closed two of my business locations and turned over the management of the third operation to a family member. I want to apply my seasoned business judgement, along with my problem-solving and opportunity-finding skills, to new areas.

If you can use the expertise of a savvy and creative professional who is skilled at handling every aspect of business management, from sales and marketing to personnel and finance, I would enjoy talking with you informally about your needs and goals. A flexible and adaptable person who feels comfortable stepping into new situations, I am able to "size up" problems and opportunities quickly through the "lens" of experience. I pride myself on my ability to deal tactfully and effectively with everyone.

I hope you will welcome my call soon to arrange a brief meeting at your convenience to discuss your current and future needs and how I might serve them. Thank you in advance for your time.

Sincerely yours,

Desmond Vaughn

DESMOND VAUGHN

1110½ Hay Street, Fayetteville, NC 28305 • preppub@aol.com • (910) 483-6611

OBJECTIVE   To add value to an organization that can use a resourceful entrepreneur and manager who offers a proven ability to start up successful new ventures and transform ailing operations into profitable ones through applying my sales, communication, and administrative skills.

EDUCATION   Earned a **B.A. degree in Sociology**, University of Pennsylvania, Philadelphia, PA. Completed numerous executive development courses in business management and sales.

AFFILIATIONS & COMMUNITY LEADERSHIP   Have served by invitation on the Board of Directors of the following organizations:

Philadelphia Business Guild	Heart Association
Olde Philadelphia Association	Philadelphia Family Life Center
Philadelphia Hospital Pastoral Foundation	New South River Association
City of Philadelphia Downtown Revitalization Commission	

Have earned a reputation as a creative strategist with the ability to transform ideas into operating realities and with the communication and leadership skills necessary to instill enthusiasm in others.

EXPERIENCE   **FOUNDER & MANAGER**. The Captain's Den, Philadelphia, PA (1991-present). Established "from scratch" this business which grew to three locations with sales in seven figures; developed a product line which I bought from sources worldwide, and developed a customer base which included discriminating purchasers from all over the east coast.

- Refined my expertise in all aspects of business management, including financial planning and reporting, hiring and training personnel, designing advertising and marketing plans, selling products valued at up to thousands of dollars, and overseeing accounts payable and receivable.
- Simultaneously acted as an **Importer** and **Management Consultant** for an English antiques business; traveled to England three times a year as an importer.
- From 1993-95, after being recruited as **Development Director** by the Methodist State Convention, took on the paid job of coordinating the pledging and collection of $1.5 million to construct a dormitory and cafeteria for the Methodist State Convention; set up all systems and procedures and managed funds until construction was finished.
- Recently closed down the center city locations of The Captain's Den, and have turned over the midtown location to a family member.

ENTREPRENEUR. Desmond Vaughn, Inc., Philadelphia, PA (1990-95). While simultaneously managing the Captain's Den, was successful in this separate entrepreneurial venture; after extensive market research to determine the viability of establishing a business in the gifts and accessories niche, set up a store in the affluent midtown district which rapidly became successful through innovative promotions, vigorous marketing, and word of mouth.

- In less than two years, the business was producing sales in the low six figures.
- Sold the business to a large chain in the gifts and accessories industry.

SALES MANAGER. Solomon's Carpet Co., Inc., Philadelphia, PA (1981-89). Took over the management of an existing business and tripled the sales volume while increasing the staff from four to 11 employees.

- Used radio and newspaper in innovative ways which boosted traffic and sales.
- Supervised a five-person sales staff and trained them in techniques related to prospecting, closing the sale, overcoming objections, and solving customer concerns.

Other experience: **CAPTAIN & COMPANY COMMANDER**. U.S. Army. Was awarded the Bronze Star and Army Commendation Medal for service in Vietnam.

PERSONAL   Offer a proven ability to manage several functional areas and projects at the same time.

Date

Exact Name of Person
Title or Position
Name of Company
Address (number and street)
Address (city, state, and zip)

All-Purpose Sales

Although he doesn't reveal this fact in his cover letter or resume, this entrepreneur lost his zest for his business when two of his employees got killed on the job. He is seeking a sales position in a large company.

Dear Exact Name of Person: (or Dear Sir or Madam if answering a blind ad.)

With the enclosed resume, I would like to introduce you to the proven leadership ability, management skills, and sales/marketing experience which I could put to work for your organization.

Through my strong sales and management skills, I built a business "from scratch" which rapidly grew into a profitable venture grossing more than $2 million last year. I am a very hard-working individual and am highly confident in my ability to sell any type of service or product to any type of individual or organization.

You will see from my resume that I offer a proven ability to prospect not only for new customers and new accounts but also for new business opportunities and new niches, markets, and segments in which to position a product and grow market share. Although I established a residential landscaping business, I rapidly perceived of new sales opportunities and became a major force in the wholesale and retail sod brokerage business. Through my ability to deal with people and establish strong personal relationships, I became a respected individual who was often called in on complex commercial projects after a low bidder or initial contractor had botched the job. I am experienced in negotiating large commercial projects.

Although I am a very successful businessman who is effective in hiring and retaining quality employees, I have decided that I wish to become involved full-time in sales and marketing, since I feel that is where my strongest abilities lie.

If you can use a dedicated person with an outstanding personal and professional reputation to enhance your growth and profitability, I hope you will give me a call to suggest a time when we might meet to discuss your needs and how I might help you. Thank you in advance for your time.

Sincerely,

William Goldman

WILLIAM GOLDMAN

1110½ Hay Street, Fayetteville, NC 28305 • preppub@aol.com • (910) 483-6111

OBJECTIVE   To contribute to an organization which can use a motivated professional with exceptionally strong sales, leadership, stress management, and customer relations skills along with proven abilities related to managing operations, boosting profitability, and solving problems.

EXPERIENCE   **PRESIDENT & SALES MANAGER.** Quality Turf, Inc., Virginia Beach, VA (1990-2000). With only a pickup truck and an aggressive sales orientation, started "from scratch" a business which grew from $54,000 in gross revenue in its first year to over $2 million last year; started out by providing residential landscaping services and then expanded and diversified into other areas as I gained knowledge, experience, and a reputation for reliability and quality.

- Once established in residential landscaping, identified an opportunity for statewide sod sales; became a broker and eventually serviced customers from Atlanta to Washington, DC, while providing quality sod and grading services to prominent golf courses.
- As a large sod wholesaler and retailer, achieved an 80% market share in the Virginia Beach market; serviced most landscapers and gardeners.
- Negotiated numerous multimillion-dollar contracts for services provided to organizations such as AT&T, the City of Virginia Beach, privately owned golf courses, Target Stores, Home Depot Stores, and large construction companies.
- Expanded the company into the tree surgery business, and personally completed extensive formal training which resulted in my becoming a Certified Arborist (tree surgeon); became a member of the International Society of Arboculture.
- Acquired a million-dollar inventory of pickup trucks, dump trucks, tractors, fork lifts, front-end loaders, tree chippers, and other equipment.
- Employed up to 40 people including three crew foremen while always acting as General Sales Manager and negotiating all commercial contracts.
- Gained extensive experience in bidding on government and commercial contracts; on numerous occasions was called in on a job after a low bidder had mishandled and often abandoned the project.

COMMUNICATIONS TECHNICIAN. U.S. Army, Ft. Bragg, NC (1987-90). Received an Honorable Discharge and several medals for exceptional performance while serving my country as a Radio Technician.

FOREMAN. Bekins Moving and Storage, Phoenix, AZ (1985-87). In my first job after high school, began working for one of the world's largest moving and storage companies, and became the company's youngest-ever full-time employee and youngest-ever foreman.

- Supervised 30 individuals involved in moving office and industrial goods.

EDUCATION   Completed extensive management and technical training sponsored by the U.S. Army. Excelled in numerous executive development programs related to sales and marketing, effective communications, and operations management.

PERSONAL   Am a highly motivated hard worker who excels in communicating with others. In sales situations, have always sold my strengths rather than my competitor's weaknesses. Believe that establishing a personal relationship based on trust is the key to sales success. Have a visionary approach to business; am able to troubleshoot problems before they arise.

Exact Name of Person
Title or Position
Name of Company
Address (number and street)
Address (city, state, and zip)

Automobile Dealership Management and Sales

After a failed attempt at retirement, this ambitious professional is attempting to take his sales background and automotive industry knowledge to a higher level by owning his own dealership. His first strategy is networking among well-placed industry colleagues. As a general rule, it's best to keep the objective on your resume versatile and all-purpose, but you will notice that this resume and cover letter are narrowly targeted to a specific purpose and industry.

Dear Sir or Madam:

Although I have tried to retire from my career in the car business, I have discovered that I don't play golf well enough to retire! I believe you will recall that the last time I saw you was, in fact, on a golf course when we played the tournament in Pebble Beach two years ago. Hope your golf game has fared better than mine in the meantime!

Although I believe you are well acquainted with my background, I am sending you an updated resume to refresh your memory. I want you to know that I am very interested in pursuing a franchise opportunity with the Lincoln-Mercury Company.

I can assure you that I have the necessary capital for this business opportunity, and I believe you know that I would be an individual who could make a success out of such a franchise. I would feel honored, too, to be a part of the Handicapped Dealers Program and feel that my success would be a credit to the fine program which you direct.

I enjoyed our brief phone conversation recently, and I hope the enclosed brings you up to date on my most recent successes and accomplishments. I hope you will contact me to suggest what you think is the next suitable step in light of my desire to become associated with this program and with the Ford franchise program.

Best regards to you and your family.

Sincerely,

Rich Arnett

RICHARD T. ARNETT ("RICH")

1110½ Hay Street, Fayetteville, NC 28305   •   preppub@aol.com   •   (910) 483-6611

OBJECTIVE   I want to contribute to an organization that can use a dynamic leader who has excelled in recruiting and training personnel, developing and implementing effective human resources policies, as well as troubleshooting difficult problems and identifying creative solutions.

EDUCATION   M.S. Business Administration, University of Arizona, Tempe, AZ.
Masters of Science in Guidance and Counseling, Yale University, New Haven, CT.
B.S. Degree, Sable University, Sable, MS.
Completed two-year Dealer Trainee Program of Chrysler-Plymouth Company.

EXPERIENCE   **PRESIDENT & GENERAL MANAGER.** Rich Arnett's Used Cars, Manhasset, NY (1999-2000). Supervised 15 individuals including six sales professionals, two finance specialists, one manager, one assistant sales manager, office personnel, and the Recon Department.
  • Founded a company which rapidly became a major competitor.

PRESIDENT & GENERAL MANAGER. Randolph Chrysler-Plymouth, Manhasset, NY (1992-99). Supervised 60 individuals who included 18 sales professionals, two finance specialists, the Used Car Manager, the New Car Manager, the Service and Parts Manager, the Service Department, the Recon Department, and the office personnel.
  • Led the company to achieve gross sales of $32 million a year, and achieved a $1 million profit-before-tax income for seven consecutive years.
  • Became recognized as a Five Star Dealer.
  • Exceeded all goals and projections for growth, market share, and profitability; for example, doubled assigned market penetration each year for three consecutive years.
  • Received "Just the Best" award and the Outstanding Dealer's Award from Chrysler for three consecutive years.

GENERAL SALES MANAGER. Falls Court Lincoln-Mercury, Manhasset, NY (1991-92). Supervised 10 sales professionals including the Used Car Manager, the New Car Manager, and the finance specialist.
  • For this dealership with a $6 million inventory and gross sales of $25 million per year, increased market penetration by 60%.
  • Was rated one of the top Lincoln-Mercury dealerships in Manhasset for CSI.

INTERIM OPERATOR & CONSULTANT. Capital Lincoln-Mercury, Vienna, VA (1989-91). Was recruited to serve as Interim Operator and Consultant until a major buy/sell was negotiated and implemented.
  • During this time, served for one year as a Consultant at two different dealerships.
  • As a consultant in Keithville: In 90 days, turned around a franchise which had been losing $100,000 a month and restored it to profitability.
  • As a consultant in Iowa City: Led a new dealership to achieve phenomenal results in profitability and sales through advertising, merchandising, and expense control.

GENERAL MANAGER. Paramount Lincoln-Mercury, Lansing, MI (1986-89). Supervised 65 individuals including one General Sales Manager, one Used Car Manager, one New Car Manager, and a New Truck Manager along with finance specialists, service and parts technicians, office personnel, the Recon Department, the body shop, and 20 sales professionals.
  • Increased CSI to the Top 10 in a group of 50 dealers within 18 months.

PERSONAL   Can provide excellent personal and professional references. Dynamic and results-oriented.

Date

Exact Name of Person
Title or Position
Name of Company
Address (number and street)
Address (city, state, and zip)

Automobile Dealership Management and Sales Management

This senior manager is similar to Mr. Rich Arnett on the previous page in that their goals are the same: to take over as manager of an automobile dealership and manage a sales force. Notice how this individual stresses his community standing as well as his willingness to relocate according to employer needs.

Dear Sir or Madam:

With the enclosed resume, I would like to make you aware of my desire to become General Manager of a Chevrolet Automobile Dealership.

As you will see from my enclosed resume, I have excelled in a track record of accomplishment with Chevrolet of Portland. I am proud of the results I achieved as Sales Manager, Finance & Insurance Manager, Used Car Manager, and General Sales Manager. My exceptionally strong leadership skills have been refined in the highly competitive environment of the automobile sales business, and I offer a reputation as a powerful leader and motivator with the ability to inspire people to perform to their highest levels of competence. You will notice on my resume that I have used my outstanding personal reputation and ability to influence others to take action in high-visibility community leadership roles when a trusted leader was needed to take on a tough job and mobilize people to accomplish difficult tasks.

I am willing to relocate according to company needs in order to accomplish my goal of becoming General Manager of a dealership. I can assure you in advance that I am confident in my ability to take a good dealership and make it great or to transform a troubled operation into a well-oiled machine. My skills as a motivator and team builder are highly respected, and I can provide outstanding references throughout the industry.

Please favorably consider my desire to take the next logical step in my career of becoming a General Manager and suggest a time when we might meet to discuss your goals and how I might help you achieve them. I will look forward to your response.

Yours sincerely,

Roderick F. MaClure

RODERICK F. MACLURE ("ROD")

1110½ Hay Street, Fayetteville, NC 28305 • preppub@aol.com • (910) 483-6611

OBJECTIVE   To benefit an organization that can use a General Manager with exceptional motivational and communication skills who offers a strong background as a sales trainer and a track record of excellence as a general sales manager, used car manager, and finance manager.

EDUCATION   Bachelor of Arts degree in History, Bryant College, Orono, OR, 1990.
Associate of Arts in General Education, Western Community College, Orono, OR, 1988.

COMMUNITY LEADERSHIP   Offer a reputation as a highly respected local leader who believes in helping my community:
1997-99: President, Portland Sports Association. Took control of a small athletic association comprised of 8 teams totaling 120 people and, in three years, transformed it into a 43-team organization with more than 700 people affiliated. Established new programs for children including flag football and persuaded city government to better equip playing fields.
1995-98: Appointed President, Portland Middle School Athletic Booster Club; organized the club from scratch, served as its first president, and created revenue-generating plans.

EXPERIENCE   *With Chevrolet of Portland, have advanced in the following "track record:"*
1999-present: GENERAL SALES MANAGER. Portland, OR. Advanced to this position after excelling as Used Car Manager and Sales Manager; was tasked with the additional responsibility of overseeing the operation of the entire sales department; continued to serve as Used Car Manager.
- Supervise 14 Sales Representatives, Finance Managers, and Sales Managers.
- Serve as director of employee training for all departments; track completion of training courses required by Chevrolet and ensure that all employees receive proper instruction.
- Achieved and maintained a Customer Service Index of #1 or #2 among all dealerships.
- New car sales consistently exceed national and territory averages.

1997-99: USED CAR MANAGER. Portland, OR. Promoted from a Sales Manager position; responsible for managing all operational aspects of the Used Car department.
- Monitored used car inventory, ensuring that the dealership didn't become overstocked; controlled the number of overaged units and ordered program vehicles.
- Performed appraisals of vehicles being traded in based on condition, black book value, and existing unsold inventory of the same or similar used vehicles.
- Due to my initiative, net profit for the used car department increased by 47%, and returned a net-to-gross profit ratio greater than 29%; the used car department was consistently ranked in the top four among all Lumpert Chevrolet dealerships.

1994-97: SALES MANAGER and FINANCE & INSURANCE MANAGER. Portland, OR. Hired by Chevrolet of Portland to serve as Sales Manager of their existing sales team; also acted as a backup Finance and Insurance Manager.
- Supervised a staff of Automotive Sales Representatives; set daily, weekly, and monthly sales goals and monitored progress towards achieving those goals.
- Maximized the dealership's profit by selling aftermarket products such as warranties.

Other experience: FINANCE & INSURANCE MANAGER. Bronson Cadillac and Franklin Lincoln/Mercury, Orono, OR. Gained expert knowledge of how cars are financed and leased. Maintained high conversion percentage while maximizing profit per retail deal.

PERSONAL   Excellent personal and professional references on request. Outstanding reputation.

Exact Name of Person
Exact Title
Exact Name of Company
Address
City, State, Zip

Automobile Rental Sales

Dear Exact Name of Person (or Dear Sir or Madam if answering a blind ad):

Notice the aggressive and dynamic first sentence of his cover letter. What employer couldn't use an employee who could improve sales and profitability? Also notice the similar nature of the Objective on his resume. It is specific without "nailing him down" to a particular industry. (He is actually seeking a change from automobile rental sales.)

Can you use a dynamic young professional with a proven ability to boost market share, achieve exceptionally high customer satisfaction levels, develop new sales opportunities, and boost profitability?

I have been excelling with Dollar Rent-A-Car in positions of increasing responsibility. In my most recent position as Regional Manager for the city of Utica, NY, I supervised 105 personnel in a region with annual sales of $8.8 million dollars. Earlier, as Area Manager for the western region of St. Louis, I launched the highly successful start-up of this new region, which quickly grew to six locations employing 49 personnel. By designing and implementing innovative and effective marketing plans, our sales increased 47% per year over a three-year period and the region achieved annual sales of $4.8 million.

As Branch Manager, I was responsible for opening a new office, which became the first location in the Southeast region to reach a monthly net profit of $40,000. Despite being a newly-launched branch with a new manager and staff, we were one of the top five branches in the region for total sales. I was promoted to this position after excelling as a Management Trainee in a branch where I had the highest inside sales of any management trainee in the region, and was promoted to Assistant Manager after only six months with Dollar.

If you can use a confident, self-motivated management professional whose exceptional supervisory, communication, and organizational skills have been proven in positions of ever-increasing responsibility, then I look forward to hearing from you soon, to suggest a time when we might meet to discuss your needs.

Sincerely,

Scott T. Sears

SCOTT T. SEARS

1110½ Hay Street, Fayetteville, NC 28305 • preppub@aol.com • (910) 483-6611

OBJECTIVE

To benefit an organization that can use an articulate, results-oriented professional with exceptional sales and management skills who offers a background in managing multiunit operations as well as a track record of success in territory development and management.

EDUCATION

Associate of Applied Science, Marketing, Utica Technical College, Utica, NY, 1998.
Completed three years of college course work towards a Bachelor of Science in Marketing, University of Kentucky, Lexington, KY.

EXPERIENCE

With Dollar Rent-A-Car, have excelled and been promoted to positions of increasing responsibility by the largest automotive rental and leasing company in North America, with sales of $5.2 billion annually:

1997-present: **REGIONAL MANAGER.** Utica, NY. Promoted from Area Manager for St. Louis, oversee all aspects of operations in this region with multimillion-dollar annual sales; provided valuable leadership in quickly turning around an unprofitable operation and showing a profit in only eight months.

- Planned and executed the expansion of branch offices from five locations to 14.
- Supervise 105 personnel including two area managers, a corporate recruiter, one sales manager, one corporate sales manager, one trainer, and an administrative assistant.
- Developed and launched new pricing, rebate, and incentive programs, increasing sales more than 23% annually, from $3.9 million to $8.8 million annually; increased net profits from $420,000 to $2.1 million over a 3½ year period.
- Serve as Director of Human Resources, conducting final interviews on all potential employees and determining labor needs and personnel budgets for 14 branch offices.
- Provided strong leadership to a young management team with diverse backgrounds during corporate restructuring, instilling them with pride in their accomplishments and a positive attitude during this difficult transitional period.
- Worked with office personnel to ensure the highest levels of customer service; our customer service scores went from below the company average to the top 5% of all regions.

1993-1997: **AREA MANAGER.** St. Louis, MO. Launched the start-up and managed all aspects of the western region of St. Louis as part of the Midwest Expansion Team; the new region overcame the costs associated with start-up and turned a profit in its first year.

- Interviewed, hired, and trained all new employees in a team that eventually grew to 49 employees at six locations; through my efforts in personnel development, nine of my hires were promoted to Branch Manager.
- Designed and implemented innovative marketing plans, achieving average growth of 47% per year over three years, and annual sales of $4.8 million.
- Achieved customer service scores in the top 10% of the entire company.

1989-1993: **BRANCH MANAGER.** Charlotte, NC. Managed the start-up of a new branch office, directing the marketing and sales strategies, training employees in the presentation of company products and services, and performing administrative tasks.

- Created, developed, and maintained strong relationships with insurance companies, auto dealerships and autobody repair shops to ensure a large base for referral customers.
- Became the first branch office in the southeast to achieve a net profit of $40,000 in one month; strong revenues placed our branch in the top five in the region.
- In my first position as a Management Trainee in 1989, was promoted after six months.

PERSONAL

Outstanding personal and professional references are available upon request.

Exact Name of Person
Exact Title
Exact Name of Company
Address
City, State, Zip

Automobile Rental Sales

This young professional has proved her sales abilities since graduating from college. Now she wishes to explore sales opportunities in numerous industries. Although she has enjoyed selling automobile rentals, she wants to "see what's out there."

Dear Sir or Madam:

With the enclosed resume, I would like to formally initiate the process of being considered for a position within your organization which can use my exceptionally strong sales, marketing, communication, and management skills.

As you will see from my resume, since earning my B.S. degree in Business Administration with a Marketing major, I have excelled in both sales and customer service. In my most recent job as a District Sales Manager, I traveled frequently while prospecting for new accounts and establishing outstanding relationships with insurance adjustors and car dealers throughout the state.

I am familiar with numerous types of software and offer a proven ability to rapidly master new programs.

After graduating with my college degree, I was promoted to increasing levels of responsibility related to customer service by a bank in Williamsville. I enjoy dealing with people and have often been commended for my gracious manners and positive approach to solving customer problems. While with First Bank, I received two awards recognizing my exceptional communication and customer service skills.

If you can use a highly motivated young professional with a strong bottom-line orientation, I hope you will contact me to suggest a time when we might meet to discuss your business needs and how I might serve them. Thank you in advance for your time.

Yours sincerely,

Marilyn P. Hall

MARILYN P. HALL

1110½ Hay Street, Fayetteville, NC 28305 • preppub@aol.com • (910) 483-6611

OBJECTIVE
To benefit an organization that can use a hard-working young professional with outstanding sales, communication, customer service, marketing, and management skills.

EDUCATION
B.S. in Business Administration and Marketing, Middlebury College, Middlebury, VT, 1995. Graduated from Smith High School, Williamsville, VT, 1990.
- Was co-captain of the Cheerleading Squad.

TECHNICAL SKILLS
Computers: Familiar with WordPerfect 6.0, 5.2, 5.1; Microsoft Word; Lotus; Windows. Offer a proven ability to rapidly master new software.
Other: Experienced in using E-Mail, 10-key, PBX Phone, copiers, fax machines, and all other office equipment.

EXPERIENCE
DISTRICT SALES MANAGER. Enterprise Rent-A-Car, Middlebury, VT (1997-present). Travel frequently while prospecting for and managing sales within a large territory in Vermont which includes Middlebury and ranges from Norwich, to Wilmington, to Williamsville.
- Aggressively prospect for new accounts; acquired excellent prospecting skills.
- Target primarily insurance adjustors and car dealerships in my sales strategies; establish long-term accounts through which customers can secure rental cars while their own automobiles are being repaired.
- Have become known for my ability to provide excellent customer service; maintain rapport with a team of professionals within the parent organization so that the promises I make will be reliably delivered.
- Maintain extensive paperwork related to sales calls, scheduling of meetings and sales calls, as well as travel records.
- Have been commended by company officials as a highly self motivated individual with outstanding communication and interpersonal skills.

CUSTOMER SERVICE REPRESENTATIVE. First Bank, Williamsville, VT (1995-97). Began with First Bank as a Teller in 1995 and was promoted into a customer service position in 1996; worked extensively on the telephone and in person while assisting customers.
- Received the bank's Communicator Award for outstanding achievements in customer service and superior communication skills.
- Was awarded a Quality Certificate for consistently high-quality production.
- Fielded customer requests for information or problem solving, and directed customers to appropriate bank personnel.
- Was gradually cross trained to promote the bank's products and services, and refined my skills in presenting financial services.
- As a Teller, was entrusted with safeguarding the vault while also assisting customers with banking transactions.

Other experience: Worked 30 hours per week while financing my college education:
FASHION CONSULTANT. Filenes, Middlebury, VT (1994-95). Assisted customers of Filenes' fashion merchandise and haute couture.
CUSTOMER SERVICE REPRESENTATIVE. Schenker, Middlebury, VT (1992-94). Refined my communication skills while operating a busy telephone switchboard.
- Cordially assisted customers with complaints and questions about returns.
- Was frequently complemented for my gracious telephone manners.

PERSONAL
Have volunteered my time with the American Heart Association and Habitat for Humanity.

Date

Exact Name of Person
Title or Position
Name of Company
Address (number and street)
Address (city, state, and zip)

Automobile Sales in Career Transition to Other Types of Sales

Employers often feel that skills are transferable to other industries. For example, if an individual excels at the sale of automobiles, it is likely that person could succeed in selling other products or services. Mr. McAteer is attempting to change industries and utilize his sales skills for the benefit of a company such as UPS or FedEx, where he can use his transportation industry knowledge while functioning in an inside sales role.

Dear Sir or Madam:

With the enclosed resume, I would like to express my strong interest in exploring career opportunities with your organization and introduce you to my proven customer service, communication, and sales skills.

As you will see from my resume, I have had a successful sales career with companies in Knoxville, including my current employer, Walsh Auto Sales. Through my experience as a Sales Manager and Sales Representative there, I have developed the proven ability to quickly build rapport with customers from many different backgrounds, while learning to deal amicably with people even in tense situations.

During my tenure as Manager of Metro Pawn & Loan, I utilized my strong organizational and sales abilities to increase profits at the Wilton Road location by an average of $1,500 per month while insuring the security and accountability of over $200,000 worth of inventory. I excelled in the role of Sales Manager as I trained more than 10 associates in techniques including overcoming objections and closing the sale.

Although I am highly regarded by my present employer and can provide excellent personal and professional references at the appropriate time, I have decided that I would like to express my sales abilities and communication skills in another industry.

If you can use a highly motivated, detail-oriented individual with a commitment to providing the highest possible levels of customer service, I hope you will contact me to suggest a time when we might meet to discuss your needs. I can assure you that I have an excellent reputation and could quickly become a valuable asset to your organization.

Yours sincerely,

Samuel R. McAteer

SAMUEL R. MCATEER

1110½ Hay Street, Fayetteville, NC 28305 • preppub@aol.com • (910) 483-6611

OBJECTIVE   To benefit an organization that can use an energetic, self-motivated individual with strong sales, sales management, organizational, communication, and customer service skills.

EXPERIENCE   **SALES MANAGER.** Walsh Auto Sales, Knoxville, TN (1998-present). Supervise one salesperson while overseeing the operation of this busy used car lot.
- Quickly build rapport with customers and assist them with the selection and purchase of a pre-owned vehicle.
- Communicate verbally and in writing with outside agencies, such as insurance companies, lending institutions, and advertising representatives.
- Complete customer contracts and perform credit checks on potential customers.
- Maintain existing accounts and carry out collection actions on past-due accounts.
- Open and close the lot, ensuring the security of all vehicles and money.

STORE MANAGER. Metro Pawn & Loan, Knoxville, TN (1997-1998). Hired as an Assistant Manager Trainee, was quickly promoted to Manager of my own location.
- Supervised a staff of 6-10 employees and performed all employee evaluations; trained the staff in sales techniques.
- Increased sales by an average of $1,500 per month; personally set new sales records.
- Interviewed, hired, and trained all new associates.
- Opened and closed the store, completing all operational paperwork and making bank deposits and change orders.
- Responsible for an inventory of more than $200,000.
- Ordered merchandise and supplies.

ASSISTANT MANAGER. King Pawn & Loan, Nashville, TN (1996-1997). Assisted the manager in the operation of this busy retail pawn shop; hired as a trainee and was promoted to Assistant Manager in two months.
- Opened and closed the store; made bank deposits.
- Supervised up to 10 employees.
- Named Salesperson of the Month on several different occasions.
- Assisted customers in the selection and purchase of merchandise; responsible for maintaining a certain level of sales each month.

AUTOMOTIVE SALES CONSULTANT. Reid Olds-Nissan, Knoxville, TN (1993-1996). Assisted customers in the selection and purchase of a new or pre-owned vehicle; demonstrated the features and selling points of the vehicle; offered a demonstration drive.
- Assisted customers in filling out loan applications and other necessary paperwork to purchase a vehicle.
- Followed up with customers after the sale; ensuring their satisfaction and obtaining referrals to friends and family members.

Other Experience: Proudly served my country for three years as an infantryman at Fort Bragg, NC.

COMPUTERS   Am familiar with the following computer software: Windows 3.1 & 95, Microsoft Word 97, Excel 97, Publisher 97, Works 97, PowerPoint 97, and Expedia.

PERSONAL   Excellent personal and professional references are available upon request.

Date

Exact Name of Person
Title or Position
Name of Company
Address (number and street)
Address (city, state, and zip)

Automobile Sales Associate

This accomplished
automotive industry sales
professional enjoys selling
cars, and his goal is to seek
a sales management
position in a major
dealership. Notice that he
asks that the prospective
employer treat his
approach as confidential.
He doesn't want to be
gossiped about in his
industry, and he also
doesn't want his current
employer to discover that
he is discreetly looking
around.

Dear Sir or Madam:

With the enclosed resume, I would like to confidentially express my interest in exploring sales management opportunities within your organization. Although I am held in the highest regard and can provide outstanding references at the appropriate time, I would appreciate your treating my interest in your company as confidential until after we have a chance to speak in person.

As you will see from my resume, I have excelled as a Sales Representative for Toyota-Jeep products, motorcycles, and top-of-the-line luxury automobiles. In every job I have held, I have set personal sales and productivity records, and I have become skilled at establishing warm working relationships with customers. I have enjoyed the product lines I have represented and have come to believe that enthusiasm is the key to effectiveness in sales situations.

The most satisfying sales challenge of my career has been selling Porsches and Mercedes, and I have learned to communicate effectively with purchasers of these luxury vehicles. I am confident that I could motivate and develop other sales professionals into top-notch performers, and it is my desire to move up to the next challenge of my career: sales management.

If you can use an enthusiastic hard charger with a proven ability to profitably impact the bottom line, I hope you will contact me to suggest a time when we might meet in person to discuss your needs. With extensive knowledge of automotive products, I offer a proven ability to succeed in a highly competitive industry and I would relish training other sales professionals to do the same.

Yours sincerely,

David M. Valera

DAVID M. VALERA

1110½ Hay Street, Fayetteville, NC 28305 • preppub@aol.com • (910) 483-6611

OBJECTIVE   To benefit an organization through my effective sales techniques along with my superior communication and "people" skills as well as my education in management and sales.

EDUCATION   Studied **Business Management** and **Salesmanship**, Louisburg Junior College. Studied accounting, business law, and business finance, Pennsylvania State University.

EXPERIENCE   **SALES REPRESENTATIVE.** Allentown Motors, Allentown, PA (2000-present). Provide extensive knowledge and assistance to customers interested in the selection and purchase of a new or used Mercedes or Porsche; trained in the Mercedes Star-Mark used car program and certified as a sales consultant for both Mercedes and Porsche.
- Expertly handle all aspects of the sale from demonstrating the vehicle to closing the sale, obtaining financing, and sales of warranty products.
- Qualified to sell all lines of automobiles from the used car inventory.

SALES MANAGER. Wallace Cycle World, Allentown, PA (1993-2000). Oversee sales department of showroom selling motorcycles, ATVs, and watercraft including maintaining showroom traffic log, performing inventory maintenance of new and used products, as well as arranging credit applications and financing for the customer through the manufacturer and local finance services.
- Provided customer service through extended warranties, credit life, and accident and health insurance.
- Recruited top-notch sales people and provided ongoing sales training and orientations of manufacturers' programs; increased sales volume by 10% from previous year.
- Planned events and compiled daily/weekly/monthly reports for the general manager.
- Created additional dealer profit through increased extended warranty sales and by offering more flexible financing.
- Increased used motorcycle sales by purchasing units from outside services.
- Improved customer relations by implementing a follow-up system for customer feedback after the point of sale.

SALES REPRESENTATIVE. Sampson Toyota-Jeep-Eagle, Allentown, PA (1992-93). Sold automobiles for this aggressive, multiline, national company.
- Was a "team captain" responsible for daily status reports on sales of each team member.
- Communicated new product information and sales techniques to team members on a daily basis; assisted team members in closing negotiations.
- Completed training to become certified leasing consultant for Jeep-Eagle.
- Attended and successfully completed quarterly seminars to obtain status as a Certified Sales Consultant for Toyota and Jeep-Eagle.
- Met and exceeded all monthly sales goals set by the general manager.

SALES REPRESENTATIVE. Valenti Ford, Allentown, PA (1990-92). Sold Ford automobiles with specialization on leasing.
- Completed coursework to become a Certified Leasing Consultant for Ford Motor Co.
- Consistently ranked in the top 10 out of a sales force of 25 representatives.

PERSONAL   Outstanding personal and professional references are available upon request.

Date

Exact Name of Person
Exact Title
Exact Name of Company
Address
City, State, Zip

Banking Services
Transitioning to High-Tech
Sales

Dear Exact Name of Person (or Dear Sir or Madam if answering a blind ad):

There are some things you can learn from this cover letter and resume. When you read the cover letter, you will see that this young woman has figured out what interests her the most career-wise, and she is taking careful aim at companies which will stimulate her technological interests and offer her an opportunity to become involved in a business which is focused on creating quality hardware or software products. She would be most happy, she thinks, if she were involved in training customers, selling quality products, or communicating in a high-tech business.

With the enclosed resume, I would like to make you aware of my desire to utilize and expand my knowledge of computer software and business applications within an organization that can use my enthusiastic personality, sales and marketing background, as well as my strong desire to work in an environment on the forefront of technology.

I am proficient with a wide range of computer software, including most versions of Microsoft Word, Excel, and PowerPoint, as well as Publisher 97, DragonDictate, and Website Developer. In my current position, I utilize numerous software packages to compile data and produce reports, newsletters, and other documents for distribution to 30 branch offices. I want to stress that **on my own initiative** and in my spare time I have mastered these software programs and then utilized them for the benefit of my employer. I have also trained others in software operation, which allowed branch managers whom I instructed to achieve maximum productivity from their use of the Mobius computer report system.

Through my rapid advancement with Bank of New York, I have been afforded the opportunity to achieve a degree of success rare for a young professional. While I am highly regarded by my present employer and can provide excellent references at the appropriate time, I feel that my strong software knowledge and excellent communication skills would be of great value to an organization with a strong technological orientation.

If you can use a highly motivated young professional whose personality and technical knowledge could surely enhance your organization, I hope you will contact me to suggest a time when we might meet to discuss your needs and how I might help you to meet them. Thank you in advance for your time.

Sincerely,

Vivian E. Perdue

VIVIAN E. PERDUE

1110½ Hay Street, Fayetteville, NC 28305 • preppub@aol.com • (910) 483-6611

OBJECTIVE
To utilize my knowledge of computer software and business applications within an organization that can use a highly motivated young professional with strong communication, sales, customer service, and technical support skills.

COMPUTERS
Proficient in the operation of a wide range of computer software including the following:
- Word Processing—Microsoft Word for Windows, Access.
- Spreadsheet —Microsoft Excel, Lotus 1-2-3.
- Multimedia—Microsoft PowerPoint.
- Desktop Publishing—Microsoft Publisher, PageMaker 6.5, Quark, CorelDraw.
- Dictation—DragonDictate.
- Web Page Design—Website Developer.
- Accounting—Peachtree Accounting; QuickBooks Pro.

EDUCATION
Bachelor of Science degree in Business Education, Smith University, Scarsdale, NY, 2000.
First National Bank's 400-hour Internship program, 1998-2000.
Bank of New York, Cohen Brown Proactive Relationship Banking course, 2000.
Bank of New York, Cohen Brown Extraordinary Sales & Leadership course, 2000.

EXPERIENCE
Was hired at Bank of New York as a temporary employee; quickly advanced to full-time and was promoted to a position of increased responsibility.
REGIONAL SALES ANALYST. Bank of New York, Huntington, NY (2000-present). Act as liaison to 30 branch offices of this large regional bank, compiling various data and preparing documents for dissemination throughout the company.
- Provide each of the 30 branches with campaign goals and weekly updates of campaign information to be distributed to the employees.
- Compile data from various sources and enter the pertinent information into a Microsoft Excel spreadsheet, generating monthly reports.
- Order analytic data and issue the information in its final form to Branch Managers, Relationships Bankers, and City Executives.
- Instruct and assist Branch Managers in operation and information retrieval via Mobius, a proprietary computer report system.
- Produce and develop new spreadsheets in Excel.
- Developed electronic forms for lending and mortgage department to be used in E-mail.

MORTGAGE LOAN PROCESSOR. Bank of New York (through Kelly), White Plains, NY (2000). Performed a variety of loan processing and clerical functions in this busy office.
- Processed incoming mortgage loans, completing the initial preparation of the application before forwarding it to the appropriate processor.
- Responsible for office accounting, writing disbursement vouchers, keeping accounts, and paying bills.
- Photocopied mortgage files that were distributed to processors for second level review.
- Sorted and delivered all incoming mail to the appropriate person.

OFFICE ASSISTANT. Smith University, Scarsdale, NY (1997-99). Worked in a clerical/secretarial capacity while I was pursuing my college education.
- Answered phones for professors; photocopied documents and ran errands.

PERSONAL
Excellent personal and professional references are available upon request.

Date

BY FAX TO: Mrs. Maryanne Snider
District Manager
Pfizer

Dear Mrs. Snider:

With the enclosed resume, I would like to make you aware of my interest in employment as a Pharmaceutical Healthcare Representative with Pfizer. I believe you are aware that Don Smith, one of your Healthcare Representatives, has recommended that I talk with you because he feels that I could excel in the position as Pharmaceutical Healthcare Representative.

As you will see from my enclosed resume, I offer proven marketing and sales skills along with a reputation as a highly motivated individual with exceptional problem-solving skills. Shortly after joining my current firm as a Mortgage Loan Specialist, I was named Outstanding Loan Officer of the month through my achievement in generating more than $20,000 in fees.

I believe much of my professional success so far has been due to my highly motivated nature and creative approach to my job. For example, when I began working for my current employer, I developed and implemented the concept of a postcard which communicated a message which the consumer found intriguing. The concept has been so successful that it has been one of the main sources of advertisements in our office, and the concept has been imitated by other offices in the company.

In addition to my track record of excelling in the highly competitive financial services field, I have also applied my strong leadership and sales ability in the human services field, when I worked in the adult probation services field. I am very proud of the fact that many troubled individuals with whom I worked told me that my ability to inspire and motivate them was the key to their becoming productive citizens.

If you can use a creative and motivated self-starter who could enhance your goals for market share and profitability, I hope you will contact me to suggest a time when we could meet in person to discuss your needs and goals and how I could help you to meet them. I can provide strong personal and professional references at the appropriate time.

Yours sincerely,

Irene S. Lane

IRENE S. LANE

1110½ Hay Street, Fayetteville, NC 28305 • preppub@aol.com • (910) 483-6611

OBJECTIVE   To offer my experience in sales, marketing, and customer service to an organization that would benefit from my aggressive style of developing customer relationships and my desire to work for an organization that seeks to maximize market share and profitability.

EDUCATION   **B.S. in Business Administration,** University of San Diego, CA 1998.
- Completed this degree in my spare time while excelling in my full-time job.

EXPERIENCE   **SENIOR MORTGAGE LOAN SPECIALIST.** First Mortgage Services, San Diego, CA (1997-present). Have continuously excelled in this position which requires excellent sales, customer service, decision making, and problem solving skills.
- In Jan. 2000 was named Outstanding Loan Officer for generating $20,000 in fees.
- Process VA, FHA, conforming, and nonconforming first and second mortgages while handling debt consolidations, refinancing, and other financial arrangements.
- Consult with attorneys, VA and FHA officials, appraisers, and other construction and lending officials in matters related to loan conveyances and loan closings.
- Research property to assess value, ensure liens, and assess credit worthiness of clients.
- Am known for my gracious style of communicating with the public and for my ability to explain technical concepts in language that is understandable to lay people.
- Have gained valuable experience in marketing services which are not well understood by the average consumer.

MORTGAGE LOAN SPECIALIST. Ramsey Mortgage, San Diego, CA (1995-97). Gained expertise in all aspects of mortgage loan processing while becoming an expert in handling slow payments and credit repairs.

ADULT PROBATION SERVICES OFFICER. CA Department of Corrections, San Diego, CA (1990-95). Because of my exceptional work performance, excellent attitude, and superior work performance, was promoted in the following track record:
1994-95: **Adult Intensive Probation Parole Officer.** Was promoted to a supervisory position which involved providing guidance and supervising a case load of 50 clients per week.
- Earned respect for my ability to establish rapport and cordial relationships with a wide variety of individuals from troubled backgrounds and with turbulent case histories.

1990-94: Adult Probation/Parole Officer. Took pride in the fact that an extremely high percentage of my caseload clients completed their probation and went on to become well adjusted and productive citizens; was frequently told that it was my leadership and motivation skills which made the difference in their lives.
- Provided supervision and guidance for up to 150 clients per month who were on court-ordered probation; completed paperwork and reports in a timely fashion.

DEPUTY CLERK. County Clerk of Superior Court, San Diego, CA (1988-90). Processed affidavits for traffic court tickets, misdemeanors, and felonies in the Criminal Division; was known for my professional style of interacting with others.

Other sales experience: Gained sales experience as an Account Representative for a company which sold sleep systems; also worked as a Sales Representative for a company marketing the Canon Facsimile line.

PERSONAL   Enjoy tackling, achieving, and exceeding ambitious goals through my ability to work effectively with others. Excel in prospecting for new business. Resourceful and high energy.

Date

Exact Name of Person
Exact Title or Position
Name of Company
Address (number and street)
Address (city, state, and zip)

Dear Exact Name of Person: (or Dear Sir or Madam if answering a blind ad.)

With the enclosed resume, I would like to formally initiate the process of being considered for a position within your organization which can use my exceptionally strong marketing, communication, and consulting skills.

As you will see from my resume, since earning my B.S. degree in Business Administration with a Marketing major, I have enjoyed a track record of success in highly competitive banking and consumer product environments. Most recently I was named the top producer in my region based on my results in establishing the most new accounts, achieving the highest loan volume, and obtaining the most referrals. In an earlier position, I consistently led my office in sales and received the Sales Leadership award as well as other honors recognizing my aggressive marketing orientation and highly refined customer service skills.

Even in summer and part-time jobs while earning my college degree, I was selected for highly responsible positions at companies including R.J. Reynolds/Nabisco, where I managed 30 employees. My summer jobs prior to college graduation helped me acquire excellent skills in merchandising, marketing, and sales.

If you can use an ambitious, results-oriented marketing professional, I hope you will contact me to suggest a time when we might meet to discuss your needs and goals and how I might help you achieve them.

Sincerely,

Jason Vetter

JASON VETTER

1110½ Hay Street, Fayetteville, NC 28305 • preppub@aol.com • (910) 483-6611

OBJECTIVE

To offer strong marketing and sales experience to an organization in need of a professional with the ability to motivate others to exceed expectations through excellent communication and consulting skills.

EXPERIENCE

ASSISTANT VICE PRESIDENT, CONSUMER BANKING. FirstBank, N.A., Seattle, WA (1996-present). In May, 2000, was ranked the Top Consumer Banker in the Central Washington Region based on my results in establishing the most new accounts, achieving the highest loan volume, and obtaining many referrals.

- Have achieved a record productivity for four years in a row.
- Assisted customers while educating them on the merits of different products such as checking and savings accounts, Certificates of Deposit, and IRAs.
- As a loan officer, met with customers and explained differences between types of loans available and made decisions on their qualifications for loans.

PERSONAL BANKER and **RETAIL MANAGEMENT ASSOCIATE.** Nations Bank of Washington, N.A., Seattle, WA (1995-1996). Achieved record productivity while completing a comprehensive management training program with this major financial institution; maintained and managed a portfolio of approximately 1,000 customers.

- Increased the size of my customer base by 30%.
- Played a key role in achieving the highest number of loan and credit card sales and the highest dollar volume of any branch in the Seattle region (April and May).
- Learned all aspects of banking from teller operations to becoming familiar with investment and loan procedures as well as account management; continued to attend training classes to refine and add to my store of knowledge.
- Emphasized quality customer service and set an example for other bank employees while helping existing customers and selling the bank's services to new ones.
- Supervised teller staff and daily operations; conducted staff sales meetings.

ACCOUNT REPRESENTATIVE. Dictaphone Corporation/Pitney Bowes, Midlands, WA (1994-95). Managed more than 300 new and existing accounts while selling communications equipment including Dictaphone, voice mail, and time management equipment in a three-county area.

- Consistently led the office in sales: received the "Sales Leadership" award for achieving 206% of my quota two months ahead of schedule and later received recognition in the "Achievement Club" for 210% of quota.
- Worked mainly with medical and legal accounts while selling systems valued from $400 to more than $100,000 in a generally long-term sales process.
- Opened more than 25 accounts.

EDUCATION

B.S. in Business Administration, Seattle State University, Seattle, WA, 1993.

- Majored in Marketing; was a member of the American Marketing Association.
- Held leadership roles in Delta Chi Fraternity including vice president and rush coordinator; was honored as "Brother of the Year"; and currently serve as a trustee on the alumni board.

Completed professional development programs related to consumer finance and consumer loans sponsored by FirstBank, 1996-present.

PERSONAL

Have volunteered with the United Way, Hospitality House, and Watauga Hunger Coalition. Knowledgeable of Microsoft Word, Lotus 1-2-3, and dBase III. Excellent references.

Date

Mr. David Smith
District Manager
Quality Booksellers
88 Independence Avenue
New York, NY 12367

**Bookseller and
Store Manager**

Dear Mr. Smith:

Mid-level managers are
often distinguished from
junior managers by their
ability to manage their
careers. In the case of
Delaine Baughman, he is
aggressively pursuing a
management opportunity
with a prestigious
bookseller who is coming to
town to compete. He's now
commuting more than 40
minutes each way to work,
and a job with the new
company would mean
only a five-minute
commute.

With the enclosed resume, I would like to make you aware of my background as
an experienced retail bookstore manager whose proven communication, organizational,
and leadership skills have been tested in a high-volume, large-format environment.

As you will see, I have been with Books-A-Million for some time and have served
in a managerial capacity in the Charleston store. Supervising 18 employees in a store
that averages $2.5 million dollars a year, I have consistently received high marks on all
employee evaluations. Since my promotion to Store Manager, I am responsible for all
aspects of personnel recruitment, staff development, and scheduling.

As Manager, I also act as operations manager, directing day-to-day functions of the
store and assigning tasks to employees. In addition to administering payroll, benefit
and personnel programs, I handle all aspects of the hiring process, and I am proud of the
low turnover I have achieved in a job market with a very high transient rate.

Although I am highly regarded by my present employer and can provide excellent references at the appropriate time, I would like to take on the challenge of a
larger store. I could benefit Quality Booksellers as they enter the Charleston market
through my enthusiasm, high energy level, and "can-do" attitude as well as through my
strong management, staff development, and organizational skills.

If you can use a manager with a strong commitment to providing the highest
possible levels of customer service and the proven ability to motivate employees to achieve
excellence, then I hope you will contact me soon. I can assure you that I have an excellent reputation within the community and could quickly become a valuable addition to
your organization.

Sincerely,

Delaine Baughman

DELAINE BAUGHMAN

1110½ Hay Street, Fayetteville, NC 28305 • preppub@aol.com • (910) 483-6611

OBJECTIVE

To benefit an organization that can use an energetic, self-motivated, and highly experienced bookstore manager with exceptional sales and communication skills as well as the proven ability to positively impact the attitude and performance of employees.

EXPERIENCE

Started with Books-A-Million as a Bookseller and was promoted in the following "track record" of increasing responsibility in this high-volume, large-format store:

1996-present: **STORE MANAGER.** Books-A-Million #4326, Charleston, SC. Advanced to this position when the increase in our sales volume prompted home office to reclassify this as a large-format store; perform all my previous duties while assuming increased responsibilities.

- Direct all aspects of operations of a large-format store averaging $2.5 million per year; supervise an average of 18 employees.
- Develop weekly schedules and prioritize daily tasks, directing each employee's work so that all assignments are accomplished in a timely and accurate manner.
- Promote the highest possible standards of customer service by ensuring compliance with Customer Service Standards and providing a strong example for other employees.
- Oversee and direct ordering, receiving, and returns, ensuring a strong in-stock position on fast-moving titles in spite of the store's small size for its volume and high turn rate.
- Solely responsible for all recruiting, interviewing, hiring, and training of staff members; administer payroll, personnel, and benefit programs; perform employee evaluations.
- Conduct coaching, counseling, and motivational sessions, maintaining employee morale and assisting employees to improve in areas of marginal performance.
- Coordinate special events; actively seeking institutional sales and arranging off-site Book Fairs and in-store author appearances to raise community awareness of Books-A-Million.

1990-96: **ASSISTANT MANAGER.** Books-A-Million #4326, Charleston, SC. Advanced to Assistant Manager from Senior Sales Clerk.

- Assisted the Manager in all aspects of the operations of this high-volume store.
- Prepared and maintained the accuracy of all management-level paperwork to include daily, weekly, and monthly sales reports; completed time sheets and schedules; price changes; book, non-book, and magazine receiving and returns logs, etc.
- Merchandised all areas of the store according to district, region, and chain guidelines; changed weekly best-sellers and power aisles; maintained full and attractive displays throughout the store.

1986-90: **SENIOR SALES CLERK.** Books-A-Million #2102, Charleston, SC. Was promoted to Senior Sales Clerk after only four months with Books-A-Million.

- Performed all the duties of a key holder, opening and closing the store.
- Provided direction to booksellers when no Managers were present.
- Stocked, shelved and merchandised all assigned areas of the store, creating effective displays and keeping all display areas full and attractive.

1985-1986: **BOOKSELLER.** Books-A-Million #4109, Charleston, SC. Responsible for customer service; ringing sales, assisting customers in locating and selecting their purchases, and special ordering titles which were out of stock.

PERSONAL

Excellent personal and professional references are available upon request.

Exact Name of Person
Exact Title
Exact Name of Company
Address
City, State, Zip

Business Equipment Sales in Pursuit of Another Product to Sell

This aggressive professional offers proven sales skills, and he loves sales. His goal now is to find another product or service to sell other than copier equipment. Notice the numerous achievements shown on his resume. Notice, too, that the cover letter does not emphasize "copiers" or the product line he has been selling but rather "sells" him and his abilities.

Dear Exact Name of Person: (or Dear Sir or Madam if answering a blind ad):

With the enclosed resume, I would like to make you aware of my interest in exploring sales opportunities within your company. Although I am excelling in my current position and am held in the highest regard, I am selectively exploring other options.

A graduate of Arizona State University, I am highly skilled in utilizing all Microsoft applications, and I am adept at creating PowerPoint presentations on a laptop computer. After graduating from Arizona State University with a degree in History, I went to work in sales for a company in California, and I quickly discovered that my strong communication and problem-solving skills were highly effective in sales and marketing situations. As a Territory Manager and Sales Associate, I established the company's largest-ever national account which generated business for the company in 48 states. I was awarded numerous honors because of my success in exceeding sales quotas.

I was recruited for my current job in 1998 as a Major Accounts Manager and Sales Representative, and in less than a year I have transformed an unproductive territory in what was considered a "secondary market" into one of the top territories in the nation. I am currently ranked #5 among 1,000 sales representatives in the U.S. and I have won numerous awards in 1999, including a trip to Hawaii which was awarded to only 10 people in the company. I was named Company Sales Representative of the Month in January, March, and August 2000 for achieving the highest sales among my peers.

In my current job I call on major accounts including hospitals, and I have established a strong network of contacts. I am skilled at utilizing every type of sales tool and technique including cold calling, networking through friends and referrals, and developing superior written proposals. I am a highly self-motivated individual who is satisfied with producing no less than the highest-quality results in any project I take on. I have thoroughly enjoyed applying my intellect and intelligence in the sales field, because I have discovered that sales is all about solving problems for people and companies.

If you can use a polished go-getter who would thrive on whatever challenge you place in my path, I hope you will welcome my call soon when I try to arrange a brief meeting to discuss your goals and how my background might serve your needs. I can provide outstanding references at the appropriate time.

Sincerely,

Jacob R. Dixon

JACOB R. DIXON

1110½ Hay Street, Fayetteville, NC 28305   •   preppub@aol.com   •   (910) 483-6611

OBJECTIVE

To benefit an organization that can use an aggressive young sales professional and highly effective communicator with the proven ability to exceed ambitious goals while maximizing profitability and assuring the highest level of customer service, support, and satisfaction.

EDUCATION

Bachelor of Arts in History, Arizona State University, Phoenix, AZ, 1995.
Studied abroad through the Arizona State University program in Valencia, Spain, 1993-94.
Extensive courses related to sales including Solution Selling II, and Advance System Selling.

COMPUTERS

Highly computer proficient with all Microsoft applications; am skilled in creating PowerPoint presentations for customers on a laptop computer; work with Microsoft and Novell Computer Networks in the process of installing new products and add-ons to computer networks.

EXPERIENCE

MAJOR ACCOUNTS MANAGER & SALES REPRESENTATIVE. Effective Business Solutions, Scottsdale, AZ (1998-present). Took an unproductive territory in what is considered a "secondary market" and have transformed it into one of the top territories in the nation in only one year.

- Am **ranked #5 among nearly 1,000 U.S. corporate sales representatives,** and am currently the top sales producer in my area after only a short time with the company.
- Have exceeded year-to-date quota by 155% of which $393,000 (or 98%) was new business.
- Have already won the **National Sales Award for 2000,** a trip to Hawaii awarded to only 10 people nationwide; previously won a trip to Colorado and was one of only 15 reps to win that trip based on second quarter sales.
- After only nine months with the company, received the prestigious **Century Club Gold Level Ring Award,** an award recognizing $200,000 in sales which normally takes an individual 1 ½ years to achieve.
- Named **Company Sales Representative of the Month in January, March, and August 2000,** for producing the highest monthly sales of all reps.
- Call on hospitals and other institutional buyers as well as businesses of all sizes while prospecting for new business and establishing highly profitable new accounts; have established a network of contacts within the medical community and hospitals.
- Call on large companies in 18 counties in Arizona; have increased market share dramatically and have significantly grown the customer base while consistently exceeding my sales quota of $33,333/month.

TERRITORY MANAGER & SALES ASSOCIATE. Better Business Information Systems, Inc., San Francisco, CA (1996-98). Prospected for new customers in eight zip code areas while servicing 400 existing accounts; became skilled in utilizing every sales tool and technique including cold calling, writing proposals, and networking through friends and referrals.

- **Established the company's largest-ever national account.**
- Exceeded year-to-date sales goals by $178,000 (218% of quota).
- Was the recipient of the **Century Club Award** for exceeding $100,000 in sales, May 1998; was awarded the President's Club Vacation for excellence in work performance, March 1998; was named a member of the **President's Club** in 1996, 1997, and 1998; received the **Nifty-Nifty Award** for exceeding $50,000 in sales for May, April, and January 1998 as well as October and April, 1997.
- Was **Salesman of the Month,** May 1998 as well as December and April 1997.

PERSONAL

Thrive on the challenge of solving customer problems. Highly motivated self-starter.

Exact Name of Person
Title or Position
Name of Company
Address (number and street)
Address (city, state, and zip)

Business Sales and Management

This successful entrepreneur started a lawn and garden business which grossed $250,000 in its fourth year. She could stay comfortably where she is, but she finds herself in a small town missing the "action" of a larger company and a larger town. She has decided to sell her business and job-hunt in a large metropolitan area, and she is seeking a position where she can utilize her sales abilities.

Dear Exact Name of Person: (or Sir or Madam if answering a blind ad.)

With the enclosed resume, I would like to acquaint you with my background and begin the process of exploring opportunities within your organization which could utilize my versatile strengths in management, marketing, and financial control.

As you will see from my resume, after graduating from Alabama University I obtained my Real Estate Broker's License and was consistently in the Top Ten in my county with sales and listings of over $5 million annually. After a sustained track record of outstanding performance, I became involved in large-scale industrial development; I initiated and directed the design of a high-tech digital global telecommunications system which required me to organize extensive collaboration and cooperation among engineers from various competing telecommunications giants. With a partner, I pioneered the concept of and then developed Alabama's first "business incubator" for start-up businesses; after we transformed the concept into a successful operating reality, I became a consultant to 25 foreign countries and a guest lecturer on entrepreneurism at Alabama University's School of Business.

Subsequently, I was recruited by a consulting firm to market and sell industrial buildings and sites for clients such as Burlington Industries, Cone Mills, Jefferson Pilot, and NationsBank. In addition to utilizing my strong negotiating and communication skills, I was involved in planning Alabama's largest commercial development, and I provided leadership in creating a state-of-the-art retirement community based on extensive input from both the public and private sectors.

Most recently I have utilized my proven visionary thinking skills and creative conceptual abilities in simultaneous jobs as a Business Manager/Property Manager and General Manager for two separate businesses. Although I am excelling in handling these responsibilities, I am eager to take on new challenges. I am single and will cheerfully relocate and travel as your needs require. With an outstanding personal and professional reputation, I offer a proven ability to take an idea and transform it into a viable operating entity.

I could make valuable contributions to your organization, and I hope you will contact me. I have a strong bottom-line orientation and outstanding references.

Sincerely,

Martha Woolcott

MARTHA WOOLCOTT

1110½ Hay Street, Fayetteville, NC 28305 • preppub@aol.com • (910) 483-6611

OBJECTIVE

To benefit an organization that can use a creative problem-solver and resourceful manager with excellent negotiating skills along with a proven ability to transform ideas into operating realities while maximizing profitability and satisfying customers.

EDUCATION

B.S. in Political Science, *magna cum laude*, Alabama University, Macon, AL, 1980. Numerous executive development courses in communication/supervision, 1980-1997.

AFFILIATIONS

Have been prominent as a leader in state, local, and business organizations:
- Appointed to a Macon County Strategic Planning Commission; was active in site selection for a major shopping center; recruited new business to the county; and am developing feasibility plans for a small industrial and business park.
- Developed Alabama's first business incubator for start-up businesses; became a leading spokesperson in the state for entrepreneurial development and also became a consultant on the federal and state level to 25 foreign countries.
- Sold 2,000 acres of land for construction of an innovative and comprehensive new retirement community after working extensively with legislators, retirement groups, and numerous public officials to sell them on the concept.

EXPERIENCE

Am excelling in management roles in two separate organizations:
1993-present: **GENERAL MANAGER.** Quality Lawn & Garden, Macon, AL. Combined my strategic planning skills with my management ability in identifying a need and a niche for this successful business; started "from scratch" a business which grossed $250,000 in its fourth year.
- Manage a diversified company which provides landscaping services to 50 new homes annually while managing a retail garden center which sells top-quality trees, flowers, and gardening supplies; also operate a related side business which rakes, bales, and markets 50,000 bales of pine straw a year.
- Hired, trained, and managed a work force of between 6-10 employees.

1991-present: **BUSINESS MANAGER/PROPERTY MANAGER.** Bryson's, Inc., Macon, AL. Represent a diversified multiplex consisting of a furniture store, grocery store, and rental properties; negotiated the multimillion-dollar sale of 200 acres of prime commercial property; developed infrastructure plans and obtained permits/inspections in spite of complicated county procedures.
- Sold prime commercial sites for a service station and an auto parts business.

VICE PRESIDENT & BROKER. XYZ Industrial Relations, Lincoln, AL (1986-91). Marketed and sold industrial buildings and sites for such clients as Burlington Industries, Cone Mills, Jefferson Pilot, and NationsBank while providing the key leadership in two major projects:
- *Project 1:* Assembled a 28,000-acre parcel of land, devised plan for infrastructure and funding and then wrote and presented a proposal to the Governor for Alabama's largest planned commercial development.
- *Project 2:* Pioneered the development of new concepts now routinely used in many retirement communities; obtained several patents on designs for handicapped bathrooms and kitchens while also inventing new concepts in financing retirement living which banks and insurance companies now accept; sold 2,000 acres of land for a new "model" retirement village after engaging public and private sector leaders in "think-tank" activities which ultimately led to their support of the project.

REAL ESTATE BROKER. Trainor Realtors, Duluth, AL (1981-86). Was consistently in the Top Ten in the county in sales and listings with over $5 million annually.

PERSONAL

Can provide outstanding personal and professional references. Single and will relocate.

Date

Exact Name of Person
Title or Position
Name of Company
Address (number and street)
Address (city, state, and zip)

Dear Sir or Madam:

With the enclosed resume, I would like to make you aware of my interest in exploring opportunities with MCI in the Columbia area. I would like to relocate to Columbia for family reasons, and I would very much like to continue my distinguished track record of employment with MCI.

As you will see from my resume, I have worked for MCI in a call center environment in Portland, OR. I began as a Sales Representative and was promoted to Customer Service Representative and Sales Manager. In my current position, I handle escalated calls on a daily basis, and I have become known for my tactful and resourceful style of dealing with the public when a customer situation requires the intervention of a manager. I have received three Customer Commendations from customers who have written to voluntarily praise my initiative and effectiveness in resolving their problems. I have also received three Outstanding Sales Awards for excellent performance in sales as well as a "MCI Values Excellence" on-the-spot award from my coworkers.

In my previous positions prior to joining MCI, I refined my communication and problem-solving skills working in human services, employment services, and medical insurance services. In those fast-paced environments, I learned to make rapid decisions under tight deadlines, and I refined my ability to work with the public. In one job in a medical insurance organization, I began as a Claims Clerk and Receptionist and was rapidly promoted to Lead Administrative Assistant in charge of five people while we worked as a team to support a 20-person sales staff.

Since joining MCI, I have excelled in all aspects of working in sales and in a call center environment. I have completed numerous training courses sponsored by MCI, and I have also completed numerous courses in my spare time in order to strengthen my customer service and management skills.

I hope you will contact me if you can use my experience and expertise in your Columbia office. I would be delighted to make myself available for a personal interview at your convenience. You may feel free to call me at my work number, which I have provided on my resume along with my home number.

Sincerely,

Lucille E. Madoff

LUCILLE E. MADOFF

1110½ Hay Street, Fayetteville, NC 28305   •   preppub@aol.com   •   (910) 483-6611

OBJECTIVE   To benefit an organization that can use a highly experienced customer service and sales professional with call center expertise who offers a proven ability to resolve customer problems.

EDUCATION   Completed two years of college courses toward Bachelor of Science degree in Psychology with minor in Personnel and Organizational Leadership, Oregon State University, Corvallis, OR.
   • Completing degree in my spare time as my demanding work schedule permits.

TRAINING   Excelled in these and other training programs at MCI's University of Excellence:

Telephone Techniques-Determining Caller Needs   Telephone Techniques-Curt to Courteous
LTD Consumer Features-Phase I & II   Telephone Techniques-Incoming Calls
Telephone Techniques-Five Forbidden Phrases   Extraordinary Customer Relations
Incoming Demand Service Representative-Sales   Developing MCI Leaders
Basic Telephony   The MCI Story
Selling Naturally   Windows/Excel: Parts I & II
MCI ION General Overview   Big Eight—NCO Certification

   • On my own initiative, have attended seminars to refine my management and communication skills which included: The Organized Employee; Telephone Skills; Non-Violent Crisis Intervention; Diamonds in the Ruff

EXPERIENCE   Have excelled in a track record of promotion with MCI, Portland, OR (1998-present).
   March 2000-present: CUSTOMER SERVICE REPRESENTATIVE & SALES MANAGER. Was promoted to oversee other customer service representatives and to provide a management presence in difficult customer situations.
   • Have received three **Customer Commendations** from customers who voluntarily wrote to MCI describing my initiative and resourcefulness in resolving their problems; have received three **Outstanding Sales Awards** for my excellent performance on a team which exceeded sales objectives in March, July, and November 2000. Also received an **"MCI Values Excellence"** on-the-spot award from my coworkers.
   • Handle escalated calls on a daily basis.
   • Assist with training of new hires; provide individual development training requested by managers.
   • Consult on customer account/billing scenarios and handle scheduling.
   • Work closely with Pic Lab to identify and correct system errors/glitches.

   1998-March 2000: SALES REPRESENTATIVE. Began with MCI in this job in which I was the primary contact with customers for new service or for changes in existing service; educated the public as I marketed Local Telephone Division (LTD) products and services, long distance, PCS wireless, and Earthlink (ISP) services.
   • Consulted on customer account/billing scenarios.
   • Consistently achieved 150% of my sales objectives monthly.

   HUMAN RESOURCES TECHNICIAN. Oregon Behavioral Services, Eugene, OR (1997-98). Worked one-on-one with children diagnosed with behavioral problems using positive reinforcement to change their behavior; documented behavior patterns and reaction to stimuli.

PERSONAL   Can provide outstanding personal and professional references. Will relocate and travel as extensively as my employer's needs require. Known as outgoing, reliable, courteous individual with impeccable character, unlimited initiative, and a desire to create value.

Exact Name of Person
Title or Position
Name of Company
Address (number and street)
Address (city, state, and ZIP)

Catering and Dining Services Manager

This is an excellent example of an all-purpose resume and cover letter. The cover letter is designed to make this individual appealing to employers in numerous industries, and the Objective on the resume highlights skills and abilities which are transferable to all types of work environments. Notice how the Personal Section of the resume emphasizes his ability to adapt easily to new environments—a subtle hint that he is in career change.

Dear Exact Name of Person: (or Dear Sir or Madam if answering a blind ad.)

Can you use an articulate, detail-oriented professional who offers outstanding abilities in the areas of sales program development and management, financial management, and the training and supervision of employees?

You will see by my enclosed resume that I have built a track record of accomplishments with Holiday Inn Management Services where I am currently the Account Director at Yale University in New Haven, CT. During my six years in this position I have reduced labor costs and increased auxiliary sales while overseeing a program with a $900,000 annual operating budget. I oversee two supervisors and a 30-person staff which provides resident dining, catering, conference, and retail dining services on a private college campus.

In addition to my business, inventory control, personnel, and human resources management responsibilities, I also am heavily involved in the development and management of promotional materials and programs. I have refined natural verbal and written communication skills while acting as liaison between corporate headquarters and the university, training and dealing with employees, and handling customer service activities.

I believe that you would find me to be an articulate professional with the ability to learn quickly and apply my organizational skills and common sense.

I hope you will welcome my call soon to arrange a brief meeting at your convenience to discuss your current and future needs and how I might serve them. Thank you in advance for your time.

Sincerely yours,

Callahan Warren

Alternate last paragraph:
I hope you will call or write me soon to suggest a time convenient for us to meet and discuss your current and future needs and how I might serve them. Thank you in advance for your time.

CALLAHAN WARREN

1110½ Hay Street, Fayetteville, NC 28305 • preppub@aol.com • (910) 483-6611

OBJECTIVE

To offer my expertise in reducing costs as well as increasing profits and customer satisfaction while displaying exceptional sales, leadership, and financial management abilities and refining organizational, training, and time management skills.

EXPERIENCE

Built a track record of accomplishments with Holiday Inn Management Services at Yale University, New Haven, CT:

SALES MANAGER & ACCOUNT DIRECTOR. (1996-present). In this role, have reduced total labor costs more than $96,000 while operating a $900,000 program providing this campus with resident dining, catering, conference, and retail dining services.

- Provided outstanding customer satisfaction in all areas of dining services with a staff of two supervisors and approximately 30 employees.
- Increased Operating Profit Contributions (OPC) from $25,000 to $90,000 and auxiliary sales to more than $228,000 by identifying opportunities, developing strategy, and implementing new plans.
- Polished managerial abilities while developing budgets and business plans along with making revisions in procedures which led to increases in sales and production.
- Managed a procurement program for more than 1,000 line items.
- Reconciled profit and loss statements and balance sheet management.
- Supervised accounts payable and receivable, payroll, and weekly financial reports sent to the corporate office while acting as liaison between the corporation and client.
- Assisted the regional sales director in the development of sales proposals by using sales and cost analysis modules.
- Used my communication skills to prepare brochures, calendars, and other promotional materials as well as in the development of a client communication manual.

FOOD SERVICE MANAGER. (1993-96). Gained exposure to a wide range of day-to-day operational activities related to campus dining, catering, and conference food services.

- Applied time management and organizational skills overseeing fiscal areas of operations which included purchasing as well as inventory, labor cost, and cash-handling controls.
- Handled additional activities ranging from vendor specifications, to menu development and implementation, to promotions and marketing, to catering, to sanitation and safety.
- Updated the automated procedures which reduced unit labor costs.
- Implemented a computerized system used to handle associate payroll, accounts payable, accounts receivable, and billing.

MANAGEMENT TRAINEE. (1993). As a food service management trainee, became familiar with customer service, scheduling, and employee training.

STUDENT MANAGER. Holiday Inn Management Services, Davis University, Augusta, SC (1992). Hired by the corporation while attending the university, was in charge of food-handling controls and supervised 10 part-time employees.

EDUCATION & TRAINING

B.A., Business Administration (minors: Marketing and Finance), Davis University, SC, 1992. Completed extensive corporate training programs in major areas of emphasis including:

Public relations	Safety training	Human resource management
Sales & cost analysis	Internal accounting systems	Labor productivity I and II
Total Quality Management 1 and II		Diversity/sensitivity training
Hazard Analysis Critical Control Points (HACCP)		Food handling/food-borne illness

CERTIFICATION

Am a licensed food handler with certification in food-borne illness.

PERSONAL

Fast learner capable of easily adjusting to new environments. Excellent references.

Date

Exact Name of Person
Title or Position
Name of Company
Address (number and street)
Address (city, state, and zip)

Commercial Products Sales

This talented individual could do many things—and has done many things, including founding a successful company. Now he has decided that he wishes to pursue a career in sales and marketing, so this resume and cover letter emphasize his dynamic personality, sales accomplishments, and marketing know-how rather than his management abilities. (He has decided that he would rather not manage other people, if he can avoid it!)

Postscript: This is a good resume to illustrate how to make the decision about whether to put the Education or Experience section after the Objective. If your experience is more impressive than your education (as his is), then put your Experience section ahead of Education on your resume.

Dear Exact Name of Person: (or Sir or Madam if answering a blind ad.)

With the enclosed resume, I would like to formally make you aware of my interest in your organization. As you will see, I have excelled in jobs which required originality and creativity in prospecting for new clients, business savvy and financial prudence in establishing new ventures, as well as relentless follow-through and attention to detail in implementing ambitious goals.

I was recruited for my current job when the company decided that it wanted to set up a new commercial division and needed someone with proven entrepreneurial skills and a make-it-happen style. Under my leadership we have set up a new commercial division which has targeted the healthcare and pharmaceutical industry as a primary customer base in addition to major financial institutions and large corporations. Although I now manage several individuals, I personally prospected for the initial accounts and I discovered that my extensive training and background related to chemicals and microbiology was of great value in interacting with healthcare industry decision makers.

Although I can provide outstanding personal and professional references and am being groomed for further promotion within my company, I have decided that I wish to transfer my skills and knowledge to the healthcare industry. You will notice from my resume that I have been a successful entrepreneur and previously started a company which I sold to a larger industry firm. I succeeded as an entrepreneur largely because of my ability to communicate ideas to others, my strong problem-solving skills, and my naturally outgoing and self-confident nature. I am certain I could excel in the healthcare industry in any role which requires extraordinary sales, marketing, and relationship-building abilities.

If my background interests you, and if you feel there is a suitable position in your organization in which you could make use of my sales and marketing strengths, I hope you will contact me to suggest a time when we might meet to discuss your goals and how I might help you achieve them. Thank you in advance for your consideration and professional courtesies.

Yours sincerely,

Parsival Flanagan

PARSIVAL FLANAGAN

1110½ Hay Street, Fayetteville, NC 28305 • preppub@aol.com • (910) 483-6611

OBJECTIVE

To contribute to an organization that can use a dynamic professional who wishes to transfer my exceptionally strong sales and marketing abilities to the pharmaceutical industry.

EXPERIENCE

MANAGER, COMMERCIAL DIVISION. Drayton Enterprises, Augusta, ME (1995-present). Was aggressively recruited by this company which wanted to establish a new commercial division targeting the healthcare and pharmaceutical industry as a primary client base; provided the leadership in developing the strategic plan for the new division which has annual revenues of more than half a million dollars; now manage several technicians and sales reps.
- Personally prospected for all the initial accounts.
- Utilized my background and extensive training in chemicals and microbiology to facilitate my sales effectiveness in the healthcare and pharmaceutical industry.
- Excelled in building relationships through creative lead generation, astute needs assessment and fulfillment, and strong skills in closing the sale.

FOUNDER/PRESIDENT. Termites Undone, Inc., Richmond, VA (1988-94). Started "from scratch" a company which was bought out by one of the largest pest elimination service companies in the country.
- Succeeded as an entrepreneur and business manager in a highly competitive industry because of my ability to communicate ideas to others, my problem-solving skills, my ability to formulate new ideas based on information obtained from multiple sources, and my outgoing and self-confident nature.
- Handled all financial matters including budgets, profit-and-loss quotas, tax planning, insurance, and purchasing.
- Acquired considerable experience in dealing with government regulatory agencies and in preparing the paperwork necessary to document programs in critical situations.

VICE PRESIDENT OF SALES AND TRAINING. Dana Exterminating Company, Inc., Augusta, GA (1980-88). Was a major force in the company's growth for over eight years; helped establish formal training and hiring policies.
- Began in sales and in my fourth year was promoted to supervisor responsible for 15 individuals, project management, as well as equipment maintenance and troubleshooting.
- In my fifth year was promoted to **Vice President of Sales & Training** responsible for setting/achieving branch goals, defining/implementing training programs, as well as overseeing safety and vehicle/equipment maintenance.

EDUCATION

More than two years of college coursework at **Maine University;** courses included biology and social sciences, accounting and economics.
- Corporate sales and technical training sponsored by leading firms.

PERSONAL

Business skills include marketing and sales, starting up new business operations, selecting and training employees, controlling inventory, purchasing materials, preparing strategic plans, dealing with regulators, accounting and financial control.

Date

Exact Name of Person
Exact Title
Exact Name of Company
Address (number and street)
Address (city, state, and zip)

Communications Sales

Dear Sir or Madam:

This young professional
has specialized in
telecommunications sales
and is seeking to explore
opportunities with other
industry firms. He is not
certain whether he wants
to take on a high-powered
sales job or pursue a sales
management position.

With the enclosed resume, I would like to introduce you to my background as an articulate young professional who offers a track record of advancement and exceptional sales, organizational, and customer service skills which have allowed me to prosper in challenging telecommunications environments.

As you will see from my resume, I am currently excelling as Regional Sales Manager in a two-state region for a large telecommunications/paging services company. When I took over this operation, our dealer accounts were lagging far behind forecasted sales levels; by creating an entirely new plan for our dealer format and implementing innovative new marketing plans, our dealer sales have more than tripled. Prior to this position, I was asked by the owner of the company to assume the leadership role in our Bedford location, which he was on the verge of closing due to its poor performance. Within a matter of months I had uncovered and resolved most of the problems contributing to the store's decline and was producing the highest profit and the largest net gain of any retail location.

In these and earlier positions, I have shown a commitment to excellence and a work ethic which resulted in unusually rapid advancement with my employers. My exceptional customer service skills, sales and problem-solving ability, and strong bottom-line orientation have contributed to my continued success and that of my employers. But I feel that it is my willingness to do whatever is required to ensure the company's goals are met that has been the key to my achievements.

If you can use an accomplished young professional with proven ability in sales, customer service, and management, then I hope you will welcome my call soon when I try to arrange a brief meeting to discuss your goals and how my background might serve your needs. I can provide outstanding references at the appropriate time.

Sincerely,

Adam Henke

ADAM HENKE

1110½ Hay Street, Fayetteville, NC 28305 • preppub@aol.com • (910) 483-6611

OBJECTIVE   To benefit an organization that can use an articulate communicator and accomplished young professional with exceptional organizational and problem-solving skills who offers a track record of success in sales, account management, personnel management, and telemarketing.

EDUCATION   Completed two years of college course work in prelaw, Leavonworth College, Alstead, NH.

EXPERIENCE   *With Northstar Communications, have advanced to positions of increasing responsibility while playing a key role in increasing sales and profitability:*

2000-present: REGIONAL SALES MANAGER. Manchester, NH. Promoted after excelling as General Store Manager and Area Sales Manager; tripled dealer sales while servicing existing accounts, developing new business, and reviving dormant accounts in New Hampshire and Vermont.

- Perform account management for more than 100 dealers in a two-state region; provide inventory management, ordering, and pricing for each store.
- Develop innovative and effective marketing plans, creating different promotions for each distinct market area; deliver and set up point-of-purchase (POP) displays.
- Track dealer's customer payments and sales figures; collect on account balances.
- Completely redesigned the dealer program, authoring new policies and procedures as well as creating and implementing new marketing concepts.
- Organized a sales seminar for clients, to increase market penetration and profitability by ensuring that all components of the sales force are presenting our services effectively.
- Reversed declining dealer sales, effecting a 55% increase in only three months; rebuilt the company's reputation and established rapport with previously dissatisfied customers.

1998-2000: GENERAL STORE MANAGER. Bedford, NH. While simultaneously serving as Regional Manager for a two-state market, orchestrated a complete turnaround in sales and profitability in the Bedford retail location by providing strong leadership, accountability, and controlling inventory and labor costs.

- Directed the sales and support staff; interviewed, hired, and trained new employees as well as developing work schedules based on sales forecasts to control labor costs.
- Maintained careful control over inventory management, tracking sales to determine appropriate stock levels and overseeing all ordering of merchandise.
- Implemented stronger loss prevention measures, including general preventive methods and documentation and accountability procedures which decreased employee theft.
- Became adept at resolving problems with difficult customers in a tactful manner.
- Updated and maintained a customer database of more than 2,000 customers; turned around this troubled operation and increased store profit by 7.25%.

1998: AREA SALES MANAGER and CUSTOMER SERVICE REPRESENTATIVE. Swanzey, NH. Hired as a Customer Service Representative, was quickly promoted to manage an established account list of 25 dealers while developing new business; set up point-of-purchase displays and delivered products throughout the Swanzey area.

- Tracked and logged repair requests, sales request and activations, and account orders; performed inventory management and collections on account balances.
- Built excellent working relationships with new and existing clients; developed an excellent rapport with several clients that had been considered "difficult."

PERSONAL   Excellent personal and professional references are available upon request.

Date

Exact Name of Person
Exact Title
Exact Name of Organization
Address
City, State Zip

Dear Exact Name: (or Dear Sir or Madam)

With the enclosed resume, I would like to make you aware of my strong interest in the job of Pharmaceutical Sales Representative. It has been my goal for some time to enter the field of pharmaceutical sales, and I believe you will see from my resume that I offer skills and experience which could make me very successful in the job.

In my current job as Unit Business Manager with Proctor & Gamble, I am excelling in an outside sales position which involves calling on the buyers for chains and retail stores and military accounts in a territory which covers 35 counties in Virginia. My territory includes 100 retail stores, 9 indirect headquarters, and three military retail commissaries. Because of my persistence and initiative, I have been responsible for numerous accomplishments including achieving the distribution of **all** new items in **all** stores; increasing the facings for **all** Proctor & Gamble brands in **all** stores. I have also achieved "gold standard placement" for **all** Proctor & Gamble brands while achieving the suggested retail price for **all** Proctor & Gamble brands in **all** accounts.

Most of my success in my current job has been due to my enthusiastic attention to detail as well as my relentless persistence of the highest goals. Especially in my military accounts, I had to compete against strongly entrenched competitors who had been in the business for more than 20 years. Persistence and relentless marketing paid off, and I have succeeded in obtaining more than my fair share of shelf space for Proctor & Gamble despite stiff competition and strongly entrenched traditions.

In my previous job as a National Account Representative with American Careers, I achieved 130% of my sales goal in my first full year while also being honored as "Job Fair Coordinator of the Year" for my efforts in planning and coordinating the Houston job fair.

I hope you will contact me to suggest a time when we might meet to discuss your needs and goals and how I might help you achieve them. I can provide excellent references, and I thank you in advance for your time.

Yours sincerely,

Sharron A. Howard

SHARRON ANN HOWARD

1110½ Hay Street, Fayetteville, NC 28305 • preppub@aol.com • (910) 483-6611

OBJECTIVE

To apply my sales and communication abilities to an organization in need of a mature young sales professional who offers a talent for training and teaching others as well as a reputation as a creative thinker and good listener with a high level of enthusiasm and energy.

EDUCATION

Bachelor's degree, Elementary Education, the College of Fairfax, Fairfax, VA, 1996.

EXPERIENCE

UNIT BUSINESS MANAGER (OUTSIDE SALES). Proctor & Gamble, Arlington, VA (1999-present). Am excelling in an outside sales position which involves calling on the buyers for grocery store chains and their retail stores in a territory which covers 35 counties in Virginia; my territory includes 100 retail stores, 9 indirect headquarters calls for grocery store chains, and three military commissaries.

- Plan and organize my time and schedule appointments for maximum profitability.
- When calling on retailers, maintain vigilant control of pricing, missing items, new opportunities to sell newly approved products, correct implementation of planogram and stock rotation, and problems or opportunities created by new competitive activity.
- When calling on indirect headquarters, am skilled in presenting new items, negotiating where that item would be placed in the appropriate category, developing pricing, ensuring a full share of shelf on planograms, and coordinating promotions with appropriate retail reductions.
- When calling on military accounts, am responsible for managing vendor stockers at each account; as a Unit Business Manager, am responsible for hiring my own vendor stockers and paying them according to how many cases they stock on the shelves. Develop incentives to encourage vendor stockers to stock as many cases as possible.
- Have excelled in selling to military accounts despite the overwhelming competition and have succeeded in obtaining more than my fair share of shelf space even though I was competing against two competitors who had been in the business for more than 20 years.

Accomplishments:
- Achieved distribution of all new items in all stores.
- Increased facings for all Proctor & Gamble brands in all stores.
- Achieved gold standard placement for all Proctor & Gamble brands.
- Achieved suggested retail price for all Proctor & Gamble brands in all accounts.

NATIONAL ACCOUNT REPRESENTATIVE. American Careers, Arlington, VA (1997-99). Achieved 130% of my sales goal my first full year and excelled in maintaining existing accounts and establishing new ones through my strong communication skills and professional approach.

- Achieved the honor of "Job Fair Coordinator of the Year" for my efforts in planning and coordinating the Houston job fair within my first six months with the company.
- Was consistently ranked in the company's "top ten" sales professionals.

SALES REPRESENTATIVE. The Fairfax Times, Fairfax, VA (1995-97). Learned to use my persuasiveness and sales abilities while calling customers on the phone and letting them know the cost of subscriptions.

SALES REPRESENTATIVE. The Puppet Barn, Fairfax, VA (1995). Refined my sales skills working independently by setting up a booth and making attractive displays and then demonstrating different puppets for sale.

PERSONAL

Highly self motivated, resourceful, and well organized with strong bottom-line focus.

Date

Exact Name of Person
Title or Position
Name of Company
Address (number and street)
Address (city, state, and zip)

**Consumer Products Sales,
Transitioning from Buying
to Sales**

This young professional
actually offers more
experience in purchasing
than in sales, but sales is
what he wants to do. He
is hoping to convince an
employer to see his sales
potential. Many
employers feel that
employees succeed
because of their highly
motivated nature, and
many employers will see
the relevance of his
buying background as an
advantage in sales.

Dear Exact Name of Person: (or Sir or Madam if answering a blind ad.)

With the enclosed resume, I would like to initiate the process of being considered for employment within your organization. Because of family ties, I am in the process of relocating to the San Diego area. Although I already have a San Diego address which is shown on my resume, it is my sister's home and I would prefer your contacting me at the e-mail address shown on my resume or at my current telephone number if you wish to talk with me.

Since graduating from the University of Iowa in 1993, I have a track record of rapid promotion with a corporation headquartered in Bladen, IA. I began as an Assistant Branch Manager and Head Buyer, was cross-trained as a Sales Representative, and have been promoted to my current position in which I manage the selling process related to 3,500 different products. In that capacity, I am entrusted with the responsibility for nearly $15 million in annual expenditures, and I maintain excellent working relationships with more than 150 vendors of name-brand consumer products sold through chain and convenience stores.

In my job, rapid change is a daily reality, and I have become accustomed to working in an environment in which I must make rapid decisions while weighing factors including forecasted consumer demand, distribution patterns, inventory turnover patterns, and vendor capacity and character. I have earned a reputation as a persuasive communicator and savvy negotiator with an aggressive bottom-line orientation.

If you can use my versatile experience in sales, purchasing, distribution, and operations management, I hope you will contact me to suggest a time when we might meet to discuss your needs and how I might serve them. I can provide excellent personal and professional references, and I assure you in advance that I am a hard worker who is accustomed to being measured according to ambitious goals for profitability in a highly competitive marketplace.

Yours sincerely,

Charles Granquist

CHARLES GRANQUIST

1110½ Hay Street, Fayetteville, NC 28305   •   preppub@aol.com   •   (910) 483-6611

OBJECTIVE

To contribute to an organization that can use a resourceful manager with proven skills in managing the selling process while prudently overseeing inventory carrying costs, maintaining excellent working relationships with vendors, and preparing strategic plans.

EDUCATION

B.S. in Business Administration, University of Iowa, Bladen, IA, 1993.
- Dr. Philip and Betsey Davis Scholarship award recipient.

EXPERIENCE

MIDLAND DOMINION DISTRIBUTORS (1994-present): Since graduating from the University of Iowa, have a track record of success and rapid promotion with Midland Dominion Distributors, a company with seven locations throughout the Midwest, headquartered in Bladen, IA:

HEAD BUYER. Bladen, IA. (1996-present). Personally handle more than half of the buying for a company which purchases up to $25 million annually in consumer products which are then distributed to the consumer through chain and convenience stores.
- Develop and sustain effective working relationships with more than 150 vendors including Hershey, Nabisco Foods, Quaker, and other vendors of name-brand juices, candy, health and beauty aids, and groceries.
- Maintain extensive liaison with sales representatives; coordinate contests and promotions for sales representatives and customers.
- Attend national trade shows and buying conventions.
- Was commended for playing a key role in my branch's being named "Branch of the Year" in 2000.
- Am responsible for prudently managing the selling process and making astute buying decisions related to 3,500 products in a highly competitive market in which rapid turnover is critical.

HEAD BUYER. Walton, IA (1995-96). Reported directly to the Vice President while handling the buying of more than $10 million worth of merchandise annually; purchased products supplied to five locations in Iowa from the Walton location.
- Established and maintained excellent working relationships with 50 vendors while purchasing juices, candy, health and beauty aids, and other consumer products.
- Was commended for my excellent decision-making ability in forecasting inventory needs and purchasing products on a timely basis at lowest cost; made weekly buying decisions.
- Maintained a close working relationship with warehouse managers to ensure inventory accuracy.
- Organized deliveries of products to locations served by the Walton branch.
- Conducted semiannual inventory of the Walton location.
- Maintained strict accountability; entered receiving documents into computer to update inventory status daily and reconciled all invoices monthly. Monitored inventory turnover.
- Learned to resourcefully troubleshoot a wide variety of inventory problems.

BUYER & ASSISTANT BRANCH MANAGER. Bladen, IA (1994-95).
Became skilled in buying groceries and tobacco products while also functioning in the role of **Sales Representative**; was cross-trained as a Route Sales Representative.

AFFILIATIONS

Member, Leadership Development Division, a national group of young executives
Member, Delta Sigma Pi, a professional business fraternity

COMPUTERS

Lotus, Microsoft Excel, Microsoft Word, Harvard Graphics, and WordPerfect for Windows

Date

Exact Name of Person
Exact Title
Exact Name of Company
Address
City, State, Zip

Dear Exact Name of Person (or Dear Sir or Madam if answering a blind ad):

With the enclosed resume, I would like to make you aware of my extensive cosmetics and cosmetology knowledge as well as my desire to put that knowledge to work for your organization in some role in which I could contribute to your bottom line.

As you will see from my resume, I have completed extensive training related to numerous premier-line cosmetics courses and seminars from cosmetics industry firms such as Lancôme, Mary Kay, Aveda, Sebastian/Trucco, and Goldwell. I am a Colorado State Board licensed Cosmetologist, and I am the graduate of a 1,500-hour Cosmetology certification course. I also hold an Associate of Arts degree in Fashion Merchandising.

Currently working as a freelance Beauty Consultant/Makeup Artist, I worked previously for Lancôme Cosmetics in California and Nevada, where I created innovative displays and merchandising concepts while coordinating fashion shows and special events to market Lancôme products. I also worked for Lancôme Cosmetics in Colorado, where I played a key role on a sales team which generated the highest sales of all military exchanges in the U.S.

In earlier experience in the cosmetology industry, I excelled as a Cosmetologist with Galliard's Hair Design in Colorado and I also worked in Nebraska as a Salon Manager and Cosmetologist. While at the Marriott Grand Hotel & Salon in Lincoln, NE, I interviewed and hired employees while managing all aspects of a salon catering to high-end customers.

If you can use my considerable sales and customer service experience, I hope you will contact me to suggest a time when we might meet to discuss your needs. I can assure you in advance that I can provide excellent references.

Sincerely,

Samantha T. Yurko

SAMANTHA T. YURKO

1110 1/2 Hay Street, Fayetteville, NC 28305 • preppub@aol.com • (910) 483-6611

OBJECTIVE　　To benefit an organization that can use an enthusiastic sales professional with exceptional communication and organizational skills who offers a track record of accomplishment as a premier-lines cosmetics advisor, consultant, aesthetician, and salon manager.

EDUCATION　　**Associate of Arts in Fashion Merchandising**, Long Beach City College, Long Beach, CA, 1990. Graduated from a 1,500-hour Cosmetology certification course, Boulder Technical Community College, Boulder, CO, 1992.
Completed numerous premiere-lines cosmetics courses and seminars, including:
- Mary Kay Beauty Seminar, 40-hour course in product line, sales, and productivity.
- Lancôme Cosmetics Beauty Seminars, 120 hours; trained in proper application, developed knowledge of product lines, learned sales and merchandising techniques.
- Redken Color Class, 80 hours; learned proper application, product lines, sales techniques.
- Sebastian/Trucco Hair Academy, 160 hours; trained in product lines, sales techniques, and proper application of Sebastian Hair and Trucco Cosmetics products.
- Goldwell Color Class & Color Analysis, 80 hours; learned hair coloring, highlighting, and color-matching techniques.

LICENSES & AFFILIATIONS　　Colorado State Board licensed Cosmetologist, 1992-present.
Member, Colorado Medical Society Alliance, 1998-present.
Member, Boulder Area Chamber of Commerce, 1999-present.
Patron, Colorado Museum of Arts, 1995-1999.
Member, National Association of Business Women's League, 1999-present.

EXPERIENCE　　**BEAUTY CONSULTANT & MAKEUP ARTIST.** Boulder, CO (1998-present). Freelance.

BEAUTY ADVISOR and **FREELANCE MAKEUP ARTIST.** Lancôme Cosmetics, California and Nevada (1998). Performed cosmetic makeovers and facials, presenting Lancôme's premier line of cosmetics to customers and training them in techniques for applying makeup.
- Created innovative and effective displays and merchandising concepts; coordinated fashion shows and other special events to present Lancôme products to potential customers.
- Developed strong relationships with clients, generating repeat customers and sales of Lancôme products; met or exceeded all store, district, and regional sales quotas.
- Monitored sales and inventory to ensure a strong in-stock position on fast-moving items.
- Provided exceptional service to Lancôme clients, averaging eight makeovers per four hour shift.

MARKETING REPRESENTATIVE. Lancôme Cosmetics, Ft. Carson, CO (1997-1998). Performed inventory control, merchandising, customer service, bookkeeping, and events promotion while professionally representing Lancôme's premiere line of cosmetics.
- Provided makeovers, manicures, facials, and Personal Image Consulting to new and existing Lancôme customers, generating sales of premiere line cosmetics.

COSMETOLOGIST. Galliard's Hair Design, Boulder, CO (1992-1997). Provided a full range of cosmetology, hair care, manicure/pedicure, and therapeutic massage services while assisting the management of this busy salon with bookkeeping, inventory control, and sales.

PERSONAL　　Excellent personal and professional references are available upon request.

Exact Name of Person
Title or Position
Name of Company
Address (number and street)
Address (city, state, and zip)

Credit Card Sales,
Executive-level
Customer Service & Sales

Senior managers and
executives often face the
problem of deciding which
of their many
accomplishments to show
on a one-page resume.
Nice problem to have!

Dear Exact Name of Person: (or Dear Sir or Madam if answering a blind ad.)

With the enclosed resume, I would like to indicate my interest in your organization and my desire to explore employment opportunities.

As you will see from my enclosed resume, in my current job as Vice President of Customer Service and Sales, I have supervised an 800-person workforce and improved customer satisfaction from 79% to 95%. Although I am held in high regard by my current employer, my wife and I have decided to relocate to the east coast to be closer to our aging parents.

If you can use an experienced sales professional with extensive quality assurance knowledge, I hope you will welcome my call soon to arrange a brief meeting at your convenience to discuss your current and future needs and how I might serve them. Thank you in advance for your time.

Sincerely yours.

Denford Hanby

Alternate last paragraph:
I hope you will call or write me soon to suggest a time convenient for us to meet and discuss your current and future needs and how I might serve them. Thank you in advance for your time.

DENFORD HANBY

1110½ Hay Street, Fayetteville, NC 28305 • preppub@aol.com • (910) 483-6611

OBJECTIVE	To add value to an organization that can use an energetic and innovative executive who offers a dynamic communication style, superior motivational skills, as well as strong sales, problem-solving, and decision-making abilities refined as a corporate executive.
EDUCATION	Completed **Graduate Management Training Program**, MasterCard, 1991. **M.B.A.**, San Diego State University, CA, 1990; Led a team of MBAs to earn honors in a state competition solving profitability problems of real companies. **B.S. in Business Administration**, Georgia State University, SC, 1983. • Received a full athletic scholarship; was captain of the track team.
EXPERIENCE	**VICE PRESIDENT, CUSTOMER SERVICE & SALES.** MasterCard, San Diego, CA (1997-present). Lead and develop strategies for one of three major customer service and sales centers located in the United States; responsible for serving over 20 million cardmembers with exclusive relationship management responsibilities for customers that hold co-branded MasterCard cards like the Travelers Group product while controlling a $36 million annual operating budget. • Supervise 800-person workforce; improved customer satisfaction from 79% to 95%. • Achieved best annual employee satisfaction scores in the company's history to date. • Improved revenue attainment by 6% in customer service "concept test."

REGIONAL SALES DIRECTOR. Sprint, Huntington Beach, CA (1994-97). After excelling as Regional Sales Director in Huntington Beach from 1994-96, was handpicked to manage the consolidation of two offices with a total of more than 300 employees which involved managing sensitive customer relations for Sprint residential customers while controlling a $35 million annual budget.
• Supervised 1,100 employees operating out of two remote customer contact centers.
• Improved revenue attainment 15% and customer satisfaction 10% while meeting a $190 million revenue objective.
• Provided the leadership which allowed the region to achieve first-place honors in tough competition with the seven other regions throughout the country.
• At Huntington Beach, improved revenue attainment 20%, customer satisfaction 5%, and productivity 30% while managing customer service and sales relationships with more than 200,000 small business customers; supervised 200 employees located in a remote business sales center operating on a $9 million budget while working as a key member of a team to achieve a $40 million corporate revenue objective; cut expenses by $300,000.

Previous MasterCard experience: Was promoted in this track record:
1990-94: **RE-ENGINEERING DIRECTOR.** Managed re-engineering project portfolio worth $3 million in savings; redesigned work flows and eliminated activities that did not add value to the process of delivering excellent customer service.
• Aggressively managed re-engineering projects, reaping over $2 million in savings; consulted with retailers on streamlining credit card operations to improve customer service.
• Developed innovative concept for resolving customer inquiries that saved $500,000.

1984-90: **CUSTOMER SERVICE DIRECTOR.** Began as a Customer Service Manager managing 85 employees, settling cardholder-retailer disputes, and controlling a $2 million budget; then was promoted to manage customer relationships with over 400,000 retail merchants nationwide to develop strategies for improving service levels and re-engineering workflows.

Date

Exact Name of Person
Exact Title
Exact Name of Company
Address
City, State, Zip

Dear Exact Name of Person (or Dear Sir or Madam if answering a blind ad):

Sales professionals are
usually lucky in that they
often have
accomplishments which can
be expressed in numbers
which can make their
achievements seem
exciting. Notice the
numbers Mr. Julian is able
to provide to show the
scope of his involvements.

With the enclosed resume, I would like to make you aware of my abilities as an experienced sales and management professional with exceptional communication and motivational abilities and a background in district-level outside sales, retail and industrial management, and staff development.

In my most recent position, I am excelling as a District Sales Representative for Century Enterprises, the largest broadline food distributor in the Southeast. During my time there, I have raised gross profit dollars by 72%, total sales dollars by 59%, and increased the customer base in my district by 185%. For these and other accomplishments, I was awarded Century Enterprises' President's Club Growth Award for fiscal 2000.

As Assistant Manager for Target in Louisville, I was in charge of all hard lines areas of a $28 million store, supervising 120 people, including 7 department managers. Areas under my direct supervision contributed nearly $10 million dollars annually in sales, and under my management the hard lines area experienced a sales increase of 20% while reducing inventory shrinkage by 70%. In a previous position as a Manager Trainee with Elite Furniture Industries, I developed spreadsheets to track productivity and quality in key parts and assemblies, and maintained databases to analyze the effectiveness of "Just In Time" processes in assembly areas.

As you will see, I have earned a Bachelor of Science in Economics from Woodside University. I feel that my strong combination of education and experience would make me a valuable addition to your organization.

If you can use an experienced sales or management professional with exceptional communication and motivational skills, I hope you will contact me to suggest a time when we might meet to discuss your needs. I can assure you in advance that I have an outstanding reputation and would rapidly become an asset to your organization.

Sincerely,

Paul W. Julian

PAUL W. JULIAN

1110½ Hay Street, Fayetteville, NC 28305   •   preppub@aol.com   •   (910) 483-6611

OBJECTIVE   To benefit an organization that can use an experienced manager and sales professional with exceptional communication, motivational, and organizational skills, as well as a background in district-level outside sales, retail and industrial management, and staff development.

EDUCATION   **Bachelor of Arts degree in Economics,** Woodside University, Monticello, KY, 1991.

EXPERIENCE   **DISTRICT SALES REPRESENTATIVE.** Century Enterprises, Lexington, KY (1996-present). Manage growth of and maintain existing accounts while developing new business in my district for this large broadline food distributor.
- Increased customer base in my district by 185% while maintaining a very high percentage of paid accounts.
- Received the Century Enterprises President's Club Growth Award for fiscal year 2000.
- Raised gross profit dollars by 72% and total sales dollars by 59% in my district.
- Quickly built a strong rapport with customers, assessing their needs, and assisting them in selecting the products that will best serve their needs.
- Demonstrate exceptional communication skills on a daily basis, presenting new products and services in a clear and persuasive manner.
- Participate in company promotions and regional trade shows.

ASSISTANT MANAGER. Target, Louisville, KY (1994-1996). Managed the hard lines area of this $28 million per year retail store; co-responsible for all aspects of store operations. Supervised up to 120 people, including 7 Department Managers.
- Contributed over one-third of the total sales in a $28 million dollar store, achieving sales of $2 million in the Candy/Food and Electronics departments and $1 million in the Stationery and Appliance departments.
- The store doubled its net income for fiscal 1993.
- Maintained a sales increase for the hard lines area of more than 20% while reducing inventory shrinkage by 70%.
- Coordinated the ordering of merchandise in basic and seasonal areas.
- Utilized the perpetual inventory system and other inventory controls to ensure a strong in-stock position on fast-moving items.
- Served as third-shift manager in charge of all shipping and receiving.

MANAGER TRAINEE. Elite Furniture Industries, Monticello, KY (1991-1994). Cross-trained in all aspects of furniture production in this busy, high-volume facility.
- Assisted the production manager in producing detailed sketches of parts and assemblies, to increase accuracy and productivity.
- Developed spreadsheets to track productivity and quality in key parts and assemblies.
- Utilized data and spreadsheets to improve quality of key components, including table tops, doors, frames, drawers, moldings, etc.
- Maintained data to analyze effectiveness of and compliance with "Just In Time" process in assembly areas.

PERSONAL   Excellent personal and professional references are available upon request.

Date

Exact Name of Person
Title or Position
Name of Company
Address (number and street)
Address (city, state, and ZIP)

District Manager,
Magazine Distribution

A round of mergers and
acquisitions in the
magazine distribution
business—with the potential
of layoffs—has caused this
manager to prepare his
resume so that he can
change fields if he finds
himself "downsized."

Dear Exact Name of Person: (or Dear Sir or Madam if answering a blind ad.)

Can you use a top-notch sales professional who offers exceptional communication and marketing skills which have resulted in increasing territory profitability?

Currently the District Sales Manager for the New York City-based McAllister News Company, Inc., I have consistently increased sales and currently handle a territory with $2 million in sales annually. While selling and distributing magazines to wholesalers throughout both North and South Carolina, I have used my analytical skills and "industry instincts" to determine trends and make changes which increased sales. Because the publishing/wholesaling business is in such a state of flux, with larger companies buying up the smaller ones, I have become accustomed to the need for flexibility and resourcefulness.

As you will see from my enclosed resume, I am a versatile professional who can easily adapt to selling different types of products or services. I am highly effective in developing new sources and expanding a territory for increased sales and profits. Known for my warm sense of humor, I can provide outstanding references.

I hope you will welcome my call soon to arrange a brief meeting at your convenience to discuss your current and future needs and how I might serve them. Thank you in advance for your time.

Sincerely yours.

Preston Blum

Alternate last paragraph:
I hope you will call or write me soon to suggest a time convenient for us to meet and discuss your current and future needs and how I might serve them. Thank you in advance for your time.

PRESTON BLUM

1110½ Hay Street, Fayetteville, NC 28305 • preppub@aol.com • (910) 483-6611

OBJECTIVE

To offer my top-quality communication and marketing skills to an organization that can use an accomplished sales professional with sales management experience who offers a track record of increasing territory profitability.

EXPERIENCE

DISTRICT SALES MANAGER. McAllister News Company, Inc., Charleston, SC (1995-present). Sell and distribute magazines to wholesalers in North and South Carolina while consistently increasing sales in this territory which has a volume of over $2 million annually.
- Analyze sales information from retail chains; create strategic plans and continuously monitor/modify distribution efforts to maximize sales.
- Have increased sales by at least 5% every year at a time when the industry was experiencing much turbulence, with larger wholesalers buying smaller ones with the result that buyer names and faces were constantly changing.
- Am extremely knowledgeable of the channels of distribution and industry structure related to magazine/book publishing and wholesaling; am highly respected for the strong negotiating and customer service skills I use to compete for shelf space in this competitive industry with tight margins.

SALES REPRESENTATIVE. Southeastern Concrete, Tampa, FL (1988-95).
Demonstrated my ability to rapidly excel in the sale of industrial products; while selling concrete, checked building permits for leads and contacted contractors, concrete finishers, and other members of the building public to arrange delivery of the product.

SALES REPRESENTATIVE. Systel Business Equipment Company, Raleigh, NC (1986-87). Cold-called businesses and nonprofit organizations to evaluate the need for copier equipment and deliver proposals for services.
- Was honored as "*Salesman of the Month*" for six out of 12 months.
- Negotiated selling prices, lease agreements, and maintenance contracts.
- Maintained accurate records of customers' equipment in order to be able to offer them upgraded equipment.

GENERAL MANAGER. Shear Salon, Tampa, FL (1983-85). Started "from scratch" and then managed a hair salon business; became skilled in purchasing supplies and in obtaining the best prices for materials through resourceful buying and skillful negotiating.
- Managed all operational areas of this thriving business including bookkeeping, payroll, merchandising, and hiring/training.

Highlights of other experience: Excelled in the highly technical field of electronics maintenance while proudly serving with the U.S. Navy.

EDUCATION

Earned an **A.A. degree in English**, Tampa Community College, Tampa, FL, 1981.
- Graduated *with honors*.

PERSONAL

Have earned the respect of both my peers and upper-level management for my outstanding sales and marketing skills. Enjoy developing territories and providing top-quality service. Am known for my warm sense of humor. Excellent references.

Date

Mr. James Brown
Regional Sales Manager
Excalibur Company
190 Decatur Road
Houston, TX 90235

Dear Mr. Brown:

Upon the strong recommendation of Ann Williams with The Bessemer Company, I am faxing you my resume.

As you will see, I have an outstanding track record in producing sales and profit for Frito-Lay Company, where I have worked since 1988. You will see from my resume that I have won numerous awards including Manager of the Year several times as well as District Manager of the Year. I believe my fine personal reputation as well as my extensive knowledge of convenience store operations in Texas could be of value to the Excalibur Company, and I would enjoy an opportunity to speak with you in confidence about employment opportunities.

At the appropriate time, I can provide exceptionally strong personal and professional references, including from Frito-Lay Company, but I would appreciate your not contacting Frito-Lay until after we have a chance to talk.

I pride myself on high standards of loyalty and integrity, and I am well known within my industry for delivering on whatever promises I make.

Please let me know if you would be interested in discussing the possibility of putting my talents, knowledge, sales skills, contacts, and background to use. In advance I send warm holiday greetings and best wishes for the New Year.

Sincerely,

Joe Vieira

JOE VIEIRA

1110½ Hay Street, Fayetteville, NC 28305 • preppub@aol.com • (910) 483-6611

OBJECTIVE	To benefit an organization that can use a loyal and dedicated sales professional who offers versatile skills in sales management, extensive knowledge of convenience store operations in Texas, as well as a "track record" of achievement in maximizing sales and profit.
TRAINING	Excelled in extensive executive development course work sponsored by Frito-Lay Company and previous employers; areas studied included merchandising, advertising, budgeting, buying, marketing, sales, inventory control, quality control, shrinkage control, and human resources administration. • Was born and raised in Austin, TX, and graduated from Austin High School.
EXPERIENCE	**DISTRICT SALES MANAGER.** Frito-Lay Company, Austin, TX (1988-present). Began with this company as a warehouseman and was rapidly promoted to Route Sales Representative; then advanced quickly into management: was named supervisor of five sales representatives and in 1992 was promoted to District Sales Manager. • From 1992-2000, built the existing territory from five to 22 routes; the parent company then divided up the huge territory I had created and I was named **Regional Sales Manager of the Year in 2000.** • Currently supervise 10 sales representatives and two spare reps. • Plan and administer a budget of $2 million annually. • In 1999, doubled projected profit for my territory; exceeded the sales budget by 20%. • In 2000, was named **National District Manager of the Year** as well as **Regional District Manager of the Year.** • Accomplished an historical sales record within Frito-Lay of $124,000 net sales for one week, and was the first and only district manager to ever exceed quarterly sales of $1 million. • Am completely familiar with convenience store operations in Texas, having made headquarters calls and presentations to buyers and owners. • Offer extensive knowledge of the chain convenience stores such as Quik Stop, Scotchman, and Short Stops. *Other experience:* • As a manager for a shoe division, opened three stores and trained the managers, assistant managers, and other personnel. • As an insurance salesman, was named **Top Salesman** for the year for the eastern Texas region.
REFERENCES	Outstanding personal and professional references available upon request.
PERSONAL	Believe in the pursuit of excellence in all areas of life, and have become skilled in motivating employees to give their best effort. Have excellent contacts throughout Texas.

Date

Exact Name of Person
Exact Title
Exact Name of Company
Address
City, State, Zip

Financial Services Sales, Credit Union Background

Dear Exact Name of Person (or Dear Sir or Madam if answering a blind ad):

Remember that your cover letter is the first impression you make in your job hunt! If you were Top Branch Employee, or received some other honor, mention it in the cover letter. A good way to approach the cover letter is to make three main points about yourself which will arouse the employer's interest in meeting you.

With the enclosed resume, I would like to make you aware of my skills and experience in the financial services field as well as my proven customer service and sales abilities. I am in the process of permanently relocating to Southington where my extended family lives.

As you will see from my resume, I have been promoted rapidly while excelling in jobs with credit unions and banks. I can provide outstanding personal and professional references from all previous employers. In my most recent position as a Financial Services Representative, I was honored as the **Top Branch Employee** in recognition of my sales accomplishments, and I was credited as the key factor in my location's earning **"Branch of the Year"** honors for the greatest level of improvement in sales and membership.

I am accustomed to the fast pace and aggressive bottom-line orientation of financial institutions, and I am known for my cheerful, outgoing personality as well as my extensive knowledge of financial products and services. On my own time while excelling in my full-time jobs, I have completed college courses and numerous professional development programs, and I am committed to earning my college degree in my spare time while continuing to advance in my field.

If you can use a highly motivated self-starter who could contribute to your bottom line with enthusiasm, please contact me to suggest a time when we might meet to discuss your needs and how I might serve them.

Yours sincerely,

Betty R. Achim

BETTY R. ACHIM

1110½ Hay Street, Fayetteville, NC 28305 • preppub@aol.com • (910) 483-6611

OBJECTIVE To offer my experience in financial services to an organization that can use a self-motivated and articulate young professional with talents for prioritizing, handling pressure, and building strong client relations based on an enthusiastic and dedicated personal style.

EDUCATION Completed 22 credit hours of general studies, Southington Community College, CT.
& TRAINING Graduated from McCallum High School, Southington, CT, 1991.
- Earned certificates in the following areas of professional development:
  - Consumer Lending, September 1998
  - Service Plus, August 1997
  - Member Services, June 1997
- Completed Notary Public course, Somerville Technical Community College, MA, 1997.

SPECIAL SKILLS *10-key calculators:* use by sight
Computers: MS Windows 95, Excel, MS Office Applications, and MS Word; type 65 wpm

EXPERIENCE **FINANCIAL SERVICES REPRESENTATIVE.** Westbrook Federal Credit Union, Somerville, MA (1997-present). Was recognized as the **"Top Branch Employee"** in recognition of my sales accomplishments which include very active and successful efforts during two credit union-wide cross selling promotions for debit and credit card products as well as for life and disability insurance sales.
- Earned recognition as an important player during team efforts which resulted in **"Branch of the Year 2000"** honors for the greatest increase in sales and membership.
- Handle New Accounts Representative duties which include opening accounts, processing applications, and informing new account holders of benefits and services.
- Open IRA accounts and sell CDs (certificates of deposit).
- Act as a Cash Operations Specialist and Teller for deposits and withdrawals as well as accepting loan payments.
- Order cash for the branch and maintain funds in the vault.
- Interview applicants for consumer loans and process their requests; administer loan closings.

MEMBERSHIP SERVICES SPECIALIST. Dreyer Federal Credit Union, Somerville, MA (1996-97). Provided fast, friendly service in an extremely high-volume and hectic branch with an emphasis on completing cash transactions for members.
- Cited for my willingness to contribute my time and knowledge to help others, was effective at cross selling credit union services and products.
- Balanced and settled ATM (automated teller machine) transactions.

COMMERCIAL ACCOUNT AND VAULT TRANSACTIONS TELLER. First National Bank of Hartford, CT (1995-96). Processed all cash orders to and from the Federal Reserve Bank and five branch banks – an amount in excess of $2 million each week.
- Handled the cash orders and commercial account deposits for such large companies as Wal-Mart, Sam's Club, and Dillards.
- As Acting Supervisor, guided the front-line staff and drive-in window tellers.

SALES ASSISTANT and **DESK CLERK.** Holiday Inn, Carlsbad, CA (1992-93).
Refined customer service, public relations, and administrative skills in a 120-room hotel.

PERSONAL Offer excellent verbal and written communication skills. Enjoy fast-paced workplace.

Date

Exact Name of Person
Title or Position
Name of Company
Address (number and street)
Address (city, state, and zip)

Dear Exact Name of Person: (or Dear Sir or Madam if answering a blind ad.)

Financial Services Sales, Series 7 Qualified

Having a wife who is interested in moving back to her hometown to be near her aging parents is what has prompted this high achiever to seek employment in a new area.

With the enclosed resume, I would like to make you aware of my interest in exploring suitable opportunities within your organization which can utilize my proven sales abilities, entrepreneurial spirit, as well as my background as a Stockbroker and Investment Counselor.

Although I am excelling in my current position with a South Carolina Bank and am being groomed for further rapid promotion, I am exploring opportunities in your area. I can provide outstanding references from my current employer at the appropriate time.

As you will see from my resume, in my current position as a Stockbroker and Investment Counselor I am responsible for 22 branch locations in nine counties and am involved in meeting with clients and potential clients to develop investment plans and strategies. I have consistently generated $800,000 a year in revenues and have been ranked for the past four years in the top four of the top sales producers at my bank. Although I came to the bank armed with my Series 6 and 63 licenses, I have recently earned my Series 7 license while excelling in my full-time job. In my prior position, I excelled as a Securities and Insurance Broker with a securities firm where I rapidly became respected for my creativity, technical knowledge, and dynamic marketing style. I am highly computer literate and am skilled at using various software programs to create graphics, charts, illustrations, and printouts.

You would find me in person to be a congenial individual who can be counted on to produce outstanding results in the most competitive situations. If you can use a dedicated professional who can provide outstanding personal and professional references, I hope you will write or call me to suggest a time when we might meet to discuss your needs and goals and how I might meet them. I can assure you that I could rapidly become a vital and contributing member of your team.

Sincerely,

Richard David Beers

RICHARD DAVID BEERS

1110½ Hay Street, Fayetteville, NC 28305 • preppub@aol.com • (910) 483-6611

OBJECTIVE	To benefit an organization that can use a hard-working and aggressive young professional with unlimited initiative and resourcefulness, strong communication and organizational skills, as well as proven sales and marketing abilities.
FINANCIAL LICENSES	Hold Series 7, 6 & 63 Securities Licenses, licensed by the NASD and the SEC. Obtained a Life & Health Insurance License. • Studied for and obtained these licenses while excelling in full-time jobs.
EDUCATION	**B.A. degree** in Sociology, New Haven University, New Haven, CT, 1987. Excelled in Ranger School, the 72-day "stress-test" management school designed to test the mental and physical limits of the military's most talented leaders.
COMPUTERS	Familiar with software including Word, WordPerfect 5.1, Microsoft Works, and Windows. Skilled in formulating different investment strategies using software programs to create graphs, charts, and printouts; adept at developing illustrations for mutual funds and annuities.
EXPERIENCE	**STOCKBROKER & FINANCIAL CONSULTANT.** Nation's Bank Investment Services, Florence, SC (1998-present). Responsible for 22 branch locations in nine counties, am involved in meeting with clients and potential clients to develop investment plans and strategies; train key individuals at the 22 branches to recognize qualified customers through profiling and by helping these customers develop financial plans. • Have consistently generated $800,000 per year in revenue through my ability to set high goals and then persistently following through with well executed plans. • Studied for and obtained my Series 7 license while excelling in this full-time job. • Ranked in the top four of the bank's top sales performers for four straight years. • Have become skilled at analyzing customer needs and developing financial plans. **SECURITIES & INSURANCE BROKER.** Dale Securities, Inc., Florence, SC (1993-98). Rapidly became respected for my creativity, technical knowledge, and dynamic marketing style while developing portfolios/plans for private pensions, retirement, and investments for individuals, family entities, and organizations. • Became known for my skill in creating packages with products including tax-sheltered mutual funds and annuities, 401(k) plans, as well as variable universal life insurance. • In the belief that "a picture is worth a thousand words," used my computer software knowledge to create printout "pictures" for investment strategy proposals. • Acquired valuable insights into the tax advantages available for different types of investors, depending on risk aversion and overall goals in financial planning. • Gained expert knowledge regarding laws governing mutual funds and annuities. • Learned how to talk about financial planning and investment concepts with all types of people, from the savvy businessperson to the person with no technical knowledge of finance. **PRINCIPLES OF MANAGEMENT INSTRUCTOR.** U.S. Army, Ft. Bragg, NC (1990-93). At the Army's largest U.S. military base, was specially selected as an instructor in the Non-Commissioned Officer's Course, a seven-week management training program. **GENERAL MANAGER.** U.S. Army, Ft. Bragg, NC (1988-90). As a squad leader in the famed 82nd Airborne Division, excelled in leading a six-person Scout Squad—an organization which had to remain continuously ready to relocate worldwide in order to respond to international crises, terrorism, conflict, or disasters; controlled an inventory valued at $125,000. • Designed and supervised the implementation of training programs.
PERSONAL	Am an extremely positive and cheerful person who adapts easily to new situations.

Exact Name of Person
Title or Position
Name of Company
Address (number and street)
Address (city, state, and zip)

Financial Services Sales, Banking Background

This young professional is using her cover letter and resume to explore other opportunities in financial services.

Dear Sir or Madam:

I would appreciate an opportunity to talk with you soon about my strong interest in receiving consideration for the position of Commercial Sales Manager. I believe I offer the enthusiasm, talent, and knowledge that make me a professional who can make important contributions to First Union National Bank in this area.

As you will see from my enclosed resume, I am presently a Client Services Manager who consistently places at the top of my peer group in internal performance evaluations. I rapidly advanced from Administrative Assistant in the consumer banking department, gained experience as a Teller, and then advanced to this position where I represent the bank while opening new accounts and selling bank products to our clients. While excelling in my full-time positions, I have worked hard in my spare time to complete my college degree.

My ability to develop interesting and informative written materials was discovered in high school when I edited the yearbook. While attending Peace College in Raleigh for my first two years of studies, I was selected to edit the college yearbook and was credited with producing an attractive and well-organized publication. I went on to earn a degree in Mass Communications from the University of North Carolina at Charlotte where I wrote for the college newspaper. I have become involved in the Junior League and am now serving this organization as the Public Relations chairman in a role which includes preparing all newspaper releases about the organization and its civic activities.

I believe that through my enthusiasm, experience, and talent I can make valuable contributions in preparing products which will enhance the bank's ability to sell services to the public and gain new clients through informative and interesting written materials.

I hope you will call or write me soon to suggest a time convenient for us to discuss how I would fit into the bank's commercial sales team. Thank you in advance for your time.

Sincerely,

Kerry Zaeske

KERRY ZAESKE

1110½ Hay Street, Fayetteville, NC 28305 • preppub@aol.com • (910) 483-6611

OBJECTIVE

To offer my strong verbal and written communication skills along with my knowledge of and experience in banking and finance to an organization that can benefit from my ability to sell financial services.

EDUCATION

B.S. in **Mass Communications,** University of North Carolina at Charlotte, NC, 1997.
- Completed this degree in my spare time while excelling in demanding full-time positions.
- Maintained a cumulative GPA of above 3.0.
- Wrote articles for the college newspaper.

Attended Peace College, Raleigh, NC, for two years of basic studies in the Liberal Arts.
- Selected by faculty advisors to edit the college yearbook during my sophomore year, applied my communication skills and creativity to write copy for and produce a well-organized and attractive publication.

EXPERIENCE

CLIENT SERVICES MANAGER. First Union National Bank, Charlotte, NC (1995-present). After a short period of time as an Administrative Assistant in the consumer banking department, was soon selected to gain experience as a Teller before advancing to this highly visible role as the public's first contact with the bank and its services.
- Consistently placed at the top of my peer group within the region according to the bank's system of internal performance ratings.
- Displayed the ability to listen to people's financial needs and requirements in order to recommend products such as Certificates of Deposit, MasterCard and VISA credit cards, and savings accounts and to open accounts.

SALES REPRESENTATIVE. Carlyle & Co., Charlotte, NC (1993-1995). Consistently met aggressive sales goals through both my patience and persistence in public relations and customer service; became known as a goal-driven, skilled professional who could be counted to always deliver customer satisfaction.

ADMINISTRATIVE ASSISTANT. First Union National Bank, Charlotte, NC (1992-93). Gained valuable experience in banking procedures and all phases of the loan process while providing clerical and administrative support to two regional vice presidents specializing in the area of consumer credit.
- Used my talent for organization and attention to detail while creating spreadsheets, typing, and maintaining files for two busy executives.
- Improved the filing system for increased efficiency.
- Refined my communication skills dealing with banking professionals on a regular basis.
- Polished my knowledge of computer operations using WordPerfect and Lotus software while typing memos and correspondence as well as handling financial record keeping.

LEGAL OFFICE INTERN. Office of the District Attorney, Charlotte, NC (1990-91). Gained valuable exposure to the workings of the law while aiding assistant district attorneys in such activities as contacting witnesses to remind them of court appearances; became familiar with the court system and legal procedures while learning to work with elected officials.
- Ensured persons pleading "not guilty" were aware of how to respond to questioning; learned to write guilty pleas.
- Earned a reputation for my maturity and judgment displayed while relating to a variety of people from all socioeconomic and age groups.

PERSONAL

Am an articulate speaker and skilled writer. Offer a creative and enthusiastic approach to project development and the organizational skills to see them to completion. Enjoy dealing with the public and making contributions to my community.

Date

Exact Name of Person
Exact Title
Exact Name of Company
Address
City, State, Zip

Financial Services Sales,
Applying for Internal Public
Relations Position

Dear Exact Name of Person: (or Dear Sir or Madam if answering a blind ad):

This young professional
feels that her strengths lie
in her strong written
communication skills. She
is attempting to put
herself in an internal
public relations position
which will allow her to use
her writing skills and
company knowledge to
sell the bank's
products.

With the enclosed resume, I would like to make you aware of my education related to Mass Communications and Marketing as well as my in-depth knowledge of the bank's financial services. I am interested in applying for the Public Relations Coordinator position recently created, and I feel I am the ideal candidate for the position.

As you will see from my resume, I am presently employed by Citizen's Bank where I am respected for my exceptional sales and customer service skills as well as for my resourcefulness and attention to detail. In August 2000 I was a Pinnacle Club Recipient, an honor given in recognition of sales achievements. I was singled out for this award specifically for my second quarter sales of bank products ranging from credit cards, to home equity lines of credit, to new savings and checking accounts. Previously I excelled in jobs in retail management and sales.

If you can use an experienced professional with strong sales and communication skills as well as high levels of drive, initiative, and energy, I hope you will contact me. I would enjoy the opportunity to talk with you in person to discuss your goals and how my background might serve your needs. I can provide outstanding references at the appropriate time.

Sincerely,

Nancy Childs

NANCY CHILDS

1110½ Hay Street, Fayetteville, NC 28305   •   preppub@aol.com   •   (910) 483-6611

OBJECTIVE

To contribute analytical, communication, and problem-solving skills as well as expertise in managing fiscal and human resources to an organization that can use a mature detail-oriented professional with high levels of initiative and self-motivation.

EDUCATION & TRAINING

B.S. degree in Mass Communications and Marketing, Indiana State University, IN, 1991.
• Completed a course in banking procedures sponsored by Citizen's Bank (1999), a Real Estate course leading to licensing by the State of Michigan (1991) and extensive training by K-Mart in management and financial operations.

COMMUNITY INVOLVEMENT

Am serving on a second task force with the Ridge County Partnership for Children and Families, Troy, MI: the current group is developing goals and guidelines for a mobile preschool unit while an earlier task force focused on the development of the organization's goals, objectives, and operational guidelines for a program called Child Care Connections.

EXPERIENCE

FINANCIAL SERVICES SALES ASSOCIATE. Citizen's Bank, Troy, MI (1998-present). Was recently honored by the bank's Pinnacle Club for second quarter sales achievements while excelling in a job which requires the adaptability to adjust to traveling between four different locations to provide financial services and sales support.
• Utilize computer systems with proprietary software programs unique to banking.
• Am known for my accuracy while balancing large amounts of funds to include weekly balancing of cash drawers and Automated Teller Machines (ATM).
• Have been cited for my attention to detail while preparing a variety of daily reports and providing exceptional customer service.
• Handle sales of a variety of bank products including credit cards, loans, credit lines, and home equity lines of credit as well as new checking and savings accounts.

RETAIL STORE ASSISTANT MANAGER. K-Mart Stores, Inc., Troy, MI (1993-97). Gained knowledge and built strong skills in all aspects of daily operations while overseeing the activities of up to 60 employees in 15 different departments.
• Became skilled in reading and understanding a variety of financial statements from profit-and-loss, to inventory, to budget statements.
• Was entrusted with the control of a successful and effective project which established and set up third-shift receiving procedures and operations.
• Utilized computers daily for inventory control, accounting, budgeting, scheduling.

HUMAN RESOURCES AND CONTRACTING MANAGER. Megaforce Temporary Services, Birmingham, MI (1992-93). Developed business contracts and met with existing corporate customer representatives in order to understand their requirements and manage an office which provided skilled and qualified temporary personnel to order.
• Developed and refined human resource management skills while interviewing and screening prospective employees and making decisions on their placement.
• Learned how to market the organization and its services to prospective clients.
• Refined time management skills in a simultaneous job as a supervisor/training specialist with Food Mart Stores: handled activities ranging from balancing registers, to making deposits, to opening or closing the store, to processing shipments, to managing funds.

PERSONAL

Have enrolled in a college Spanish class and am the only person on the bank staff who speaks enough Spanish to help the approximately 300 non-English speaking customers.

Date

Exact Name of Person
Exact Title
Exact Name of Company
Address
City, State, Zip

Financial Services Sales, Credit Union Background

Dear Sir or Madam:

With the enclosed resume, I would like to make you aware of my considerable background and track record of accomplishment in financial services, sales, customer service, and collections.

A background related to financial services sales, collections, customer service, and credit counseling is what this individual is offering prospective employers. If you are wondering what a Summary of Qualifications Section would look like, notice the one on her resume.

As you can see from my enclosed resume, I have over seven years of professional experience. I have held positions as a Member Specialist, Account Manager, Full Service Banker, Front Desk and Accounting Clerk, and Sales Associate. My experience has enabled me to develop good communication, management, and supervisory skills which are essential in today's business world.

My personal strengths include dependability, a positive attitude, and the ability to quickly learn new procedures and techniques. I am a self-starter who enjoys becoming involved with new challenges, people, and situations. I deal with problems through a combination of tact and diplomacy, and I function well under stress and pressure. I feel my experience and training would make me a valuable addition to your organization.

If you can use an experienced banking and finance professional, I look forward to hearing from you soon, to arrange a time when we might meet to discuss your needs. I can assure you in advance that I have an outstanding reputation and would quickly become a valuable asset to your company.

Sincerely,

Joyce L. Zegas

JOYCE L. ZEGAS

1110½ Hay Street, Fayetteville, NC 28305 • preppub@aol.com • (910) 483-6611

OBJECTIVE
To contribute to an organization that can use my experience in financial services, sales, customer service, banking, and collections.

SUMMARY OF QUALIFICATIONS

- Establish and maintain rapport with individuals of diverse backgrounds and experience levels.
- Timely and responsive to deadline requirements.
- Able to work independently and as a team member.
- Responsible, reliable, and efficient.

EDUCATION
Bachelor of Science degree in **Business and Management**, University of Maryland University College, College Park, MD, 1997.
Associate of Arts degree in **Management Studies**, University of Maryland University College, College Park, MD, 1993.

- Completed two years of college level study in Accounting, Michigan State University, Bloomfield Hills, MI, 1991.

EXPERIENCE
SALES REPRESENTATIVE & MEMBER SPECIALIST. Winthrop Federal Credit Union, Detroit, MI (1999-present). Perform a wide range of customer service, sales, banking, and financial services in this busy credit union environment.

- Provide information to current and new members concerning membership eligibility, products, and services, including loan products and membership benefits.
- Process and complete all new account transactions, payroll deductions, direct deposits, transfer forms, and share draft orders.
- Sell all of the credit union's financial products and services to members.
- Gained expert knowledge of second mortgage products.
- Set up rental safe deposit box records and assist in gaining access to boxes.
- Balance cash box with Teller Policy guidelines.
- Interview and process loan applications.
- Recognize and capitalize on opportunities to up-sell member loan products and services; advise members of loan decisions.
- Disburse loan funds when necessary, forwarding paperwork to loan center in a timely manner.

ACCOUNT MANAGER. National Bank, Detroit, MI (1996-1998). Provided a variety of credit counseling, customer service, and collections services for this large national bank.

- Demonstrated exceptional communication and customer service skills while collecting on delinquent credit card accounts by offering payment alternatives and payment plans.
- Documented preferred payment arrangement in customer's account file.

FULL SERVICE BANKER. Savannah Bank & Trust, Savannah, GA (1995-1996). Delivered quality customer service while performing various duties as a Customer Service Representative, Teller, and Head Teller.

- Ran a cash drawer, balanced main vault, performed general bookkeeping, ordered money, opened new accounts, conducted interviews, and took loan applications.

PERSONAL
Excellent personal and professional references are available upon request.

Date

Exact Name of Person
Title or Position
Name of Company
Address (number and street)
Address (city, state, and zip)

**Firearms Sales,
Pawnshop Owner and
Firearms Dealer Background**

This entrepreneur found
himself in a job hunt
because his wife graduated
from college and her job
took them to a new city. He
decided to try to represent
one of the product lines
which he used to purchase
when he owned his own
business.

Dear Sir or Madam:

With the enclosed resume, I would like to introduce the proven sales skills and extensive firearms industry knowledge which I could put at the disposal of your company.

As you will see, I recently sold a gun store which I transformed from an unprofitable company saddled with debt into a very profitable business with an excellent reputation.

As a former dealer, I am very familiar with your company's products, and I have dealt personally with salesmen and sales representatives from all manufacturers and distributors. I strongly believe that my sales skills and congenial personality were the keys to my success as a dealer, and I am certain I could be a highly effective representative of your products.

I have grown up around guns since I was a child. Before my father became a Baptist minister, he owned the largest firearms business in eastern KY, and I helped him with everything in the store. I have used the products of every manufacturer.

I attend gun shows frequently and have developed an extensive network of contacts and friends within the industry who know me and my fine personal reputation. I feel certain that I could make significant contributions to your bottom line through my expert product knowledge, outstanding personal reputation, and exceptional sales abilities. I am writing to you because I am familiar with your company's fine reputation, and I feel it would be a pleasure to become associated with your product line.

If you can use a dynamic and hard-working individual to complement your sales team, please contact me to suggest a time when we might meet to discuss your needs and how I could help you. I am married with no children, and I can travel as extensively as your needs require. Thank you for your consideration, and I look forward to hearing from you.

Sincerely,

Robbie J. Goins

ROBBIE J. GOINS

1110½ Hay Street, Fayetteville, NC 28305 • preppub@aol.com • (910) 483-6611

OBJECTIVE
To contribute to an organization that can use an experienced sales professional with expert knowledge of firearms products along with a network of outstanding relationships which I have developed with firearms dealers, manufacturers, and distributors who know of my fine reputation and trust me personally.

EXPERIENCE
Since 1989-present, have been associated with Carolina Firearms Sports, Inc.:
GENERAL MANAGER & SALESMAN. Carolina Firearms Sports, Inc., Matthews, SD (1989-present). In 1991, bought this company after working for the company as a Salesman for two years; continued as General Manager after selling the business in 1999.
- When I purchased the company, it was unprofitable and in debt; I relocated the company to a better market and utilized effective sales and management techniques to transform an ailing organization into a highly profitable and respected company which I sold in 1999.
- Combined my expert knowledge of manufacturers and distributors with my marketing sense in determining the correct inventory for the store; carried more than 1,000 individual guns and accessories needed by shooters.
- As a dealer, have become very familiar with the products, product lines, and sales policies of all manufacturers including Smith and Wesson, Ruger, Weatherby, Colt, Browning, and Winchester.
- Worked with distributors including Outdoor Sports Headquarters, Inc., Nationwide, Bill Hicks, Go Sportsman, Bangers, and Acusport.
- On a daily basis, used my common sense in solving uncommon problems.
- Strongly believe that my sales skills and congenial personality were the keys to my success in this business.

Other experience:
- **MANAGER.** Traders Antiques, Vass, SD (1984-89). Managed all aspects of a small furniture refinishing business; personally handled sales and customer service.
- **SALESMAN.** Furniture Traders, Rowland, SD (1982-84). Upon graduation from high school, became employed by a furniture refinishing business and rapidly discovered that I have exceptional sales and customer relations skills.
- **GUN STORE ASSISTANT.** Quaker Neck Gun Exchange, Greenville, KY. As a young boy, grew up around guns since my father, who later became a Baptist minister, owned the largest firearms business in eastern KY.
- **LAW ENFORCEMENT OFFICER—Reserve.** (1988-97). As an unpaid volunteer, served as a reserve Law Enforcement Officer helping to enforce the law and keep the peace.

MEMBERSHIPS
Member, National Rifle Association; Member, Capel Baptist Church.

HOBBIES
Hunting, shooting, reloading, and collecting.

EDUCATION
Completed numerous courses in Law Enforcement, Matthews Technical Community College, Matthews, SD.

PERSONAL
Can provide outstanding references inside and outside the firearms industry. Am married with no children; will travel extensively if needed. Excel in establishing strong relationships.

Date

Exact Name of Person
Title or Position
Name of Company
Address (number and street)
Address (city, state, and zip)

Food Industry Sales and Purchasing

In the first paragraph, this junior professional makes it clear that he is relocating to Seattle. Although his background will be of interest to food companies, his experience in sales and purchasing is transferable to other fields. Notice that, although he has a license to sell Life and Health insurance, he doesn't plan on approaching the insurance industry, so his license is shown in a low-key fashion in the Personal section of his resume rather than in a separate License section.

Dear Exact Name of Person: (or Sir or Madam if answering a blind ad.)

With the enclosed resume, I would like to make you aware of the considerable sales and purchasing experience which I could put to work for your company. I am in the process of relocating to Seattle, and I believe my background is well suited to your company's needs.

As you will see from my resume, I have been excelling as the purchasing agent for a large wholesale food distributor with a customer base of schools, restaurants, and nursing homes throughout the western states. While negotiating contracts with vendors and handling the school lunch bid process, I have resourcefully managed inventory turnover in order to optimize inventory levels while maximizing return on investment. I have earned a reputation as a prudent strategic planner and skillful negotiator.

In a prior position as a Sales Trainer and Sales Representative with a food industry company, I increased sales from $250,000 to $1.3 million and won the Captain Max award given to the company's highest-producing sales representative.

With a B.S. degree, I have excelled in continuous and extensive executive training in the areas of financial management, purchasing, contract negotiation, and quality assurance.

I can provide outstanding personal and professional references at the appropriate time, and I hope you will contact me if you can use a resourceful hard worker with a strong bottom-line orientation. I am in the Seattle area frequently and could make myself available to meet with you at your convenience. Thank you in advance for your time.

Sincerely,

Benjamin Brainerd

BENJAMIN BRAINERD

Until 12/15/00: 1110½ Hay Street, Fayetteville, NC 28305   (910) 483-6611

After 12/16/00: 538 Pittsfield Avenue, Seattle, WA 89023   (805) 483-6611

OBJECTIVE

To benefit an organization that can use my exceptionally strong sales and marketing skills as well as my background in purchasing, inventory management, and contract negotiation.

EDUCATION

Bachelor of Science Degree, Denver University, Denver, CO, 1980.
- Majored in Health and Physical Education
- Minor in Business Administration

Graduated from W.G. DuBois High School, Denver, CO.
- Was named one of the "Ten Most Outstanding Seniors."
- Was selected to receive the Cayman Sportsmanship Award during my senior year. This award is presented annually to only one athlete in the Denver area.
- Earned varsity letters in football, basketball, and baseball.

EXPERIENCE

PURCHASING MANAGER. Culloughby Co., Denver, CO (1993-present). For this wholesale food distributor with a customer base of schools, nursing homes, and restaurants throughout the western states, purchase $750,000 of canned, dry, and staple goods.
- Am responsible for turning the inventory and maximizing return on investment (ROI); have resourcefully developed methods of purchasing products in a timely manner in order to optimize inventory turnover and ROI.
- Have earned a reputation as a skilled negotiator in the process of negotiating contract pricing as well as other terms and conditions with vendors.
- Have acquired eight years of experience with school lunch bid process; conduct product availability research, secure guarantee bid pricing, handle bid quoting.
- Utilize a computer with Target software for purchasing activities.

SALES REPRESENTATIVE. Mason Brothers, Denver, CO (1986-1993). Sold portion control meat and seafood to established and newly developed accounts.

SALES REPRESENTATIVE & SALES TRAINER. Bryan Foods, Bodega Bay, CA (1979-1986). Excelled in numerous positions of responsibility related to sales and sales management during my eight years with this company.
- As a Sales Representative, boosted annual sales from $250,000 to $1.3 million.
- As "Equipment and Supplies Specialist," initiated sales efforts in the western California region and helped produce sales in excess of $200,000 during the first quarter of the 1985 fiscal year.
- As "Sales Representative," produced growth of over $900,000 in annual sales revenue between 1979 and 1984, which resulted in my winning the "Captain Max" Award, presented to the company's most outstanding salesperson.
- Managed and coordinated divisional sales meeting; trained sales personnel.

Other experience:
- As **Co-Manager** of a seafood restaurant in Denver, was in charge of hiring, training, scheduling, and supervising all employees.
- Worked as a **Sales Representative and Staff Manager** for Pilot Life Insurance Company in Los Angeles; sold life and health products and served as Staff Manager.

PERSONAL

Can provide outstanding references. Have been licensed to sell **Life and Health** insurance.

Date

Exact Name of Person
Exact Title
Exact Name of Company
Address
City, State, Zip

Furniture Sales, Transitioning to Outside Sales Position as a Manufacturer's Representative

After a career in a family furniture business, this gentleman found himself in a job hunt when the business closed. When he decided that he most enjoyed sales as a functional area, he then determined that he would be happy in a job as a manufacturer's representative of the kinds of furniture lines his store used to sell. He used this resume and cover letter to approach furniture manufacturers. P.S. He can omit paragraph four when approaching a company outside the furniture industry.

Dear Exact Name of Person: (or Dear Sir or Madam if answering a blind ad):

With the enclosed resume, I would like to make you aware of my extensive sales background and my interest in putting my expertise to work for your company.

As you will see from my resume, I have established a reputation as an articulate, personable, and persuasive communicator while functioning as Sales Manager and President of a small family-owned business which was recently sold. I have decided that I wish to embark on a full-time career in sales, and I am a proven sales performer. With an instinctive sales personality fortified by years of on-the-job training, I played a valuable role in building and maintaining the company's reputation for value and an emphasis on quality customer service. I have trained and developed numerous effective sales professionals.

Although I am single and would relocate according to your needs, I believe I could be of enormous use to a company which desired to employ my sales skills in the Shreveport and surrounding area. I offer an outstanding business reputation and would have a ready-made ability to network with key decision makers in the region.

You will notice from my resume that I offer an extensive background of knowledge and contacts related to the furniture and textile industry. I am knowledgeable of the product line and reputation of most furniture and appliance makers, and I am certain I would be highly effective in a manufacturer's representative role.

I hope you will welcome my call soon to try to arrange a brief meeting to discuss your goals and how my background might serve your needs. I can provide outstanding references at the appropriate time.

Sincerely,

Kenneth Soifer

Alternate Last Paragraph:
I hope you will write or call me soon to suggest a time when we might meet to discuss your needs and goals and how my background might serve them. I can provide outstanding references at the appropriate time.

KENNETH SOIFER ("KEN")

1110½ Hay Street, Fayetteville, NC 28305   •   preppub@aol.com   •   (910) 483-6611

OBJECTIVE

To contribute to an organization in need of an articulate, personable sales professional with expert knowledge of the effective methods of buying, merchandising, displaying, and selling furniture and of the value of providing quality service for a positive bottom-line impact.

EDUCATION

Earned a B.A. in Business Administration, Shreveport College, Shreveport, LA.

EXPERIENCE

SALES MANAGER & PRESIDENT. Smithson & Associates, Shreveport, LA (1988-present). In my first job after college, joined my family's business—a well-respected downtown furniture, hardware, and appliance retailer—and became thoroughly knowledgeable of all aspects of customer service and sales. Became highly respected by clientele interested in buying quality products at reasonable prices; sell furniture which ranged from promotional to medium high-end products.

- **Sales management:** Train and manage numerous sales representatives; personally lead the store in sales and personally handle the large-volume sales of up to $15,000 and more since those purchases usually involve financing arrangements.
- **Diverse product line:** Am thoroughly familiar with products from manufacturers which include:

  Furniture: Huntington House, Pioneer, Colony House, Standard, Bemco, Carolina, Florida, and Webb living rooms, dining rooms, and bedroom furniture
  Appliances: Magic Chef, White-Westinghouse, and Gibson
  Floor covering: Sentry Rug Co. and Armstrong linoleum
  Other: Holiday Lamp lamps and Lyon-Shaw outdoor furniture
- **Affiliations:** Hold membership in the Shreveport Chamber of Commerce, Servistar Corp., and other trade associations for retailers and furniture industry firms.
- **Excellent credit and accounting policies:** Play a highly visible role in helping the business maintain an excellent reputation for providing customers with value while selling good products at fair prices. Skillfully manage accounts payable.
- **Collections:** Handle the delicate issue of making collection calls and dealing with customers who are behind in their payments which are being financed internally.
- **Vendor relations:** Make decisions on which manufacturers can provide the best quality products for the cost and carry out purchasing activities; negotiate terms.
- **Customer service:** Recognized for my ability to establish trust with potential customers, ensure they receive one-on-one attention to their needs and financial circumstances and that they receive the highest quality of service.
- **Business management:** Became president in 1998 after several years as vice president; became skilled in the hiring, termination, and training of new employees.
- **Extensive trade contacts:** Attend numerous trade shows and am highly skilled in finding small manufacturers who can produce the type of goods which will appeal to the clientele we service.
- **Negotiating skills:** Played the key role in negotiating the sale of the business and the physical building in September 2000.

AFFILIATIONS

Hold memberships in organizations which include the Shreveport Chamber of Commerce and furniture and hardware trade associations as well as the Knights of Columbus.
- Am a member of the Administrative Council of my church (United Shreveport Church).

PERSONAL

A native of Shreveport, graduated from Lawrence High School. Am single and available for travel and/or relocation. Enjoy a reputation for dedication, integrity, and high standards.

Date

Exact Name of Person
Exact Title
Exact Name of Company
Address
City, State, Zip

**Home Sales,
Manufacturing Homes
Environment**

After the experience of
founding and managing a
small business, this
individual found a satisfying
home in the environment of
manufactured home sales.

Dear Exact Name of Person: (or Dear Sir or Madam if answering a blind ad):

With the enclosed resume, I would like to make you aware of my background as an articulate, experienced sales professional with exceptional motivational, problem-solving, and financial skills that have been tested in challenging sales management and entrepreneurial environments.

As you will see from my resume, I am currently excelling as Sales Manager and General Manager for the Granville location of one of the region's manufactured home dealers. In addition to providing leadership, training, and motivation to a sales force of five personnel, I also oversee all financial aspects of the operation of this busy local dealership. Through careful hiring and training of new representatives, I have built a cohesive team of effective sales professionals, resulting in gross profits increasing by 30% each month since I became General Manager. Earlier as Sales Manager for Edgewood Homes in Dayton, my dynamic sales ability and staff development skills resulted in first-year gross profits of $375,000, while my growing knowledge of financing and credit practices allowed me to structure deals to maximize profits for the company.

Prior to entering the manufactured home sales industry, I demonstrated my keen business acumen and strong bottom-line orientation while founding and operating two successful businesses. With both Appleton Lawn Care and Dayton Seal Manufacturing, I oversaw all aspects of setup, marketing, management, financial, and accounting functions, and both of these ventures showed a profit within their first year of operation.

Although I am held in the highest regard by my present employer and can provide outstanding references at the appropriate time, I am interested in selectively exploring other opportunities in sales management. However, I would appreciate your keeping my interest confidential until after we have had the chance to meet in person.

I hope you will welcome my call soon when I try to arrange a brief meeting to discuss your goals and how my background might serve your needs. I thank you in advance for your time and professional courtesies.

Sincerely,

Latasha Emanuel

LATASHA EMANUEL

1110½ Hay Street, Fayetteville, NC 28305 • preppub@aol.com • (910) 483-6611

OBJECTIVE

To benefit an organization that can use an articulate, experienced manager with exceptional communication, problem-solving, and supervisory skills who offers a background of excellence in motivating and directing a sales force to achieve dramatic results.

LICENSE

Licensed Manufactured Home Salesperson for the state of Ohio, 1996-present.

EXPERIENCE

SALES MANAGER & GENERAL MANAGER. Ted Elliott Home Sales, Granville, OH (1999-present). Oversee all operational aspects of the business and direct a sales force of five personnel while managing a million-dollar inventory of manufactured homes.
- Have raised gross profits to an average of $60,000 per month.
- Built a reputation as an articulate communicator and skilled motivator who could be counted on to increase sales and produce dramatic results in referral business.
- Increased profits at the Sales Center by 30% every month since becoming General Manager of the location.

MANAGER. Edgewood Homes, Dayton, OH (1996-1999). In my first job in manufactured housing sales, supervised three sales professionals and an administrative staff of two employees while increasing the company's gross profit to $375,000 during my first year in this position.
- Became skilled at taking over a reluctant customer from another salesperson, effectively overcoming their objections, and closing the sale.
- Developed an extensive knowledge of credit and finance practices which allowed me to creatively structure loan packages to maximize profit for the company.
- Interviewed, hired, and trained new employees for the sales center, providing in-depth instruction in sales techniques, customer service, closing the sale, and financing.

OWNER & GENERAL MANAGER. Appleton Lawn Care, Mentor, OH (1991-1996). Founded this landscaping business and quickly grew it into a successful enterprise earning profits of $80,000 annually; handled marketing, management, and accounting functions.
- Examined job sites, estimating the cost of labor and materials needed to complete the work in order to prepare an accurate and competitive bid for each job.
- Interviewed, hired, trained, and supervised six employees.
- Processed accounts receivable/accounts payable and prepared billing statements for all accounts as well as weekly employee payroll and quarterly payroll taxes.
- Followed up with commercial accounts to ensure that customers were satisfied with the services provided; quickly resolved any customer complaints.

OWNER & GENERAL MANAGER. Dayton Seal Manufacturing, Dayton, OH (1989-1991). Started this new business "from scratch" and quickly built it into a successful venture with a first-year gross profit of $64,000.
- Interviewed, hired, trained, and then supervised a staff of three employees.
- Personally handled all advertising, marketing, sales, and promotion for the business, as well as overseeing all financial aspects of its operation.

PERSONAL

Known as an articulate sales professional and skilled motivator who can be counted on to produce outstanding results and inspire exceptional performance from the sales force. Have built a strong network of repeat and referral customers. Excellent personal and professional references on request.

Date

Exact Name of Person
Title or Position
Name of Company
Address (number and street)
Address (city, state, and zip)

Home Comfort
Products Sales

Dear Sir or Madam:

Although it's usually best
not to communicate your
preferences in an initial
cover letter, this
professional will not
consider opportunities
which are not located in
middle Tennessee or
north Georgia, where he
and his wife want to live
and retire. He intends to
"screen out" offers based
on that main criterion.

Can you use an experienced sales professional with a history of success in training others and setting sales records while applying my knowledge of inventory control and record keeping in the process of establishing new accounts and building repeat business? I would especially enjoy discussing with you how I might serve your needs in the east/middle Tennessee or north Georgia areas. My extended family is located in those parts of the country, and I have many contacts and acquaintances throughout that region.

I have been a record-setting representative for Greystone, Inc., in Pinehurst, NC. After winning recognition as the top producer for 1998, 1997, 1995, and 1993, I have reached the $1.5 million in annual sales level for fiscal 2000. I regularly service approximately 160 accounts in an area which covers Raleigh-Cary, Pinehurst, and Southern Pines, and which extends as far west as Albemarle.

Prior experience includes dealing with both the general public and building contractors with Lowe's, selling heating and air-conditioning supplies and equipment, and managing outside sales for another refrigeration supply business. I am skilled at conducting sales meetings and coordinating awards programs.

I hope you will welcome my call soon to arrange a brief meeting at your convenience to discuss your current and future needs and how I might serve them. Thank you in advance for your time.

Sincerely yours,

Claude Ingersoll

CLAUDE INGERSOLL

1110½ Hay Street, Fayetteville, NC 28305 • preppub@aol.com • (910) 483-6611

OBJECTIVE

To contribute to an organization that is in need of an experienced sales professional who offers knowledge related to sales management, inventory control, report preparation, and training others.

EXPERIENCE

REGIONAL SALES MANAGER. Greystone, Inc., Pinehurst, NC (1991-present). Consistently among the region's top producers, achieved a sales volume of over $1.5 million for fiscal year 2000 for this home-comfort products company; train and coach two junior sales representatives.

- Was honored as the region's top sales professional in 2000, 1998 1997, 1995, and 1993.
- Excelled in earning the respect and trust of professionals in the building and electrical industries through my skills in every phase of making contact, demonstrating products, and closing the sale.
- Demonstrated excellent planning skills by researching a company's needs and requirements prior to my initial call.
- Serviced approximately 160 accounts in an area ranging from Albemarle, to Sanford, to Cary and Raleigh, to Fayetteville, to Southern Pines and Pinehurst.
- Used my abilities as a communicator and my product knowledge to conduct sales meetings where employees learned effective techniques for selling the company's product line.
- Spend a great deal of my time calling on the end users of my company's products to ensure their satisfaction with our products.
- Became involved in the design and installation of display systems while selling to lighting showrooms, electrical wholesales, building supply stores, and plumbing wholesalers.

Highlights of prior experience in the sales field, Raleigh, NC:
Lowe's. Further developed my salesmanship abilities and knowledge of customer relations while dealing with both building contractors and the general public.
- Gained experience in stocking, inventory control, and computer operations.

Merritt-Holland. Sold heating and air conditioning equipment to customers throughout the eastern part of North Carolina.
- Was selected to oversee the details of coordinating special awards such as trips for high-volume sales personnel.
- Managed a wide range of advertising programs including newspaper, radio, and yellow pages advertising.
- Applied my organizational skills to arrange and coordinate dealer sales meetings.

Longley Supply Co. Established a sales territory which included Lumberton, Hamlet, and Laurinburg as well as Raleigh; sold heating and air-conditioning equipment and supplies.
- Handled the details of arranging and then hosting dealer conventions.

W.L. Smith Refrigeration Supply. As the Outside Sales Manager, was in charge of pricing and inventory control for five stores.
- Conducted regular monthly inventories and rotated stock between the stores.

EDUCATION & TRAINING

Attended courses in professional sales techniques, stress management, and positive self-suggestion as well as a 10-week Dale Carnegie course in human relations.
Studied heating and air conditioning at Pinehurst Technical Community College, Pinehurst, NC.

PERSONAL

Am a results-oriented professional. Offer a high degree of expertise in the qualities that add up to "salesmanship." Am skilled in establishing and maintaining effective relations.

Date

Exact Name
Exact Title
Exact Name of Company
Exact Address
City, State, Zip

Industrial Products Sales
and Sales Management

A short cover letter such as
this one can be highly
effective. This accomplished
sales manager could
transfer his skills and
knowledge to numerous
industries. "Short and
sweet" could describe this
cover letter which makes
powerful points about how
he has developed new
territories, improved
margins, and boosted
profit.

Dear Exact Name:

With the enclosed resume, I would like to introduce myself and the substantial
sales and marketing background I could put to work for you.

As you will see, I offer a proven track record of outstanding results in producing a
profit, improving the profit margin, developing new accounts, increasing market share,
satisfying customers, and expanding territories. In my current position, I have
developed a new territory while training and managing an eight-person sales
staff. I am contributing significantly to the company's bottom line through my results
in delivering a 40% profit margin. Prior to being recruited for my current position,
I was part of a four-person team which boosted sales 15% at a plant in Toronto.

I am known for my ability to creatively and resourcefully apply my considerable
knowledge, and I am always on the lookout for new ways to refine my own selling
techniques. I am confident of my ability to produce a highly motivated team of sales
professionals.

If you can use my talents and knowledge, please contact me and I will make myself available for a meeting with you to discuss your needs and how I might help you. I
can provide outstanding personal and professional references.

Sincerely,

Rodney Lewis

RODNEY LEWIS

1110½ Hay Street, Fayetteville, NC 28305 • preppub@aol.com • (910) 483-6611

OBJECTIVE

To become a valuable member of an organization that can use an outgoing and highly motivated sales professional who offers a proven ability to produce a profit, improve the profit margin, develop new accounts, satisfy customers, as well as motivate employees.

EDUCATION

Received Bachelor of Arts degree in **Psychology**, University of Miami, Miami, FL, 1986. Have excelled in numerous sales and sales management training programs sponsored by major industrial suppliers.
- Pride myself on my ability to creatively and aggressively apply any and all sales training.
- Have especially benefited from advanced training related to product marketing, cold calling and other sales skills, and techniques for increasing sales, profits, and motivation.

EXPERIENCE

SALES MANAGER. TrueTest Supply Network, Macon, GA (1995-present). Was recruited by key marketing officials in the parent company for this job which has involved developing a new territory as well as hiring and supervising an eight-person sales staff.
- In addition to my management responsibilities, am actively involved in sales; call on colleges, major retailers, hospitals, military accounts, and large industrial facilities.
- Sell virtually any product needed for the daily operations; provide products ranging from cleaning supplies to televisions, VCRs, refrigerators, nuts and bolts, and light bulbs.
- Have trained and organized the eight-person sales team so that it is now a sales machine known for outstanding product knowledge, customer service, and resourcefulness.
- Taught my sales peers how to improve profit in each sale by at least 5%.
- Have learned how to "work smart" in order to increase sales and sales calls by 32%.
- Trained sales personnel to establish aggressive goals and then helped them learn the practical tools which would help them achieve those goals.
- Am contributing significantly to the company's bottom line through my ability to deliver a 40% profit margin.

SALES MANAGER. Braxton & Co., Chicago, IL, and Toronto, Canada (1993-95). Was recruited to join a four-person sales team responsible for increasing by 5% the sales of a plant in Toronto which was affiliated with a company with total annual sales of $368 million.
- Greatly exceeded management expectations and our targeted goals; increased sales by 15% instead of the projected 5%.
- Retrained sales personnel in Canada in all aspects of their jobs; significantly improved their ability to prospect for new commercial and retail accounts and refined their ability to close the sale.
- Personally established numerous new commercial accounts and dramatically expanded the territory which the company had been servicing.

SALES CONSULTANT & SALES REPRESENTATIVE. Dallas, TX (1986-93). Worked for one of the country's leading sales/marketing consulting firms; acted as a management consultant under contract with numerous companies that wanted expert help in expanding their territories, boosting sales, and improving profitability. Called on and established new retail and commercial accounts.

PERSONAL

Am skilled at dealing with people and earning their confidence. Hard working, dependable, honest. Am always seeking new opportunities to improve my sales presentation skills. Known for my ability to creatively apply the knowledge I already have. Will relocate.

Date

Exact Name of Person
Title or Position
Name of Company
Address (number and street)
Address (city, state, and zip)

Dear Sir or Madam:

Inside Sales, Diversified Background in Furniture and Construction Industries

This young professional has proven that she can excel in sales in different types of environments. Notice how she emphasizes her history of always exceeding sales quotas. Tip: When prospective employers look at your resume, they think that the past is the best predictor of the future. A track record of achievement in one environment often is predictive of an ability to succeed in a different type of setting.

With the enclosed resume, I would like to make you aware of my background as an articulate professional with exceptional communication and organizational skills who offers a track record of accomplishments in sales and customer service.

Currently in an inside sales position with Mason-Build, Inc., I work with general contractors and builders from Metairie to Baton Rouge while handling sales and providing outstanding customer service. An outgoing person, I have natural sales ability which I have refined through 10 years of sales experience, and I have developed a strong rapport with residential and commercial customers. I am skilled at estimating jobs for concrete masonry and my extensive knowledge of construction and building supply allow me to work closely with general contractors and home builders, preparing cost estimates for concrete masonry units and related building supplies.

In an earlier position as a furniture sales representative for Heilig-Meyers Furniture, I further polished my selling skills while assisting customers with the selection and purchase of home furnishings and accessories. My outstanding customer service abilities allowed me to quickly build a solid base of repeat and referral clients, and I always exceeded the sales quotas set by my supervisors.

Although I am highly regarded by my present employer, I am interested in exploring opportunities with your company. Please, however, do not contact my current employer until after we talk.

If you can use an experienced sales and customer service professional who offers exceptional communication and organizational skills, I hope you will contact me. I can assure you in advance that I have an excellent reputation and would quickly become an asset to your organization. I can provide excellent references from all previous employers as well as from Mason-Build, Inc.

Sincerely,

Hannah J. Colvin

HANNAH J. COLVIN

1110½ Hay Street, Fayetteville, NC 28305 • preppub@aol.com • (910) 483-6611

OBJECTIVE
To benefit an organization that can use an articulate, enthusiastic sales professional with an outgoing personality as well as exceptional communication and organizational skills who offers a proven ability to establish and maintain effective working relationships.

EDUCATION
Completed college computer courses at Morton Community College, Metairie, LA.
Graduated from Pine Forest High School, Baton Rouge, LA, 1984. Business subjects studied included Basic Business, Typing, and Office Machines.

EXPERIENCE
INSIDE SALES REPRESENTATIVE and **CUSTOMER SERVICE REPRESENTATIVE.** Mason-Build, Inc., Baton Rouge, LA (1998-present). For this concrete masonry company, estimate commercial and residential jobs and provide exceptional customer service and sales support.
- Have established relationships with builders including Castle Construction and Talcott-Bern as well as other companies doing business from Metairie to Baton Rouge.
- Develop rapport with clients, ascertaining their needs and estimating the cost of concrete masonry units and related building supplies.
- Work closely with general contractors, subcontractors, and home builders, utilizing my extensive knowledge of construction and building supplies to provide assistance.

FURNITURE SALES REPRESENTATIVE. Heilig-Meyers Furniture Co., Baton Rouge, LA (1997-1998). Assisted customers in the selection and purchase of home furnishings and accessories as a salesperson for this local retail furniture outlet.
- Consistently exceeded all sales quotas.
- Built a strong base of repeat and referral customers based on my natural sales ability and exceptional customer service skills.

SALES ASSISTANT & CUSTOMER SERVICE REPRESENTATIVE. Williams Products Company, Baton Rouge, LA (1989-1997). Assisted the sales, dispatch, and production operations while performing customer service and receptionist duties for this local manufacturer and supplier of masonry products.
- Provided job estimates over the phone to business and residential customers, as well as acquiring dodge reports from the Internet and assisting with certifications.
- Created, updated, and maintained files for all new and existing accounts.
- Reviewed all invoices on outbound shipments and keyed contract hauler freight data into the computer, developing a template in Lotus 1-2-3 to record this data.
- Produced daily production reports, processed payroll, and coordinated safety committee activities for the production department.

SHIPPING AND RECEIVING CLERK. Lee Furniture, Metairie, LA (1986-1988). Verified invoices against purchase orders to ensure accuracy; performed data entry of invoices and purchase orders on an IBM S/36 mainframe computer.
- Assisted store supervisors while also maintaining and updating purchase order files.

AFFILIATIONS
Former member, American Business Women's Association, Baton Rouge, LA.

PERSONAL
Received the Parent in Education Award, Edwards Elementary School, Baton Rouge, LA.
Can provide excellent personal and professional references.

Date

Exact Name of Person
Exact Title
Exact Name of Company
Address
City, State, Zip

Dear Exact Name of Person (or Dear Sir or Madam if answering a blind ad):

I would appreciate an opportunity to talk with you soon about how I could contribute to your organization through my experience in office operations, computer operations, bookkeeping, and customer service. Although I am excelling in my current job and am a highly valued employee, I am interested in selectively exploring office positions with a top-notch company that can use a versatile and adaptable professional. I would appreciate your holding my interest in your company in confidence at this time.

As you will see from my resume, I worked as a Bookkeeper for a department store prior to my current position as an Inside Sales Coordinator. In my current job I am continuously involved in providing the highest level of customer service while troubleshooting and resolving a wide range of problems which occur routinely in the process of ordering building supplies. I am responsible for sales of approximately $350,000 monthly, and I am highly regarded for my dedication to our customers.

Known for my strong initiative and leadership, I thrive in situations in which I am challenged to learn new tasks and functions in my spare time. For example, at Beechwood Building Supply, I the company's most versatile employee, as I was cross-trained in all office operations and functioned as the "internal expert" in troubleshooting some of the company's computer programs.

I am highly computer literate and have utilized a computer daily to process orders, research products, prepare bids, handle special orders, and research accounting problems.

You would find me in person to be a highly congenial individual who prides myself on my ability to get along with people at all organizational levels. I offer an outstanding personal and professional reputation and can provide excellent references at the appropriate time. If you can use a hard-working and dedicated individual to join your team, I hope you will contact me to suggest a time when we could meet in person. I would like you to know that I am a permanent resident of Fayetteville and am not associated with the military.

Yours sincerely,

Valerie Ann Abraham

VALERIE ANN ABRAHAM

1110½ Hay Street, Fayetteville, NC 28305   •   preppub@aol.com   •   (910) 483-6611

OBJECTIVE

I want to contribute to an organization that can use a hard-working and versatile professional with extensive customer service experience, bookkeeping and accounting skills, as well as a strong bottom-line orientation and proven sales abilities.

EDUCATION

Graduated with high honors from Elkland High School, Tacoma, WA.
Completed extensive training sponsored by my employers in sales, accounts management, purchasing, inventory control, computer operations, and other areas.
In my spare time, am enrolling in an intermediate computer operations course, Anchorage Technical Community College.

EXPERIENCE

INSIDE SALES COORDINATOR. Houghton Building Center, Anchorage, AK (1997-present). Because of my strong reputation in the building supply field, was recruited for this job which involves continuous customer service and problem solving.

- Achieve average monthly sales of $350,000 to $400,000.
- Constantly utilize my communication and problem-solving skills in providing outstanding customer service; coordinate with customers by telephone and on two-way walkie-talkies throughout the day.
- Vigilantly monitor the customer's order to assure accuracy and on-time delivery.
- Organize and maintain an extensive volume of customer files.
- Utilize a computer daily to make accounting adjustments, process orders, prepare bids, handle special orders, and research accounts.

INSIDE SALES COORDINATOR. Alaska Builders (formerly Beechwood Building Supply), Anchorage, AK, (1990-97). Trained and managed two sales coordinators while also coordinating with five outside sales representatives on building material orders; performed liaison with dispatchers, contractors, and outside sales representatives.

- Coordinated with Duke Hill, Corning, Sierra, Inc., Masters, Northern, Alaska Pacific, and dozens of other construction and building industry firms.
- Handled sales of building materials to cash customers and walk-in traffic; over the years, became an accounts manager to dozens of customers who preferred dealing with me each time they ordered.
- Consistently achieved monthly average sales of $350,000 to $400,000.
- Prepared building estimates utilizing a computer; negotiated prices with contractors; organized and maintained customer files.
- Became known for my cheerfulness and willingness to be cross-trained in other areas including bookkeeping, computer operations, and most office operations; on my own initiative, taught myself to use several computer programs and gradually became the "internal expert" on troubleshooting software problems.

BOOKKEEPER. Beacon Department Store, Tacoma, WA (1988-90). Before making the decision to permanently relocate to Alaska, performed customer service, bookkeeping, and accounting for a department store.

- Prepared forms used by sales associates; prepared and proofed merchandise club books; was responsible for $5,000 cash till.
- Answered a four-line switchboard.
- Balanced cash sales, charge sales, and accounts receivable ledger books; made daily bank deposits; handled monthly billing of 500 furniture accounts.

PERSONAL

Am very computer literature and rapidly master new software.

Date

Exact Name of Person
Title or Position
Name of Company
Address (number and street)
Address (city, state and zip)

Dear Exact Name of Person: (or Dear Sir or Madam if answering a blind ad.)

With the enclosed resume, I would like to express my interest in joining your agency as an Investment Counselor, Licensed Insurance Agent, or Agency Manager.

As you will see from my resume, I have excelled in a track record of advancement with Sundale Financial Services. I began with the company as a Sales Representative and achieved Leader's Conference Qualification in my first year. Promoted to Sales Manager and then to Agency Manager, I was recognized at the Management Leaders Council for leading the Palo Alto office to one of the top 15 among 139 sales offices in the west. I hold licenses to sell insurance and annuities in California and also hold the Series 6 and 63. I am respected for my knowledge of financial services as well as my proven ability to develop outstanding client relationships based on trust and quality service. I quote and write insurance applications for Auto, Life & Health, and Fire including Homeowners, Renters, Boatowners, Personal Liability Umbrella, Inland Marine, and Commercial.

With a B.S. degree, I have also received extensive training in numerous aspects of insurance sales and products.

While working for Sundale Financial Services, I have played a key role in helping this agent become a Legion of Honor Agent on multiple occasions, and I have become knowledgeable of all aspects of managing an insurance agency for maximum profitability. We continually re-underwrite our book of business to remain profitable, and we maintain vigilant quality control of our multiline business in order to maintain a quality book of business.

If you can use my versatile talents and abilities, I hope you will contact me to suggest a time when we might meet in person to discuss your needs. Thank you in advance for your time.

Sincerely,

Daniel T. Traywick

DANIEL T. TRAYWICK

1110½ Hay Street, Fayetteville, NC 28305 • preppub@aol.com • (910) 483-6611

OBJECTIVE To become a valuable member of an organization that can use an outgoing and highly motivated financial services professional who offers a proven ability to produce a profit, develop new accounts, satisfy customers, as well as train and motivate employees.

EDUCATION Received Bachelor of Science degree in **Business Administration** and a Bachelor of Arts degree in **Political Science**, University of California at Los Angeles, CA, 1983.
Currently completing Certified Financial Planner Course.
Excelled in numerous training programs sponsored by Sundale Financial Services.

LICENSES Licensed to sell insurance and annuities in CA; also hold the series 6 and 63.

EXPERIENCE **Have advanced to increasing responsibilities with Sundale Financial Services,** Palo Alto, CA (1994-present).
1999-present: AGENCY MANAGER. Have been responsible for recruiting, training, and developing the sales force in the Palo Alto area.
- Coordinated target market approach of individuals to meet the needs of various groups in our market.
- Recognized at Management Leaders Council for leading the Palo Alto office to top 15 out of 139 sales offices in western US.
- Created, developed, and conducted training sessions to impart knowledge of variable life, variable annuities, and mutual funds.
- Am respected for my expert knowledge of financial services as well as for my proven ability to develop outstanding client relationships based on trust and quality service.

1996-99: SALES MANAGER. Became skilled in recruiting, managing, and motivating a sales force while guiding the office to one of the top 20 of 140 offices.

1994-96: SALES REPRESENTATIVE. Learned the insurance business at the ground level and excelled rapidly; developed leads and cultivated clients while providing financial needs analysis to prospects in order to help them prioritize financial planning needs of insurance, accumulation, and retirement programs.
- Achieved Leader's Conference Qualification in my first year with the company.
- National Quality Award Recipient, 1995 and 1996.

GENERAL MANAGER/COMPTROLLER. Fairview Enterprises, Wilmington, NC (1990-1994). Was recruited by this family business to serve as its General Manager and Comptroller; oversaw the operations of a chain of three restaurants, each of which had a unit general manager.
- Directed management team of food service operations primarily focusing on cost control, marketing, and financial operations in order to maximum profit while increasing sales and market share.
- Played the major negotiating role in the discussions which resulted in the company's being bought out by a larger restaurant chain.

CITY EXECUTIVE. Oakland, Inc., Oakland, CA (1987-90). Produced exceptional growth in both commercial and consumer loans deposit operations in order to reduce risk and improve profitability.

AFFILIATION Palo Alto Association of Life Underwriters; Board of Directors 1998-present.

Date

Attention: Anne Smith
BY FAX TO: (910) 483-2439

Dear Ms. Smith:

Later on in this book, you
will see resumes of sales
professionals trying to
break into pharmaceutical
sales. This individual has
succeeded in medical sales
and is approaching a
competitor.

With the enclosed resume, I would like to formally apply for the position with Smith-Kelley Pharmaceuticals, which you and I discussed yesterday.

As you will see from my resume, I am excelling in my current position as a Medical Sales Representative with Ogden Pharma, Inc. While developing this territory "from scratch," I have successfully launched new products and have opened and stocked pharmacies from New York to Massachusetts. In 1998 I was inducted into the President's Club, won two sales contests with monetary awards, and was one of the company's three top producers while being ranked #1 in my district. I have consistently won sales awards and contests since I began with the company in 1997 and am proud of the excellent relationships I have established within the medical community.

I can provide outstanding personal and professional references at the appropriate time, but I would appreciate your not contacting my employer until after we have a chance to talk more about the position which we discussed earlier yesterday. I am single, will relocate according to the company's needs, and would cheerfully welcome overnight travel.

If Smith-Kelley can use a dynamic sales professional with a proven ability to "make it happen," I hope you will call or write me to suggest a time when we might meet to discuss how I might help Smith-Kelley achieve its goals. While working with Ogden Pharma, I have become acquainted with some of the Smith-Kelley sales representatives who work in my territory. Through them, I have learned about Smith-Kelley and have gained an appreciation of their products and reputation, and I feel that I could rapidly become a valuable addition to the Smith-Kelley team.

Yours sincerely,

Jenifer Nichols

JENIFER NICHOLS

1110½ Hay Street, Fayetteville, NC 28305 • preppub@aol.com • (910) 483-6611

OBJECTIVE

To offer my proven track record of success in sales as well as my enthusiastic and positive attitude to an organization that can use a dedicated professional with a proven track record of results in launching new products, developing outstanding relationships, and maximizing market share.

EXPERIENCE

MEDICAL SALES REPRESENTATIVE. Ogden Pharma, Inc., Brighton, MA (1997-present). While successfully launching new products, developed this territory "from scratch" while also opening and stocking pharmacies from New York to Massachusetts; have distinguished myself as one of the company's top producers.

- Was inducted into the prestigious President's Club for 1998; was one of the company's overall top three producers in 2000 and was consistently the top producer in my district; won two sales contests with monetary awards.
- Introduced this company's product line to physicians and pharmacies in southeastern Massachusetts; through repeated sales calls have established an excellent working relationship with the medical community and continually strive to build sales in my territory.
- Have acquired expert knowledge of cough and cold products.
- Was promoted to Field Sales Supervisor and selected to assist the Manager in recruiting and field training of new employees.
- Participated in the planning for and conducting of district sales meetings.
- Was awarded a 110% pin in 1999.
- Earned the honor as the 1998 "Sales Rep of the Year."
- Won a trip to the Bahamas in a 1998 product promotion campaign.

COUNTER MANAGER. Hamilton's, Cambridge, MA (1995-97). Earned a transfer from Allston to the larger Northpark Mall store as a Clinique Counter Manager in a location with six consultants and $500,000 in annual sales.
- Gained experience in other operational areas including product demonstration, execution of special events, conducting monthly inventories, and preparing weekly work schedules.

COUNTER MANAGER. Ivey's, Allston, MA (1992-95). After only five months as a Sales Associate, was promoted to supervise two sales associates at a location with an annual gross of $250,000 in sales.
- Conducted statistical analyses of inventory and sales figures, planned and carried out special events, and determined merchandising strategy while exceeding sales goals.

Highlights of earlier experience: Learned the unique business of cosmetics sales as a Consultant for major products including Clinique, Estee Lauder, Flori Roberts, Aramis, Germaine Monteil, and Fragrances.

EDUCATION

Completing a **Bachelor of Science in Psychology,** Northeastern University; Dec. 2000. Studied **Nutrition** at Boston University.
Graduated from **Fashion Merchandising and Management** Program at Fashion Institute of Technology, New York, NY.

PERSONAL

Offer thoroughness and accuracy while handling paperwork. Am responsible, well organized, and work well with the public and my coworkers. Enjoy a reputation for being punctual.

Date

Exact Name of Person
Title or Position
Name of Company
Address (no., street)
Address (city, state, zip)

Dear Exact Name of Person: (or Dear Sir or Madam if answering a blind ad.)

I would appreciate an opportunity to talk with you soon about how I could contribute to your organization through my extensive experience in medical sales and marketing, medical billing, and nutritional consulting.

Fluent in English and Spanish, I hold an undergraduate degree in Nutrition and Dietetics **cum laude**, and I have worked as a full-time Nutritionist and Marketing Consultant for both the Beech-Nut and Quaker Oats Companies. In those jobs, I visited hospitals, doctors, health centers, and supermarkets to promote products and conduct special marketing events. I am a skilled public speaker and have coordinated numerous conferences and publicity activities.

I have also excelled in sales and sales management positions with a major pharmaceutical company. I began with the company in 1987 as a Medical Marketing Representative and progressed rapidly into sales management responsibilities which involved training up to eight medical sales professionals. With my naturally outgoing personality and extensive background in the sciences and nutrition, I became one of the company's most valuable employees and most visible spokespersons.

You will see from my resume that I am a hard worker. While excelling in my full-time positions mentioned above, I worked part-time during the evenings and on the weekends for nearly ten years handling all medical billing for a six-doctor medical practice. I had a fully equipped office in my home, and I am very experienced in utilizing WordPerfect and medical billing software including Medifast.

You would find me to be a personable and well-educated individual who relates well to people and who adapts easily to new organizational environments. I can provide excellent personal and professional references.

I hope you will call me soon to suggest a time when we might meet to discuss your current and future needs and how I might serve them. Thank you for your time.

Sincerely yours,

Soraya Zahran, LDN

SORAYA ZAHRAN, LDN

1110½ Hay Street, Fayetteville, NC 28305 • preppub@aol.com • (910) 483-6611

OBJECTIVE

To contribute to an organization that can use an experienced young professional who offers an education as a dietitian along with experience in medical marketing and administration.

EDUCATION

Bachelor of Science in Nutrition and Dietetics, **cum laude**, University of Puerto Rico, 1984. Completed graduate-level internship in Dietetics, 1984-85.

EXPERIENCE

NUTRITIONIST & MARKETING MANAGER. Quaker Oats Company, Puerto Rico (1990-99). As the company's internal nutritionist, coordinated visits to hospitals and health centers in order to present lectures on nutrition, dietetics, and other subjects; explained the benefits of Quaker products in the outpatient setting.
- Trained sales professionals and suppliers regarding product knowledge.
- Marketed Quaker products through visits to doctors' and nutritionists' offices.
- Coordinated and participated in conventions in order to promote products.
- Trained and supervised outside publicists in developing marketing materials.

MEDICAL MARKETING MANAGER. Sterling Products, Intl., Puerto Rico (1987-90). For a major pharmaceutical company, marketed medical and pharmaceutical products to public and private hospitals; began with the company as a Medical Sales Representative and then progressed into sales management; supervised eight sales representatives.
- Became one of the company's most productive sales professionals as well as a highly visible and trusted spokesperson respected for my extensive expertise related to over-the-counter drugs.
- Developed special events at medical conventions to promote the company's products; coordinated all special publicity and promotional activities.
- Trained company as well as customer personnel on new products.
- Visited prospective new clients to present products; was known as a skillful negotiator with the ability to close the sale.
- Visited doctors, hospitals, and pharmacies to promote the company's products.

NUTRITIONIST & MARKETING MANAGER. Beech-Nut Nutrition Corporation, Puerto Rico (1986-87). As a Nutritionist, visited hospitals, health centers, doctors' offices, and supermarkets in order to explain the advantages of Beech-Nut products.
- Promoted products for babies and infants and expectant mothers; designed special promotions with supermarkets and stores which generated extensive sales.
- Marketed products and trained sales/marketing sales professionals for the company in both Puerto Rico and the Dominican Republic.

CHIEF OF DIETETIC SERVICES. Hospital Gubern, Puerto Rico (1985-86). Supervised a department with 12 employees; oversaw the training and scheduling of all employees.
- Performed nutritional assessments of hospital patients; provided dietary instructions to patients being discharged.
- Purchased nutritional products and food; integrated products into the hospital menu.

COMPUTERS, LANGUAGES

Extremely computer literate; skilled in using WordPerfect and Medifast for medical billing. Fluent in both English and Spanish.

PERSONAL

Have a U.S. Social Security Number. Extremely self-motivated individual. Adapt easily.

Date

Dear Sir or Madam:

With the enclosed resume, I would like to make you aware of my background as an articulate, reliable professional with exceptional communication and organizational abilities as well as experience in merchandising, sales, and customer service.

Recently, I have been excelling as a Merchandising Specialist for Effective Merchandise, Inc. In this position, I serviced a variety of large corporate accounts, including Hanes, Bali, Playtex, Kodak, and Pepperidge Farms, resetting stock and ensuring that their products were prominently and effectively displayed. I worked in major retail outlets such as Wal-Mart, Sears, J.C. Penney, Belk, Roses, and Harris Teeter, removing product lines that were being replaced and correctly merchandising new products according to planograms provided by the corporate customer. In earlier positions with Lawrence & Company and Quality Retail Services, I merchandised health and beauty aids and pharmaceutical products for Bayer, Proctor & Gamble, Clairol, Max Factor, and other major accounts.

Earlier I served as a Book Merchandiser for Book Time, Inc., restocking book displays in K-Mart, CVS, and Kerr Drug locations. I pulled time-sensitive materials, such as monthly romances (Harlequin, Silhouette, etc.) off the shelf and replaced them with current releases. In addition, I quickly developed a general knowledge of authors, as well as fiction, nonfiction, children's books, and medical titles, which allowed me to more efficiently merchandise book products.

As you will see from my enclosed resume, I have completed several years of college-level course work at the University of Virginia and at Richmond Technical College in Richmond, VA. I also studied for and received a Nurse's Aide certification, and completed numerous technical training courses in radio operation and repair as part of my military training. I feel that my ability to quickly master new concepts, educational background, and practical experience would make me a valuable addition to your operation.

If you can use an enthusiastic, hard-working professional whose highly developed merchandising, sales, and customer services skills have been proven in challenging situations requiring tact and diplomacy, I look forward to hearing from you soon. I assure you in advance that I have an excellent reputation and could quickly become an asset to your organization.

Yours sincerely,

Francis J. Gulati

FRANCIS J. GULATI

1110½ Hay Street, Fayetteville, NC 28305　•　preppub@aol.com　•　(910) 483-6611

OBJECTIVE

To benefit an organization that can use an articulate, hard-working professional with experience in merchandising, sales, and customer service in addition to oral communication skills.

EDUCATION & TRAINING

Have completed college-level course work at institutions including the following:
- University of Virginia, general studies courses, 1993-95.
- Richmond Technical College, general studies and nursing courses, 1992.

Successfully completed intensive military training in radio operation and repair, U.S. Army.
Received a Nurse's Aide certificate after Red Cross and hospital training in CPR and safety.

EXPERIENCE

MERCHANDISING SPECIALIST. Effective Merchandise, Inc. (1997-present). Service a wide variety of corporate accounts, including Hanes, Bali bras, Playtex, Kodak film, and Pepperidge Farms, ensuring that their merchandise is presented in full and attractive displays in prominent locations and merchandised properly according to corporate guidelines.
- Reset stock in major retail outlets such as Wal-Mart, Sears, J.C. Penney, Belk, and Roses, removing product lines being replaced and correctly merchandising new product.
- Read planograms to ensure proper placement of product, and change all shelf labeling to correctly reflect the new merchandise.
- Change endcap, slat wall, and spinner displays, stocking all display areas as full as possible, fronting and blocking displays to present a full and attractive appearance.

MERCHANDISING SPECIALIST. Lawrence & Company (1996-97). Reset stock and restructured existing displays in order to add new products, merchandising health & beauty aids, household/domestics, and pharmaceutical products at a number of major retail outlets.

BOOK MERCHANDISER. Book Time, Inc. (1996). Merchandised book displays for a number of major retailers, including K-Mart, CVS, and Kerr Drugs, pulling older titles from the shelf, prominently displaying newer titles, and creating endcap and table displays.
- Pulled time-sensitive materials, such as monthly romance series (Harlequin, Silhouette, etc.) and replaced the old titles with current releases.
- Read merchandising planners in order to ensure proper placement of all titles.
- Developed a general knowledge of authors, as well as fiction, nonfiction, children's books, and medical, which allowed me to merchandise books more efficiently.

HEALTH & BEAUTY MERCHANDISER. Quality Retail Services, Inc. (1995). Serviced Wal-Mart, CVS, K-Mart, and Target stores, merchandising health & beauty aids and pharmaceutical products for accounts such as Bayer, Proctor & Gamble, Clairol, Max Factor.
- Reset stock and created displays of new merchandise, using a planogram to ensure that all products were correctly merchandised.
- Checked expiration dates on pharmaceutical products such as vitamins.

Other Experience: **AUDITOR.** Merchandise Data, Inc. (1993-1994). Used a hand-held inventory computer/scanner to conduct integrity audits of major retailers; primary responsibility was to conduct quarterly audits of local Wal-Mart stores.

PERSONAL

Pride myself on my positive attitude and determination. Have a strong desire to learn. Can develop extensive product knowledge and present this knowledge to others.

Mortgage Sales and Consulting, Semi-Functional Resume

One interesting feature of this resume is that it is in a semi-functional format, which may interest those of you who are curious about functional resumes. Even his cover letter is set up in a functional format, so that he can identify key areas of competency to prospective employers.

Dear Sir or Madam:

With the enclosed resume, I would like to inquire about employment opportunities in your organization and make you aware of my extensive background related to sales and marketing, customer service, and management.

Sales, customer service, and marketing background

As you will see from my resume, I have most recently excelled in handling sales and customer service responsibilities in both the financial services and automobile sales field. In my earliest positions as an Auto Sales Representative, I refined my communication and negotiating skills and then advanced in a track record of accomplishment as a Sales Manager and then General Sales Manager. In my current job in the financial services field, I am excelling as a Mortgage Consultant in a highly competitive marketplace, and I am known for my excellent communication and negotiating skills.

Experience in contracting and purchasing

In a previous job, I refined my decision-making and problem-solving skills as an Assistant Contract Officer. I was authorized to approve contracts under $500,000 for the procurement of goods and services, and I was commended for my ability to maintain excellent working relationships while overseeing strict quality assurance related to the expenditure of public money.

Military and security background

As a young airman in the Air Force, I proudly served my country and was entrusted with one of the nation's highest security clearances: Top Secret. After military service, I worked in the law enforcement and corrections field and continued to serve my country in the National Guard in administrative capacities.

I can provide outstanding references at the appropriate time, and I would enjoy an opportunity to talk with you in person about your needs. If you can use a versatile young professional who is accustomed to excelling in multifaceted complex assignments, I hope you will contact me. Thank you in advance for your time.

Yours sincerely,

Mark R. Graham

MARK R. GRAHAM

1110½ Hay Street, Fayetteville, NC 28305 • preppub@aol.com • (910) 483-6611

OBJECTIVE

I want to contribute to an organization that can use an accomplished sales professional who offers a proven ability to establish strong working relationships, generate profitable bottom-line results, and provide outstanding customer service.

EDUCATION

College: Completed three years of college at these institutions: studied **General Studies** and **Sociology**, Boston College, MA; studied **Business Administration**, Northeastern University, MA; and studied **Business Administration**, Boston Business College, MA.
Military Training: Completed technical training and professional development courses sponsored by the U.S. Air Force; areas studied included administration and operations management.
Sales: Completed numerous courses related to sales and customer service sponsored by my employers.

EXPERIENCE

Sales and Financial Field:
MORTGAGE CONSULTANT. New England Mortgage, Brookline, MA (1997-present). As a mortgage consultant for a regional mortgage brokerage company, am providing services related to debt consolidation while also refinancing VA, FHA, conforming, and nonconforming loans.

GENERAL SALES MANAGER. Peter David Used Cars, Lexington, MA (1995-97). Was recruited by the founder of the company to serve as his General Sales Manager; supervised up to 10 sales professionals including assistant sales managers.
• Trained sales professionals in winning techniques related to sales and customer service.
• Helped my sales staff become skilled at "closing the sale" and negotiating final details.

SALES MANAGER. Revere Chrysler-Suzuki, Lexington, MA (1994-95). Was credited with being a major force in helping the company achieve gross sales of $32 million a year along with an extremely healthy after-tax income.
• Resigned from this job when I was recruited by my former employer, Peter David, to become his General Sales Manager.

Corrections and Law Enforcement Field:
CORRECTIONAL OFFICER. (1987-94). Worked in a 1,000-man corrections facility in Maryland State Penitentiary, Potomac, MD, and in the Bethesda City Jail, Bethesda, MD.

Contracting and Finance Field:
ASSISTANT CONTRACT OFFICER. Defense Control Administrative Services, Bethesda, MD (1984-87). Was authorized to approve contracts under $500,000 for the procurement of goods and services for the U.S. government; refined my communication and negotiating skills while fine-tuning the details of complex contracts.

Military Service:
ADMINISTRATIVE SPECIALIST. Strategic Air Command, Andrews AFB, MD (1980-84). Held a Top Secret security clearance and was entrusted with receiving Top Secret documents and other classified documents. Was promoted rapidly from Airman to Sergeant.

PERSONAL

Enjoy helping others and being in business situations in which my product knowledge can help consumers make a wise decision about products and services. Have proven my ability to provide the finest customer service in a highly competitive marketplace.

Nutrition Products Sales, Food Industry and Insurance Background

After trying insurance sales and food industry sales, Mr. Aziz decided that he feels "at home" in the food industry. Therefore, his Objective mentions his food industry background.

Dear Sir or Madam:

With the enclosed resume, I would like to make you aware of my interest in exploring employment opportunities within your organization in some capacity in which you could utilize my considerable sales experience.

As you will see from my enclosed resume, I offer an extensive background in both sales and the food service industry, which began with my first job at eight years of age! Early in my career I excelled as a Sales Manager and Processing Plant Manager for a company which sold food industry items to various restaurants and food industry establishments. In another position as an independent contractor, I maintained sales of more than a quarter million dollars annually to food service establishments. Then for nearly ten years, I sold a diverse product line to accounts which included community refreshment stands, convenience store chain operations, public school cafeterias, and concession stands.

In my current position, I am managing a variety of administrative operations for a company which has a product line in the nutrition field. Although I am held in high regard in my current position and can provide excellent references at the appropriate time, I am interested in employment opportunities which can make more extensive use of my sales and marketing abilities.

I hope you will contact me soon to suggest a time when we might meet to discuss your needs.

Sincerely,

Paul A. Aziz

PAUL A. AZIZ

1110½ Hay Street, Fayetteville, NC 28305   •   preppub@aol.com   •   (910) 483-6611

OBJECTIVE   I want to contribute to an organization that can use an experienced sales professional with an extensive food industry background who offers a proven ability to achieve high goals related to market share, profitability, customer satisfaction, and sales.

EXPERIENCE   **CORPORATE MANAGER & SALES MANAGER.** NutriHerb, Inc., Montpelier, VT (1998-present). For this company which promotes a diet/weight loss/energy-enhancing product line, administer the computer operations functions for a 1,500-member customer base.
- Monitor day-to-day sales performance, and prepare a variety of reports for management which highlight key performance areas and sales trends.
- Provide oversight for shipping and receiving functions, data processing and clerical activities, as well as accounts payable.
- Have become proficient with Windows 2000.
- Am achieving significant increases in sales in 2000 compared to 1999.

INDEPENDENT INSURANCE AGENT. Avery Insurance Agency, Montpelier, VT (1996-98). Was a licensed broker with Vermont Department of Insurance recognized companies.
- Established myself as a top producer in the VT market with Blue Cross Blue Shield/VT and other companies; promoted over-65 products as well as individual and group plans to restaurants and small business, etc.

ROUTE SALESMAN. Montpelier Cigar and Candy, Inc., Montpelier, VT (1987-95). Excelled in all aspects of handling a sales route calling on accounts which included community refreshment stands, convenience store chain operations, public school cafeterias, and concession interests.
- Represented a diverse product line which included candy, grocery products, general merchandise, novelty items, and tobacco products.
- Sold an extensive inventory of paper and supply items to restaurants, grills, and institutional food service entities.

ROUTE SALESMAN. Chester Sales, Chester, VT (1983-87). Achieved sales of more than $250,000 annually to food service establishments.

Other experience: Grew up in the food industry and had my first job in a restaurant at the age of eight years old. Later on, as a **Sales Manager** and **Processing Plant Manager** for Flint Foods in Montpelier, sold food industry items including perishable foodstuffs as well as the fixtures, fittings, and supplies needed for daily operations to a customer base comprised of various restaurants and food industry establishments.

EDUCATION   Completed Mechanical Drafting and Engineering curriculum, 3.5 GPA, Montpelier Technical Community College, Montpelier, VT, 1983.
Studied Business Administration Curriculum, Chester Community College, 1977-79.

PERSONAL   Am a highly self-motivated individual with a proven ability to "talk the lingo" of the restaurant and food service industry. Can provide excellent references. Am a proven sales professional with the ability to help customers resolve their problems, which is one key to success in sales. Excellent references are available on request.

Date

Exact Name of Person
Title or Position
Name of Company
Address (no., street)
Address (city, state, zip)

Nutrition Products and Services Sales

This letter is directed to an employment agency which has placed an advertisement in the newspaper. Since Ms. Wagner is relocating from the east coast to the west coast, she will utilize all available methods of contacting prospective employers.

Dear Exact Name of Person: (or Dear Sir or Madam if answering a blind ad.)

I am writing in response to your ad in the *Los Angeles Times*. I am planning to relocate to the Los Angeles area and am sending you a copy of my resume so that you can assist me in my search for a challenging and rewarding position in this area.

As you will see from my resume, I have been successful in a management position with the nationally known Nutrition for Life organization. Despite the fact that this corporation has declared bankruptcy and more than 800 locations have had to close, I have been able to not only keep my Raleigh, NC, locations open but have increased sales. In 2000, I edged out some tough competition to earn the respected "Manager of the Year Award" from among approximately 1,600 other professionals.

My degree is in Psychology and Sociology and I offer additional experience as a Social Worker. After demonstrating that I could handle a case load of 120-150 clients and consistently complete my cases ahead of schedule, I was promoted to Eligibility Specialist in the Department of Social Services.

I have managed a staff of up to 25 and all aspects of operations in a facility which reached the $900,000 level in annual sales and serviced as many as 300 clients a week.

I am an enthusiastic, energetic, and well-organized professional. I offer a talent for getting the most from employees and finding effective ways to keep things running smoothly and productively—even under very unsettled circumstances.

I hope you will welcome my call soon to discuss how you might be able to help me in my job search in your area. Thank you in advance for your time.

Sincerely yours,

Veronica Wagner

VERONICA WAGNER

1110½ Hay Street, Fayetteville, NC 28305 • preppub@aol.com • (910) 483-6611

OBJECTIVE   To offer my superior communication and motivational skills to an organization that can use an experienced management professional who has demonstrated a bottom-line orientation and a talent for selling concepts and services through an enthusiastic and energetic style.

EXPERIENCE   **GENERAL MANAGER** and **CUSTOMER SERVICE MANAGER**. The Matthews Group (Nutrition for Life), Raleigh and Goldsboro, NC (1988-present). Continue to set sales records and steadily increase the customer base despite the fact that the parent corporation declared bankruptcy in 1993 and more than 800 locations nationwide were forced to close.

- Singled out as **"Manager of the Year for 2000"** from among 1,600 qualified professionals nationwide, displayed knowledge of every aspect of Nutrition for Life operations.
- Increased sales by more than 50% during reorganization following a corporate takeover.
- Handled a wide range of functional activities ranging from setting sales and service goals, to developing business plans, to recruiting/training/supervising employees.
- Oversaw daily operational areas including financial management, inventory control, and customer follow up procedures.
- Handpicked for my effectiveness in running the Raleigh site, was selected to open the Goldsboro location and hold the position of interim area manager.
- During a two-month period prior to opening the Goldsboro center, hired and trained personnel and set up their operation.
- Applied my knowledge of marketing techniques while developing campaigns which used successful clients in radio ads and placed "lead boxes" throughout the city.
- Supervised up to 25 employees in a facility which saw from 250 to 300 clients a week and made $900,000 in its peak years before corporate reorganization.
- Maintained a $500,000 to $600,000 level with approximately 140 clients a week and about 12 employees in 1994.
- Through personal attention and rapport with clients, built a strong customer base which continues to generate about four new clients a week.

ELIGIBILITY SPECIALIST. Department of Social Services, Raleigh, NC (1986-87). Through my ability to communicate effectively with others and quickly establish rapport, was effective in working closely with agency clients to assess their needs and using established guidelines to determine their eligibility for various types of aid.

- Was promoted after managing a case load of from 120 to 150 clients and displaying my ability to organize and deal with a heavy schedule by always completing my cases on schedule and pitching in to help other social workers with theirs.
- Investigated approximately 60 cases a month through a combination of office and home visits to obtain information to determine eligibility for aid.

EDUCATION   **B.S., Psychology and Sociology,** University of Wisconsin, River Falls, WI, 1984.

- Earned recognition in "Who's Who Among American College Students" on the recommendation of Sociology Department faculty members.
- Maintained a 3.8 GPA and was one of the top two students in my graduating class.
- Received "Special Honors" and "Highest Academic Honors" upon my graduation.
- Founded and then served as president of the university's Sociology Club; planned and coordinated a wide range of campus activities for the Student Activities Committee.
- Completed independent study in Europe on the use of alternative medicines.

COMPUTERS   Experienced with all Microsoft products including Word, Excel, and Access.

PERSONAL   Am an energetic and enthusiastic individual with a flair for handling human, material, and fiscal resources. Contribute to my community in assisting the homeless and disadvantaged.

Date

Exact Name of Person
Exact Title
Exact Name of Company
Address
City, State, Zip

**Outside Sales,
Furniture and Food
Industries**

A versatile background with
experience in the food and
furniture industries should
attract the interest of
employers in a variety of
industries. This
professional is hoping to
find a challenging position
in outside sales.

Dear Exact Name of Person (or Dear Sir or Madam if answering a blind ad):

With the enclosed resume, I would like to make you aware of the considerable sales skills and experience I could offer your organization.

As you will see from my resume, I offer excellent communication and public relations skills which I have refined in a track record of success in sales and customer service situations. In the furniture industry and the food distribution industry, I have excelled in establishing a client base and assisting customers while introducing new products and services, negotiating and explaining business and service contracts, and providing follow-up after the sale. I am very poised at dealing with the public.

My administrative skills are also highly refined. In a previous job I was involved in preparing correspondence, maintaining a database, and assisting in all aspects of office operations for an engineering and housing organization. I am familiar with many popular software programs and offer a proven ability to rapidly master new applications.

I can provide outstanding personal and professional references at the appropriate time, and I would be pleased to make myself available to talk with you in person about your needs and how I might serve them. You would find me in person to be a congenial individual, and I have succeeded in my working career so far through persistence, resourcefulness, and excellent "people skills." I hope you will contact me if my background interests you.

Yours sincerely,

Christa Kumpf

CHRISTA KUMPF

1110½ Hay Street, Fayetteville, NC 28305 • preppub@aol.com • (910) 483-6611

OBJECTIVE

To benefit an organization that can use an articulate young professional with exceptional communication and organizational skills who offers a versatile background as an administrative assistant and sales professional.

EDUCATION

Completed more than two years of college course work in General Studies, Lincoln Junior College.

Obtained a certification in Food Service from the Department of Health, Lincoln Technical Community College, Lincoln, NE, 1997.

COMPUTERS

Familiar with popular operating systems and software including: Windows 95, Microsoft Word and Excel, and Lotus 1-2-3; knowledgeable in Pascal and BASIC programming languages, and possess the ability to quickly master proprietary systems.

EXPERIENCE

OUTSIDE SALES REPRESENTATIVE. MacDougal Foods, Lincoln, NE (1998-present). Serviced existing accounts and developed new business, offering in-home delivery of groceries to residential customers for this large regional food service company.

- Established a clientele in my territory through exceptional customer service and communication skills; quickly build a rapport with customers from diverse backgrounds.
- Effectively introduce products and services to clients, demonstrating my knowledge of the product and presenting the benefits of home delivery in a positive light.
- Provide exceptional service, following up after the sale in order to ensure satisfaction and increase customer retention.
- Adept at tactfully deflecting customer objections and closing the sale; maintain an 80% closing ratio on all telemarketing leads.
- Negotiate and compose business contracts by hand and explain the terms, limitations, and protections covered in the instrument to the consumer.
- Operate a variety of business machines, including a 10-key calculator and fax machine.

SALES REPRESENTATIVE. Parker Food Service, Blair, NE (1998). Serviced existing customers and developed new accounts while working in commission sales for this local food service company.

- Effectively introduced products and services, demonstrating knowledge of the product.
- Negotiated and composed business contracts, explaining the terms, limitations, and protections covered in the instrument to the consumer.

SALES REPRESENTATIVE. Rhodes Furniture, Lincoln, NE (1995-1998). Performed customer service, sales, inventory control, and other duties for this large furniture store; quickly mastered several proprietary software systems used by the company.

- Assisted the customer in the selection and purchase of home furnishings, presenting the benefits and advantages of the product.
- Utilized proprietary software systems to check account status and credit limit on existing accounts, and run credit inquiries on potential new accounts.
- Checked stock levels, placed customer special orders and store orders, and processed returns, using the company's proprietary inventory control software.

PERSONAL

Excellent personal and professional references are available upon request.

Date

Exact Name of Person
Title or Position
Name of Company
Address (number and street)
Address (city, state, and zip)

**Outside Sales,
Seeking Sales
Management Role**

This young professional is
seeking a position which
will combine sales and
management
responsibilities.
Tip: If you're wondering
when and how to mention
your GPA, here's the rule. If
your GPA was 3.3 or higher,
it's generally to your
advantage to mention it on
your resume. Do *not*
mention your GPA if it was
below 3.3. Notice in the
Education Section of the
Resume, this professional
points out that she excelled
academically while working
up to 20 hours weekly.
Prospective employers are
likely to think she has well-
developed time
management skills.

Dear Sir or Madam:

With the enclosed resume, I would like to make you aware of my background as an articulate professional who offers a strong bottom-line orientation as well as exceptional sales ability and natural leadership skills which have been proven in challenging positions in outside sales and management.

As you will see from my resume, I am currently excelling as Manager and Outside Sales Representative for a local business. I joined this company at its inception as an Accountant but was quickly asked to take on additional responsibilities due to my natural leadership and exceptional sales ability. As Manager I trained and now supervise a staff of five Sales Associates, setting goals for each employee which have resulted in quintupling the store's business since we opened. While calling on new and existing accounts I have grown our business into one of the top five for commercial feed sales in the southeast region.

I have earned a Bachelor of Arts in Accounting from University of Alabama, where I further honed my time management skills, maintaining a **3.4 cumulative GPA** while working 20 hours per week in various sales positions throughout my collegiate career. Although I am highly regarded by my present employer and can provide outstanding personal and professional references at the appropriate time, I feel that my aggressive bottom-line orientation and exceptional sales ability make me a natural candidate for a career in pharmaceutical sales.

If you can use an experienced sales and management professional with the proven ability to build strong customer relationships and increase sales, I hope you will write or call me soon to suggest a time when we might meet to discuss your needs and goals and how my background might serve them. I can provide outstanding references at the appropriate time.

Sincerely,

Yvette Varisco

YVETTE VARISCO

1110½ Hay Street, Fayetteville, NC 28305   •   preppub@aol.com   •   (910) 483-6611

OBJECTIVE

To benefit an organization that can use an articulate, experienced sales and management professional with exceptional communication and leadership abilities who offers a background of excellence in outside sales, management, customer service, and accounting.

EDUCATION

Bachelor of Science in **Accounting**, University of Alabama, Birmingham, AL, 1992.
- Demonstrated excellent time management skills, maintaining a **3.4 cumulative GPA** despite working an average of 20 hours per week while attending college full-time.

Completed two years towards my Bachelor's degree at Birmingham Community College prior to transferring to the University of Alabama.

EXPERIENCE

MANAGER and **OUTSIDE SALES REPRESENTATIVE.** Hollis, Inc., Columbia, SC (1999-present). Hired to handle the bookkeeping for this start-up business, was quickly promoted on the basis of my exceptional salesmanship and natural leadership skills to assume additional responsibilities, managing the store and calling on customers.
- Develop new business and generate increased sales from existing accounts; build a rapport with customers through my outgoing personality and exceptional sales ability.
- Trained and now supervise an inside sales force of five associates, instructing them in customer service, operation of the computer system, and all other functional areas.
- Conduct monthly sales meetings and set sales goals for each associate.
- Create effective marketing strategies and promotions for use in television, radio, print, and billboard advertisements.
- Plan and organize events such as rodeos and horse shows, obtaining sponsorships from local businesses and coordinating site selection, advertising, etc.
- Initiated all accounting procedures for the store; process accounts payable/receivable, sales tax preparation, payroll taxes, and bank reconciliation.
- Designed record-keeping and inventory practices for the store; responsible for inventory control and ordering.
- In a short time, have built this business into one of the top five performers in commercial feed sales for the entire southeast region, with annual sales that are currently more than five times their initial level.

FARM MANAGER. Marcus Farms, Columbia, SC (1997-1999). Directed all aspects of the management of this large boarding facility, to include managing and training the staff, coordinating overnight transportation, management of the breeding program, scheduling veterinarian appointments, public relations, and accounting.

STAFF ACCOUNTANT. Monroe Environmental Services, Inc., Birmingham, AL (1995-1997). Provided the full range of accounting services to this busy waste disposal company.
- Prepared detailed analyses of balance sheet accounts, performed monthly closing of assigned companies' revenue, and recorded payroll, intercompany transactions, employee receivables, and monthly accruals.
- Updated and maintained waste inventory data, as well as preparing quarterly reports.

COMMERCIAL & RESIDENTIAL PROPERTY ACCOUNTANT. The Burrows Company (Realtors), Mobile, AL (1992-1995). Oversaw all financial reporting for 52 commercial properties; performed bank reconciliation, disbursed mortgage payments, managed investment accounts, and prepared financial statements.

PERSONAL

Outstanding personal and professional references are available upon request.

Date

Exact Name of Person
Exact Title
Exact Name of Company
Address
City, State, Zip

Parts Sales,
Recently Resigned Position in
Order to Relocate

Notice the Objective on her
resume. It flows, and it
mentions her skills as well
as her ability to work hard
in a dedicated fashion.
Tip: Usually the Objective is
the only sentence on the
resume, since "I" is
assumed before most of the
verbs on your resume. (If
you put "I" in front of every
verb on your resume, you
would have "I" fifty times
on a one-page resume!)

Dear Exact Name of Person (or Dear Sir or Madam if answering a blind ad):

With the enclosed resume, I would like to make you aware of my interest in seeking employment with your organization.

As you will see, I am a versatile individual who has excelled in corporate and government environments. In my most recent position as a Sales Representative, I earned promotion to higher and higher levels of responsibility while excelling in sales and earning corresponding promotion increases in my commission structure. I was also cross-trained in all the responsibilities of the Parts Manager, supervising up to seven people in her absence. I voluntarily resigned my position several months ago when my husband's relocation to Asheville required my full-time work in selling our home in Raleigh and managing our relocation process. I can provide excellent references from that employer, who has strongly encouraged me to return to Spalding. I have decided, however, to seek employment in the more immediate Asheville area.

Prior to my sales job in the automotive industry, I earned promotion to increased responsibilities with the Sheriff's Department in Charlotte. In addition to planning and organizing public auctions of personal and real properties, I supervised the sale of assets by deputies. I composed a variety of legal documents and worked closely with deputies as I advised deputies of legal protocol in serving criminal and civil papers. I acquired many skills and competencies usually possessed by a paralegal and legal assistant.

With a reputation as a highly intelligent individual, I once won one of 100 four-year scholarships given statewide, and then I used the scholarship funds to study a variety of courses at Charlotte Technical Community College.

Known for my strong personal initiative, I have become a valued and respected employee in every job I have held. I can assure you that I am a conscientious worker with outstanding problem-solving ability, and I always seek resourceful ways to contribute to my employer's reputation and profitability. If you can use my versatile abilities, I would enjoy an opportunity to talk with you in person. I hope you will welcome my call soon when I try to arrange a brief meeting.

Sincerely,

Joanne K. Moriwaki

JOANNE K. MORIWAKI

1110½ Hay Street, Fayetteville, NC 28305 · preppub@aol.com · (910) 483-6611

OBJECTIVE

I want to contribute to an organization that can use a versatile and outgoing professional who has excelled in environments which required outstanding sales, customer service, and public relations skills as well as dedicated hard work and attention to detail.

EXPERIENCE

AUTO PARTS SALES REPRESENTATIVE. Spalding Ford, Raleigh, NC (1998-2000). Earned promotion to increasing responsibilities because of my dedicated hard work and superior results; began as a Parts Secretary and after 10 months moved into sales. While in sales, worked at the front counter for a year and then gained experience on the back counter.
- Was cross-trained in and performed the responsibilities of the Parts Manager in her absence, supervising up to seven employees.
- Became skilled in sales and became especially skilled in selling Ford parts.
- Excelled in sales and earned maximum award points based on an incentive system; continuously earned promotion and increases in my commission structure.
- Utilized the ADP computer system for parts location and cataloging, stock orders, claims processing, and inventory control.
- Operated forklift to load and unload engine blocks, transmissions, and other heavy inventory.
- Voluntarily resigned this position when my husband accepted a new job in Asheville; have been encouraged to return to Spalding by the owner and management but I am seeking a job in the Asheville area.

Promoted in this progression with Sheriff's Department, Charlotte, NC:
CIVIL EXECUTIONS CLERK. (1994-98). Handled extensive legal paperwork as well as financial collections; processed and collected Civil Writs of Execution and State and County Tax Warrants.
- Was placed in charge of the county desk sergeant's station in his absence.
- Processed 200 new executions and tax warrants monthly; collected $145,000 in an 11-month period after calculating monies owed (collected more monies than predecessor).
- Planned and organized public auctions of levied personal and real properties, and then supervised the conduct of sales by deputies.
- Performed background checks on judgement debtors to assist deputies in locating them and their properties; verified property ownership for deputies; assigned executions.
- Handled data entry of executions/tax warrants into the county's mainframe computer.
- Composed and typed sheriff's legal documents including Notices of Hearing, Reports of Sale, and Orders; performed title searches as well as criminal and background checks.
- Supervised the inventories of businesses and personal estates which the sheriff closed under order of seizure; advised 18 deputies of protocol in serving criminal/civil papers.

LEGAL CLERK/DATA ENTRY SPECIALIST. (1989-94). Performed data entry related to most legal processes handled by the sheriff's office including civil and criminal summons, criminal warrants, subpoenas, and notices; operated a two-way radio base unit to assist deputies and also graciously assisted the public and handled telephone inquiries.

EDUCATION

Received a four-year scholarship which was one of 100 given statewide in 1979; used the scholarship to complete courses at Charlotte Technical Community College.
Scored a 92 on the rigorous DCI Terminal Certification Course, 1994, sponsored by the NC Department of Justice, SBI Division of Criminal Investigation.
Obtained Writs of Execution Certification, Institute of Government, Chapel Hill, 1995.

Date

Personnel and
Executive Recruiting

This successful sales
professional has decided
to use his cover letter and
resume to explore
opportunities in numerous
industries. He has sold
both products and
services, and he enjoys
both situations. He has
identified three cities
where he would like to
live, and he is targeting
employers in those cities.

Dear Sir or Madam:

With the enclosed resume, I would like to make you aware of my background as a results-oriented professional with exceptional sales and management skills. As you will see from my resume, I have excelled in positions which involved selling both products and services.

In my current job as Sales/Account Manager with Executive Personnel, I am highly successful in developing and maintaining national sales accounts. Part of my discipline in my job is to cold-call 150 companies daily for the purpose of developing new clients and meeting monthly sales quotas.

I have also succeeded in retail store management. In my prior position with American Eagle, I began in a trainee role after graduating from college in 1994, and I was promoted rapidly into a store management position. In that capacity I oversaw all aspects of store operation while managing inside sales, inventory control, and personnel development. I earned a reputation as an articulate manager with a strong customer service orientation.

If you can use a positive, results-oriented professional with a strong bottom-line orientation and exceptionally strong recruiting and sales skills, then I look forward to hearing from you soon to arrange a time when we might meet to discuss your needs. I can assure you in advance that I have an excellent reputation and would rapidly become a valuable asset to your company.

Sincerely,

Terell Jacobs

TERELL JACOBS

1110½ Hay Street, Fayetteville, NC 28305   •   preppub@aol.com   •   (910) 483-6611

OBJECTIVE

To benefit an organization that can use an articulate, experienced manager with exceptional recruiting, sales, and leadership skills who offers a strong bottom-line orientation and the proven ability to train and motivate personnel and increase the profitability of operations.

EDUCATION

Earned **Bachelor of Science in Criminal Justice**, minor in Sociology, University of South Carolina, SC, 1994.
Completed numerous professional development and training courses sponsored by American Eagle/Outfitters Group, including:

Executive Development Program	Behavior-based Interviewing
Fundamentals of Recruiting	Consumer Responsive Selling
Preventing Sexual Harassment	Valuing and Managing Diversity
Rightful Discharge Procedures	Security and Shrinkage

EXPERIENCE

SALES/ACCOUNT MANAGER. Executive Personnel, Charleston, SC (1997-present). Have excelled in developing and maintaining national sales accounts by cold-calling prospects and selling the advantages of using Executive Personnel for corporate human resources needs.

- Work with major U.S. corporations; half of my established accounts are New York Stock Exchange publicly-traded companies.
- Manage a budget of $200,000 annually.
- Develop strategy for corporate recruiting by selling our client companies one of our Career Fair Packages.
- Work from personal lead base to contact 150 people per day and meet monthly sales quota; have always exceeded my monthly quota.
- Coordinate career fairs, which includes setting up and managing the logistics involved in making hotel and catering arrangements.
- Train and manage new sales associates.

STORE MANAGER. American Eagle, Greensboro, NC (1995-97). Responsible for overseeing all aspects of store operation. Performed several tasks daily including inside sales, inventory control, and personnel development.

- Consistently met or exceeded weekly sales quotas.
- Formulated business plans to strengthen store performance.
- Trained new employees and provided refresher skills training to existing employees in order to create a sense of team pride which resulted in increased sales.
- Focused on strong merchandising, carefully managed profit and loss, and restored sales programs in order to achieve high profit margin.
- Developed exceptional recruiting, staff development, training, and motivational skills while controlling profit and loss and overseeing store operations.

PERSONAL

Exceptional references provided upon request. Offer extensive experience with all kinds of people. Effective communicator with an aggressive bottom-line orientation. Proven ability to train and manage others.

Date

Exact Name of Person
Title or Position
Name of Company
Address (no., street)
Address (city, state, zip)

**Pharmaceutical Sales,
Resume Requested by a
Competitor**

A company has approached
this individual and
requested a resume, so the
first paragraph of the cover
letter alludes to the fact
that the resume is being
provided in response to
their expression of interest.
Notice the last paragraph of
the cover letter. Mrs.
Murray-Dunn mentions that
she would enjoy learning
about how they would use
her considerable skills and
experience!

Dear Sir or Madam:

Thank you for your recent expression of interest in my background, and I am faxing with this cover letter an updated resume which describes my current job as a Pharmaceutical Sales Representative for Farmingdale-James. In my current job servicing chain drug stores and doctors' offices in 30 cities, I am consistently ranked among the company's top producers in my efforts to increase market share, develop new accounts, and boost sales of Vanceril and Proventil H.F.A. I believe my rapid success as a Pharmaceutical Sales Representative has been due in large part to my background as an R.N., and I have come to be regarded by all the doctors and pharmacists with whom I work as a trusted advisor and Marketing Consultant.

As you will see, I have lived in Syracuse all my life, except for a few years after high school when I worked as a model for Elite Models in New York City. After my stint in modeling, I earned my Bachelor's degree in Business Administration in 1987 and then graduated from nursing school as an R.N. in 1993. In a job with Quality Care prior to my current position, I traveled to surrounding counties handling a patient case load and training new nurses. In a previous job, I worked for Everett Medical Center, where I advanced to increasing responsibilities as a Staff Nurse in the Medical Intensive Care Unit, Emergency Department, and Coronary Care Unit.

With a reputation as a doer and achiever, I have worked since I was 16 years old. As a high school junior and senior, I assisted in managing a skating rink and handled sales, concessions, special events, as well as opening and closing the business. I have also excelled as a Sales Representative with a local 50-year-old business which operates all over the east coast handling mostly commercial and industrial accounts. I have negotiated contracts, prospected for customers, and resolved problems in fair and diplomatic ways.

Although I am excelling in my current job and am highly regarded by the company, I would enjoy learning how your company could make use of my considerable marketing and sales abilities. I am sure my extensive contacts and outstanding reputation within the medical community could be of value to you. You would find me in person to be a congenial individual who interacts with others with poise and professionalism. I hope you will contact me soon to suggest a time when we could meet to discuss your needs and how I might be of service to you.

Yours sincerely,

Shonda Murray-Dunn

SHONDA MURRAY-DUNN

1110½ Hay Street, Fayetteville, NC 28305   •   preppub@aol.com   •   (910) 483-6611

OBJECTIVE

To contribute to an organization that can use a persuasive communicator and proactive professional who combines outstanding sales and marketing abilities, including pharmaceutical sales experience, along with professional nursing experience and a degree in Business Administration.

EDUCATION

Pursuing Master of Clinical Psychology studies, Syracuse University, Syracuse, NY, 1997-present.

Hold **Associate of Applied Science in Nursing degree**, Syracuse Technical College, Syracuse, NY, 1993; excelled in extracurricular and academic activities:
- Earned **Dean's List** distinction, 1990-93.
- Was honored by selection as Marshall, Class of 1992.
- Received a faculty appointment to the Curriculum Committee and Steering Committee.
- Was named Class Historian, 1991-93.

Bachelor of Business Administration degree, cum laude, minor in Accounting and Economics, Ithaca College, Ithaca, NY, 1987; prior to graduating from Ithaca, studied Pre-Law for two years at the State University of New York at Oswego.

Graduated from Syracuse Academy, Syracuse, 1981.

EXPERIENCE

PHARMACEUTICAL SALES REPRESENTATIVE. Farmingdale-James, Syracuse, NY (1997-present). Manage a 30-city territory while servicing existing clients and developing new accounts.
- Because of my background as an R.N. with extensive medical knowledge and a thorough knowledge of medical terminology, quickly earned the respect of my clients; have become a respected Marketing Consultant and trusted advisor to pharmacists and doctors.
- Represent Vanceril (DS), Claritin, and Proventil H.F.A. to chain drug stores and doctors' offices.

Sales accomplishments: Am ranked second in the district in total sales of Proventil H.F.A and second in percentage sales growth; ranked 3rd in total sales of Vanceril Double Strength.

CASE MANAGER. Quality Care, Syracuse, NY (1996-97). Traveled to surrounding counties while handling a 25-patient case load; involved in training new nurses.
- Became skilled in time management while providing quality patient care while coordinating the efforts of physicians, ancillary medical personnel, and community resources.

Excelled in the following track record of progression to increasing responsibilities, Everett Medical Center, Syracuse, NY:

1996: STAFF NURSE, CORONARY CARE UNIT. Handled all aspects of patient care in a critical setting to include assessment, implementation of orders, treatment, and continuous monitoring of acutely ill, and pre/post surgical coronary care patients.

1994-1995: STAFF NURSE, EMERGENCY DEPARTMENT. Handled all aspects of patient care in a critical care setting while implementing triage protocol, assessing conditions and assisting with treatment, and continuously monitoring various conditions of medical, pre-surgical, and trauma-crash patients including MVAs, burns, ODs, gun shot wounds, DKAs, asthmatics, MIs, head injuries, DVT, seizures, and others.

1993-94: STAFF NURSE, MEDICAL INTENSIVE CARE UNIT. Operated as a Float Nurse for the Surgical Intensive Care Unit, the Coronary Care Unit, and the Cardiac Surgery Intensive Care Unit; provided quality nursing care in a critical care setting.

Date

Exact Name of Person
Title or Position
Name of Company
Address (number and street)
Address (city, state, and zip)

**Pharmaceutical Sales,
Seeking Internal Promotion**

Don't forget that
sometimes your best
chance to "get ahead" in
your career is to explore
opportunities with your
current employer. That's
what this professional is
doing. He is using a resume
and cover letter to formally
apply for a sales
management position.
Notice that even the
Objective mentions the
company by name, to make
the employer feel that the
resume was developed
specifically for that
purpose.

Dear Exact Name of Person: (or Dear Sir or Madam if answering a blind ad.)

With the enclosed resume, I would like to make you aware of my strong desire to contribute to the Goldman-Fremont Company and Waldemar in a sales management role. As my resume demonstrates, I have distinguished myself as a Sales Representative, and I feel my next major contributions could be in sales management.

I have won numerous awards for sales excellence including the Vice President's Award, Pacesetter Award, Wound Management Award, as well as a trip to Hawaii. I am proud of my ability to expertly and enthusiastically use the company's marketing tools to increase revenue. For example, I recently utilized Solutions in Home Care to persuade a major health care organization to increase its use of Waldemar to 80%, and I have executed numerous hospital conversions to the Premier Contract. I am skilled in Customer-Oriented Selling Skills ("COSS") and have used that consultative selling style to establish strong relationships which generated impressive bottom-line profits.

Single and able to travel as extensively as your needs require, I feel I could excel in a sales management role, and it would be an honor to be in the position of training, educating, and coaching sales representatives who could achieve the highest profitability goals and top corporate rankings. I have become skilled at utilizing every marketing tool provided by the company, and I am confident I could teach other sales representatives to profitably apply those proven techniques. I have succeeded in adding value to my customers, and in maximizing revenue for Waldemar, through the resourceful application of those tools.

I would enjoy an opportunity to talk with you in person about my desire to assume a sales management position within Waldemar, as I am certain I could be most valuable to the company in such a role.

Yours sincerely,

Allan B. Epstein

ALLAN B. EPSTEIN

1110½ Hay Street, Fayetteville, NC 28305 • preppub@aol.com • (910) 483-6611

OBJECTIVE

To benefit the Goldman-Fremont Company in a sales management position so that I can apply my knowledge of corporate marketing products and technical expertise related to Waldemar while training and developing enthusiastic and top-performing sales professionals.

EDUCATION

Bachelor of Arts in Business Management, Colorado State University, Denver, CO, 1990.
- Completed numerous sales seminars and marketing workshops sponsored by Thomas Borthwick, Inc. and Goldman-Fremont Company.
- Have been trained to use Solutions in Home Care and other marketing tools, and have become skilled in applying those marketing tools for maximum bottom-line results.

EXPERIENCE

SALES REPRESENTATIVE. *Have excelled in handling sales responsibilities within both the Thomas Borthwick, Inc. environment and then in the Goldman-Fremont Company, as my parent company changed as a result of acquisitions.*
1995-present. Waldemar (A Goldman-Fremont Company). As a Sales Representative with the Wound and Skin Care Group, conduct sales and service activities to all levels of health care providers throughout 30 counties in Colorado.
- In 2000, am managing a territory of $1.3 million while also marketing the ostomy line in addition to wound and skin care products.
- In 1999, converted a 10-chain home health agency to more than 90% usage of Waldemar products, resulting in a $100,000 increase in revenue for Waldemar; utilized the company's Solutions in Home Care; previously used Solutions in Home Care to persuade a major health care organization to increase its use of Waldemar to 80% from a minimal percentage utilization. Executed numerous hospital conversions in 1999.
- In 1998 was up $124,000 and was ranked 24th out of 160 sales reps; in 1997, was up $150,000 in sales and won a trip to Hawaii while being ranked 13th in the country.
- Provide in-service staff training and CEU-accredited training to staff.
- Am skilled in targeting sales to chains as well as hospitals, nursing homes, and home health agencies, and am known for my ability to establish rapport with enterostomal therapists, material managers, as well as directors of nursing and clinical directors.

1990-95: Phillimore Laboratories (a subsidiary of Thomas Borthwick, Inc.). As a Sales Representative, introduced and sold a line of wound care, skin care, and infection control products to area hospitals, nursing homes, and home health agencies.
- Acquired extensive training and on-the-job experience in Customer-Oriented Selling Skills ("COSS").
- Built a customer base from 35 accounts generating $150,000 in sales to 115 accounts generating over $400,000 in sales; established professional relationships with a wide variety of health care providers and maintained them through constant follow up.
- Represented products ranging in price from $25 to $950 per case while marketing a 95-item product line which included patient incontinent products, wound management products, patient bathing products, routine handwashing products, instrument and scope decontamination products, environmental decontamination products, surgical products, and hemostatic agents.
- Called on emergency rooms, cardiac care units, intensive care units, operating rooms, physical therapy units, and infection control departments.
- Received numerous sales awards including the Vice President's Award (twice), the Pacesetter Award, and the Wound Management Award.

PERSONAL

Single and able to relocate and travel extensively according to company needs. Enjoy golf.

Date

Exact Name of Person
Title or Position
Name of Company
Address (number and street)
Address (city, state, and zip)

Pharmaceutical Sales, Seeking Other Industry Opportunities

This Pharmaceutical Sales Associate seeks to explore opportunities in other companies. Notice that this individual has already made a career change into pharmaceuticals from a career as a Mathematics Teacher.
Tip: Want to see how to show off **Volunteer Experience**? Notice the third job on her resume, where she directed a volunteer organization.

Dear Sir or Madam:

With the enclosed resume, I would like to make you aware of my interest in contributing to your organization through my experience as a Pharmaceutical Sales Consultant along with my extensive network of relationships and contacts within the medical community.

You will see from my resume that I am currently promoting cardiovascular and pulmonary products, and I have excelled in establishing relationships with doctors who normally do not see pharmaceutical sales representatives. My background as an Operating Room Technician and Urology Technician has helped me greatly in rapidly becoming successful in the pharmaceutical sales field. I also hold a B.A. in Chemistry.

If you can use a knowledgeable and tested medical sales professional, I hope you will contact me to suggest a time when we could meet. Although I can provide excellent personal and professional references at the appropriate time, I would appreciate your not contacting my current employer until after we have a chance to meet. Thank you in advance for your time.

Sincerely,

Grace T. Kurland

GRACE T. KURLAND

1110½ Hay Street, Fayetteville, NC 28305   •   preppub@aol.com   •   (910) 483-6611

OBJECTIVE

To benefit an organization that can use a persuasive communicator and proactive professional who combines outstanding sales and marketing abilities, including pharmaceutical sales experience, along with professional experience as a member of an Operating Room surgical team.

EDUCATION

Bachelor of Arts in Chemistry, University of Colorado at Colorado Springs, Colorado Springs, CO, 1997.
- Emphasis in Organic Chemistry. Coursework relied heavily upon knowledge of Qbasic, Mathcad, Microsoft Office, Microsoft Excel, Microsoft Access, and Microsoft Word.

Completed 24 semester hours of study in the **Russian Basic Course,** Defense Language Institute, Monterey, CA, 1992-93.
- Developed conversational proficiency in the Russian Language.

Completed **United States Army Operating Room Specialist Course,** Ft. Sam Houston, TX, and Ft. Leavenworth, KS, 1990-91.
- Coursework included Anatomy and Physiology as well as Operating Room Procedures and Preparation.

EXPERIENCE

PHARMACEUTICAL SALES CONSULTANT. Longmont HealthCare Sales (Welleman Pharmaceuticals). Lawrence, KS (1998-present). Have consistently achieved personal and corporate sales objectives while promoting cardiovascular and pulmonary products.
- **Cardiovascular** products: Promote Zestoretic, Sular, and Zestril, which is the #1 Ace inhibitor.
- **Pulmonary** products: Promote Accolate, and through aggressive promotion have experienced no sales decrease despite the recent release of a much-publicized similar drug.
- Have been able to schedule appointments with doctors who normally refuse to see pharmaceutical representatives.

MATHEMATICS TEACHER. Parkston County Schools, Kansas City, KS (1997). Taught and evaluated four 30-student, seventh-grade classes in Geometry and Algebra; prepared instruction materials, supervised classroom and maintained discipline while also conferring with school administration officials, teaching staff, and parents.

FAMILY SUPPORT GROUP COORDINATOR. 3rd Battalion, 10th Special Forces Group (Airborne), Ft. Carson, CO (1995-97). Directed a volunteer organization with the mission of supporting deployed soldiers and their families.
- Forecasted, planned, and organized both routine activities and special events in support of the organization and its members.
- Provided liaison between Family Support Group members and Fort Carson agencies.
- Supervised and trained Family Support Group staff (six personnel) and representatives (four personnel).

OPERATING ROOM and UROLOGY TECHNICIAN. U.S. Army MEDDAC, Fort Ord, CA (1993-94). Served as a member of Operating Room surgical team performing scrub and other support services for simple to highly complex procedures.

PERSONAL

Interests include playing basketball, volleyball, and softball; travel; and family.

Date

Printing Sales, Recently Relocated to a New Area

This accomplished professional resigned her job in order to relocate near her family, and she is seeking a job in a geographical area in which she has no contacts and no network to fall back on. A great resume and cover letter will introduce her to prospective employers and acquaint them with her track record of promotion and considerable knowledge of the printing business.

Dear Sir or Madam:

With the enclosed resume, I would like to express my interest in exploring employment opportunities with your organization and make you aware of my versatile experience related to print production, media planning and buying, as well as sales and customer service.

With a reputation as a well-organized individual capable of managing multiple priorities, I most recently excelled in a track record of achievement with a communication company in Burbank, CA. After working for the company from 1989-91 as a Customer Service Representative, I was again recruited by this employer in 1997 and offered the position of Production Coordinator for the Education Division, which served the high-end needs of universities and colleges. In that capacity I coordinated print production of catalogs, brochures, viewbooks, and other publications, and I excelled in all aspects of customer service and client relations. In 1999, when the company was experiencing financial turmoil due to lagging sales, my employer asked me to move from production management into sales. After taking over the accounts of three experienced sales professionals, I quickly increased sales volume in the region to three times the level achieved by my predecessors. I was widely credited with salvaging lost accounts and restoring client confidence in the company. Although I was held in the highest regard and can provide excellent references at the appropriate time, I recently resigned my position in order to relocate permanently to Maryland to be near family.

You will see that I offer considerable experience in sales and marketing. In one previous job as a Group Leader and Production Coordinator for LithoMark, I trained and supervised three employees while playing a key role in implementing a new concept of cross-functional work teams. In that job, I worked closely with sales/marketing to develop and implement marketing plans while coordinating production of print materials for the Hotel Division. On my own initiative, I developed procedures which streamlined the division's work flow.

If you can use a hard worker with a proven ability to manage multiple priorities and produce top quality work under tight deadlines, I hope you will contact me to suggest a time when we might meet to discuss your needs. I would certainly enjoy the opportunity to talk with you in person.

Sincerely yours,

Laura Rodriguez

LAURA RODRIGUEZ

1110½ Hay Street, Fayetteville, NC 28305   •   preppub@aol.com   •   (910) 483-6611

OBJECTIVE

To contribute to an organization that can use a versatile professional who is experienced in producing top-quality results under tight deadlines while applying my expertise in media planning/buying, print production, sales, and customer service.

EDUCATION

Extensive professional training related to printing management, team building and team management, quality improvement, the printing process, media planning and buying, and the advertising process.
Strong background in the printing process; knowledgeable of color and paper selection.

COMPUTERS

Proficient with Quark, Photoshop, Illustrator, PageMaker, Microsoft Word, and other software; knowledgeable of scanning, digital pre-press, and film output.

EXPERIENCE

Was recruited by this former employer in 1997, and then excelled in the following track record of accomplishment in both the sales and production management areas; recently resigned my position in order to relocate to MD, and can provide outstanding references:

1999-2000: SALES REPRESENTATIVE. Viewpoint Communications, Burbank, CA. At a time when the company was experiencing financial difficulties because of its poor sales performance, I was asked to move from the production area into sales; was the production coordinator *and* was the first woman in the company's history ever to be placed in a sales job, and I tripled sales for the company in my first nine months.
- Salvaged lost accounts and then expanded revenue from those accounts.
- Demonstrated my ability to establish and maintain effective long-term relationships.
- Was commended for salvaging the company's reputation with numerous clients.

1997-99: PRODUCTION COORDINATOR. Viewpoint Communications, Burbank, CA. Was recruited by this former employer to coordinate its Education Division accounts comprised of universities and colleges; expertly coordinated multiple simultaneous priorities with as many as 40 major projects in progress at any one time.
- Coordinated print production of catalogs, brochures, viewbooks, and other print jobs.
- Became widely respected for my creativity, and many of the projects I managed won awards from the Print Industry Association of California (PIAC).
- It was truly an honor to be recruited for this management job in the Education Division, because the job required a professional who could produce the highest quality work under extremely tight deadlines; excelled in all aspects of customer service.

Other experience:
GROUP LEADER & PRODUCTION COORDINATOR. LithoMark, Burbank, CA (1991-97). Trained and supervised three employees, and played a key role in implementing a new concept of cross-functional work teams as Group Leader; was commended for my ability to motivate and inspire others.
- Worked closely with sales/marketing to develop and implement marketing plans.
- Coordinated production of print materials for the Hotel Division; on my own initiative, developed procedures which streamlined the division's work flow.

CUSTOMER SERVICE REPRESENTATIVE. Viewpoint Communications, Burbank, CA (1989-91). Played a key role in developing a new Hotel Division, and then coordinated the production of print materials; maintained communication between client and sales.

PERSONAL

Single and willing to relocate and travel as needed to meet the needs of my employer.

Exact Name of Person
Title or Position
Name of Company
Address (no., street)
Address (city, state, zip)

Dear Exact Name of Person: (or Dear Sir or Madam if answering a blind ad.)

**Production
Background, Seeking to
Transition into Sales**

If you look at his
resume, you might ask,
"What's a nice production
manager doing in a *Real-
Resumes for Sales*
book?" This professional
is seeking to get out of
the production
management
environment and into
sales, and he is hoping
his background of
accomplishments in
production management
will open doors with
employers who have
sales positions requiring
an intelligent hard
charger with an M.B.A.
Notice the third
paragraph of his cover
letter where he sells
his potential for sales.

With the enclosed resume, I would like to make you aware of my interest in exploring employment opportunities within your company in a position in which you could utilize my strong sales, marketing, communication, and management skills.

As you will see, I hold an M.B.A. as well as a B.S. degree. I have excelled in a "track record" of rapid promotion with my current and previous employers because of my ability to solve problems, "sell" others on the solutions to those problems, and motivate people to work hard in achieving organizational goals.

Although my recent successes have been in the manufacturing and production arenas, I have achieved top-notch results by utilizing my strong sales, marketing, communication, and strategic thinking skills. For example, as a key member of my plant's strategic planning group during a recent downsizing, I led personnel to meet aggressive sales-per-employee goals while playing a key role in repositioning the plant to achieve cost savings of $1.8 million in FY 2000. I have also excelled in working with material suppliers to create and implement highly efficient new systems for inventory control and shipping/receiving. As the head of a Matrix Team, I led and motivated employees in initiating improvements which led to greatly improved internal communications.

While working for my previous employer, I received the President's Award two years in a row for leading the company in the area of cost savings. I believe my strong communication and "sales" skills were the keys to that bottom-line accomplishment, and I have earned a reputation as a persuasive communicator and negotiator. I am respected for my ability to work well with others at all organizational levels.

If you can use an ambitious and aggressive producer who could positively impact your bottom line, I hope you will contact me to suggest a time when we might meet to discuss your needs. Although I can provide outstanding personal and professional references at the appropriate time, I would appreciate your holding my interest in your company in confidence until after we talk.

Sincerely yours,

Matthew Bianucci

MATTHEW BIANUCCI

1110½ Hay Street, Fayetteville, NC 28305　　•　　preppub@aol.com　　•　　(910) 483-6611

OBJECTIVE

To benefit an organization that can use an accomplished and versatile manager who has excelled in handling senior-level responsibilities for manufacturing and production management while achieving and exceeding aggressive sales and customer satisfaction goals.

EDUCATION

M.B.A., Brookfield College, Brookfield, IL, 1995.
B.S. degree, major in Business Administration and minor in Management, Lake Michigan Christian College, Evanston, IL, 1988.
Completed extensive training sponsored by my employers in ISO/QS9000 Quality Systems documentation, MOPAR Supplier Symposium Training, Management Information Systems.

EXPERIENCE

<u>Automotive Industry:</u> *Have excelled in the following track record of promotion to executive-level responsibilities with Ace Products, La Grange, IL, 1994-present:*
1998-present: PRODUCTION CONTROL MANAGER. After promotion to this position, was a key member of the strategic planning group that planned, implemented, and managed the company's downsizing and strategic repositioning in FY 98; greatly strengthened my strategic thinking and problem-solving abilities while repositioning the company to reap cost savings of $1.8 million for FY 2000.
- Report directly to the Plant Manager; directly supervise 16 individuals while managing a $4 million annual MRO budget as well as a monthly inventory of $2.2 million.
- Oversee functions including forecasting, planning, and scheduling; customer service; inventory turnover; raw materials warehousing; material storage and issuance systems; as well as inbound and outbound traffic.
- Am excelling in this position while being measured according to ambitious objectives related to freight claims, customer delivery performance, inventory turn, premium freight, and other areas.
- Satisfy a sophisticated customer base which includes Chrysler, Ford, GM, Toyota, and Isuzu as well as suppliers to the automotive plants and special sealing products groups.
- **Accomplishments:** Led the Production Control division through QS9000 accreditation. During the 1998 downsizing due to a sales volume decline, managed the department so that it achieved sales-per-employee goals. Implemented systems and procedures to error-proof the shipping and receiving processes; implemented a FIFO system for stock rotation. Worked with material suppliers to create Just-In-Time (JIT) and KANBAN.

1995-98: PRODUCTION CONTROL SUPERVISOR. Achieved cost savings of $198,000 for FY 98 and $224,000 for FY 97 while authoring procedures for Production Control and Shipping/Receiving.
- Transformed stockroom layout and controls for FIFO and inventory accuracy.
- Led the Matrix Team which initiated improvements in internal plant communications.
- Managed 10 people while overseeing raw material scheduling and JIT systems as well as shipping and receiving operations including the bar code system for inventory, cycle counting, inventory reporting and accuracy, material handling, and consignments.

<u>Pharmaceutical Industry:</u> *Previously excelled in a track record of promotion with Willett, Inc., a pharmaceutical company in Evanston, IL:*
1993-95: GRANULATION SUPERINTENDENT. Managed and controlled manning and equipment during a major expansion while also designing and maintaining regulatory system for FDA compliance.

PERSONAL

Can provide outstanding personal and professional references.

Date

Exact Name of Person
Title or Position
Name of Company
Address (number and street)
Address (city, state, and zip)

Property Rentals
Sales Management

Although the Objective on the resume is versatile and all-purpose, just in case she wishes to job-hunt outside the property management field, this junior professional likes what she does and is simply looking for advancement to greater responsibilities.

Dear Exact Name of Person: (or Dear Sir or Madam if answering a blind ad.)

With the enclosed resume, I would like to indicate my interest in your organization and my desire to utilize my management skills for your benefit.

As you will see from my resume, I offer extensive experience in property management and am known for my strong bottom-line orientation. You will notice that I have handled all aspects of property management including administration, maintenance management, public relations, inspection and inventory control, as well as collections and delinquency management.

I hope you will welcome my call soon to arrange a brief meeting at your convenience to discuss your current and future needs and how I might serve them. Thank you in advance for your time.

Sincerely yours,

Dianne Jones Weaver

Alternate last paragraph:
I hope you will call or write me soon to suggest a time convenient for us to meet and discuss your current and future needs and how I might serve them. Thank you in advance for your time.

DIANNE JONES WEAVER

1110½ Hay Street, Fayetteville, NC 28305 • preppub@aol.com • (910) 483-6111

OBJECTIVE	I want to contribute to an organization that can use a highly motivated self-starter who offers strong public relations and communication skills along with experience in managing people, property, finances, and daily business operations.
EXPERIENCE	**PROPERTY MANAGER.** Bladenboro Apartment Community, Canby, OR (1997-present). While managing this large apartment complex, raised and maintained occupancy by 17% in a 6-month interval.

- Collect rent, make deposits, and balance books at end of each month.
- Prepare activity, occupancy, and market reports for Broker-in-Charge and property owner.
- Maintain a monthly operating budget and explain any variances; manage a budget of $82,000.
- Coordinate with contractors and oversee all maintenance on units; lease apartment, process applications, and expedite lease agreements.

Began with The Affiliated Real Estate Consortium in 1992, and excelled in handling both sales/marketing and property management responsibilities on a large scale:
PROPERTY MANAGER. The Affiliated Real Estate Consortium, Property Management Department, Canby, OR (1992-1997). Excelled as a property manager for one of the area's most well-known real estate/property management firms; was responsible for an inventory of between 180 to 200 residences.

- *Maintenance Management*: Supervised maintenance activities; coordinated and scheduled staff and independent contractors; obtained estimates for work to be performed and monitored major repairs as work proceeded.
- *Public Relations*: Screened potential residents and conducted rental showings.
- *Inspections and Inventory*: Conducted biannual inspections of every property and conducted house inventories; ordered goods and materials as needed.
- *Administration*: Prepared reports for top management while also preparing lease renewals, inspection reports, and other paperwork.
- *Court Liaison*: Handled evictions and represented the company in small claims court.
- *Negotiation*: Mediated between owners and tenants as needed in situations where disputes arose over damages, security deposits, or rent owed.
- *Accomplishments*: Made significant contributions to office operations through my talent for organizing office policies and procedures; brought more than 125 new properties into management.

REALTOR. The Johnson Agency Realtors, Canby, OR (1990-92). Became a $1.2 million dollar producer within 12 months!

- Gained valuable skills in sales, marketing, and contract negotiating while acquiring expert knowledge of most aspects of the real estate business.

OFFICE ADMINISTRATOR. Killeen Real Estate Corp., Killeen, TX (1989-90). Handled a wide range of activities for this real estate company.

- Processed sales contracts and revisions; verified sales prices, financing, option pricing, and lot premiums with approved documents; deposited and accounted for all earnest money received; prepared sales, closings, and construction reports; maintained land files including settlement statements and title insurance commitments.
- Compiled information on approved houses for start of construction; handled building permits, color selections, and related matters; ordered trusses, brick, and cable; issued job assignments and construction schedules; assembled and evaluated plans and specifications for use by real estate appraisers.

PERSONAL	Can provide outstanding personal and professional references on request.

Date

Mr. William Monroe
Gruber Properties
222 McPherson Church Rd.
Charlotte, NC 27803

Real Estate Sales

Dear Mr. Monroe:

This young professional is in a career change. He has recently relocated back to his hometown to help his mom settle the estate of his deceased dad, and he is seeking a career change from store management to real estate sales. Notice that he is using the "direct approach" in his job hunt: he is approaching a select number of employers for whom he would like to work.

I would appreciate an opportunity to talk with you soon about how I could contribute to your organization through my sales and management experience along with my formal education and technical training related to real estate.

As you will see from the enclosed resume, I am licensed by the North Carolina Real Estate Commission as a sales person and am currently completing Brokers Certification courses. I completed the "North Carolina Fundamentals of Real Estate Course" at The Charlotte School of Real Estate.

My resume also will show you my "track record" of achievement in sales and management. Although I was born and raised in the Charlotte area and am living here permanently, most recently I worked in Ft. Lauderdale and Jacksonville, FL, as a Store Manager for Camelot Music. I managed other employees, decreased inventory shrinkage, opened new stores, converted acquisition stores to Camelot systems and procedures, and was specially selected to manage a new "superstore" of more than 10,000 square feet.

I am sending you this resume because, after conducting extensive research of real estate companies, your company is the one I would most like to be associated with. I hope you will find some time in your schedule for us to meet at your convenience to discuss your needs and goals and how I might serve them. I shall look forward to hearing from you, and thank you in advance for your time.

Yours sincerely,

Michael Jenkins

MICHAEL JENKINS

1110½ Hay Street, Fayetteville, NC 28305 • preppub@aol.com • (910) 483-6611

OBJECTIVE   To contribute to an organization that can use a resourceful and congenial sales professional with excellent customer relations skills who offers a proven "track record" of accomplishment in both sales and operations management.

REAL ESTATE
- Licensed by North Carolina Real Estate Commission.
- Currently completing Brokers Certification courses.
- Completed "North Carolina Fundamentals of Real Estate Course" at the Charlotte School of Real Estate.

**EXPERIENCE
SUMMARY**
- Eight years of restaurant and retail management experience.
- Skilled in hiring, training, scheduling, and maintaining sales staff dedicated to superior customer relations.
- Proven commitment to meeting deadlines and serving customers.
- Exceptionally strong analytical and problem-solving skills.
- Known for my positive attitude and cheerful disposition.

EXPERIENCE   **STORE MANAGER.** Camelot Music, Jacksonville, FL, and Ft. Lauderdale, FL (1993-2001). Earned a reputation as a skilled store manager who was equally effective in starting up new retail operations, "turning around" existing stores experiencing sales and profitability problems, and managing "superstores."
- After managing three Camelot Music retail stores in Jacksonville and Ft. Lauderdale, was selected to manage a new 10,000 square foot freestanding "superstore."
- Was responsible for opening new stores and converting acquisition stores to Camelot's procedures, methods, and systems.
- Devised and implemented effective merchandising techniques.
- Specialized in maintaining superior inventory conditions.
- Achieved consistent sales increases and ranked among the chain's highest volume stores.
- Diminished shrinkage and substantially increased profits.
- Implemented effective off-site sales locations utilizing radio and television as well as popular musicians and bands at successful local events.

Other experience:
After earning my Associate of Arts degree, excelled in restaurant management and was selected for management training programs.
- Worked in Hardee's and was selected for their corporate training program; was selected as co-manager of a Hardee's at Myrtle Beach.
- Worked in Quincy's Restaurant as an assistant manager after completing their corporate training program.

EDUCATION   **Associate of Arts** (A.A.) degree in Restaurant and Hotel Management, Baltimore's International Culinary College, 1987-89.
- Completed renowned management training programs with established restaurants, Hardee's and Quincy's.
- Completed high school at Hargrave Military Academy and Flora McDonald Academy.

PERSONAL   Am an accomplished guitarist and musical collector. Excellent health. Single.

Date

Exact Name of Person
Exact Title
Exact Name of Company
Address
City, State, Zip

**Retail Manager Seeking
Outside Sales Position**

This mid-level manager is involved in an aggressive career change from retailing into "who-knows-what." Here's a tip for those of you trying to change careers: Instead of abandoning everything you know for an entirely new field, try to find a niche within your industry. In Mr. Acampora's case, he is trying to get out of the weekend hours required by retailing. What he will do first in his job hunt is approach vendors with whom he worked with a view to representing their lines. This kind of job will keep him in retail without retail hours. (The reason he wants out of retail hours is that he is trying to finish his M.B.A before he hits 40 years old.)

Dear Exact Name of Person (or Dear Sir or Madam if answering a blind ad):

With the enclosed resume, I would like to make you aware of my interest in becoming associated with your fine product line in a sales role. Although I have excelled in retail management for the past 13 years with Macy's, I have decided that I wish to change careers and embark on a career in sales. I am particularly interested in your product line and would like to explore suitable opportunities with you.

Until a few weeks ago, I excelled in a track record of advancement with the Macy's organization, where I started as a management trainee and advanced into a senior management position in charge of 25 individuals. After earning my undergraduate degree in Business Administration with a minor in Economics, I was attracted to the Macy's organization because of its tradition of regarding its managers as profit centers and treating them essentially as entrepreneurs.

Although I was excelling in my job and held in high regard, I recently made the decision to resign from Macy's for two reasons: first, I wanted to spend a few weeks caring full-time for my widowed mother, who had undergone a serious operation, and second, I had decided that I wished to pursue a career in sales. I left on excellent terms and can provide outstanding personal and professional references within the Macy's organization including from my immediate supervisor, Bob Kleinstein, who would gladly welcome me back at any time.

While performing my buying function at Macy's, I became aware of your fine products and I would enjoy discussing with you the possibility of my representing your products to retailers such as Macy's.

I am single and would cheerfully travel as your needs require. If you feel that my skills and background might be of interest to you, I hope you will contact me to suggest a time when we might meet in person to discuss your needs.

Sincerely yours,

Nells Acampora

NELLS ACAMPORA

1110½ Hay Street, Fayetteville, NC 28305 • preppub@aol.com • (910) 483-6611

OBJECTIVE   To benefit an organization that can use an experienced manager who offers a background in managing budgets and performing financial analysis, buying and controlling inventory, supervising personnel, and handling public relations.

EDUCATION   **Bachelor of Arts, Business Administration major with a minor in Economics**, Newark College, Newark, NJ, 1987.
Pursuing M.B.A in my spare time from Davidson University, Davidson, NJ.
Completed extensive management training sponsored by Macy's.

EXPERIENCE   Excelled in a track record of promotion at Macy's Department Store in Newark, NJ; recently resigned from Macy's in order to devote my full time to caring for my widowed mother in the aftermath of a serious operation, and to seek a career outside retailing.

- Resigned under excellent conditions; can provide an outstanding reference from Bob Kleinstein, my immediate supervisor, and from numerous other Macy's executives.

1995-2000: SENIOR MERCHANDISE MANAGER. Was promoted to manage 25 sales associates while controlling a $5 million inventory; this position placed me in charge of this large-volume Children's Department; also managed the Home and Infant Departments.

- Interviewed and hired new sales associates.
- Consistently increased department sales by a minimum of 5% annually.
- In the Macy's environment, the Senior Merchandise Manager is in an essentially entrepreneurial role and, unlike in most department stores, the Senior Manager undertakes the buying function; performed extensive liaison with suppliers and manufacturers who acted as vendors to Macy's.
- Prepared business plans four times a year; reviewed goals monthly.
- While performing in the role of Senior Manager/General Manager, have been extensively involved in leadership and public relations roles in the community; worked with the YMCA to coordinate a "Kid of the Year" event.

1994: PROJECT MANAGER. Because of my reputation as an excellent communicator and public speaker, was selected to take on a special project related to implementing a new Designer Implementation Program; as coordinator of this program, traveled extensively to talk with store managers.

- Was commended for my ability to articulate the concepts of this new program in ways managers could understand.

1993: MANAGER. Men's Clothing and Men's Accessories.
1992: MANAGER. Infant Department.
1991: MANAGER. Housewares Department.
1989-91: MANAGEMENT TRAINEE. Was attracted by Macy's outstanding management training program and by the opportunity as a manager to function in an essentially entrepreneurial role with broad decision-making abilities after advancing into management.

MERCHANDISE MANAGER. Penney's, Newark, NJ (1985-89). Worked part-time at Penney's for two years while completing my college degree which I earned in 1987.

- Received the Manager's Award for achievement in hourly productivity.

PERSONAL   Am seeking a career outside retailing primarily so I can attend classes two nights a week in pursuit of my M.B.A. Work well under pressure and am known for attention to detail. Proficient with Word. Single; will travel extensively. Excellent references.

Date

Exact Name of Person
Title or Position
Name of Company
Address (number and street)
Address (city, state, and zip)

Retail Area Manager

Dear Sir or Madam:

If you have been promoted ahead of your peers, or "ahead of schedule," according to company tradition, go ahead and say so! In the "conceptual statement" for her first job, this young professional points out that she was promoted quickly into a job "usually reserved for someone with much more experience." Notice her "personal guarantee" in paragraph three of her cover letter. This is designed to inspire confidence in prospective employers!

I would appreciate an opportunity to talk with you soon about how I could contribute to your organization through my exceptionally strong "track record" in management and sales.

As you will see from my resume, I have been promoted rapidly in every job I have ever held because of my proven leadership ability and willingness to assume responsibility. A self-starter and fast learner, I have excelled most recently in retail management and was promoted to Sales Area Manager by the Army & Air Force Exchange Service after beginning as a stocker and advancing rapidly to reorder associate. As Sales Area Manager I supervised a department of 13 employees and became skilled in hiring and interviewing.

I believe that my exceptionally strong management "track record" is due to a combination of natural ability, excellent training which I received from my employers, and a "hard-charging" personality that thrives on a fast pace. I offer a talent for training and motivating people, and experience has taught me how to handle "problem" employees and how to motivate marginal workers. I guarantee you can trust me to produce outstanding results with little or no supervision.

I hope you will welcome my call soon to arrange a brief meeting at your convenience to discuss your current and future needs and how I might serve them. Thank you in advance for your time.

Sincerely yours,

Patricia Cresswell

PATRICIA CRESSWELL

1110½ Hay Street, Fayetteville, NC 28305 • preppub@aol.com • (910) 483-6611

OBJECTIVE   To offer my proven management, organizational, and sales skills to an organization that can use a fast learner and hard worker who thrives on serving customers and solving problems in a fast-paced, competitive environment in which I am handling lots of responsibility.

EDUCATION   Completed extensive executive development training sponsored by Army & Air Force Exchange Service (AAFES) in these and other areas:
- Managing a department of employees
- Ordering/reordering merchandise throughout the U.S.
- Using the AAFES computer system for retail sales, accounting, and control
- Was selected to attend specialized OSHA training for supervisors

EXPERIENCE   **SALES AREA MANAGER.** Army & Air Force Exchange Service (AAFES), Germany (1995-2000). Began with AAFES as a stocker and after two months was promoted to Reorder Associate; after less than ten months in that job was selected as Sales Area Manager, a position usually reserved for someone with much more experience.
- Received a cash bonus and Excellence Awards for superior performance, 2000 and 1999.
- Was recommended through a formal letter from my supervisor for selection as Sales and Merchandise Manager because of my trustworthiness, ability to motivate a team, and willingness to tackle any responsibility.
- Supervised a department of 13 employees and learned how to adopt a neutral attitude with "problem" employees; became skilled in hiring and interviewing.
- Acquired considerable skills related to merchandise ordering, shipping, and markdowns.
- Was commended on my flair for creating eye-catching displays.
- Learned valuable techniques for maximizing the turnover of seasonal merchandise.
- Continuously assured correct merchandise pricing and stocking; set plan-o-grams.
- Gained extensive experience with retail hard lines.

ASSISTANT MANAGER. Biscuit Kitchen, Dallas, TX (1995). Learned "the ropes" of managing a fast food service business.

STORE MANAGER. The Pantry, Inc., Houston, TX (1991-94). Always exceeded sales and inventory turnover goals, and earned a bonus with every paycheck I received from this company; responsible for making daily deposits of up to $8,000.
- Learned to do every job in this store including cashiering, ordering merchandise, controlling inventory, cleaning the store, hiring/firing/training employees, closing the store, and completing extensive paperwork.

ASSISTANT MANAGER. The Pantry, Inc., Houston, TX (1987-89). Was groomed for eventual store management, and became knowledgeable about every job
in this convenience store.
- Acted as cashier and made deposits; learned to order inventory and stock shelves; prepared plan-o-grams; trained and scheduled employees; handled all the paper work required of shift managers; was responsible for vendor check-ins; sold gas; handled customer relations.

COMPUTERS   Rapidly master new software and have used numerous AAFES programs to check mail, assess inventory levels in the warehouse, and determine location of products in route to their final destination.

PERSONAL   Sincerely thrive on a fast pace and work well under deadlines and pressures. Enjoy applying my talent for organizing and training people. Am a self-starter and can be trusted to do an outstanding job with little or no supervision. Am skilled at producing team results.

Date

Exact Name of Person
Exact Title
Exact Name of Company
Address
City, State, Zip

Retail Buying Transitioning into Marketing

Dear Exact Name of Person (or Dear Sir or Madam in answering a blind ad):

This successful professional found herself in a job hunt one day when her employer announced that it was relocating the buyers to the head office, 100 miles away. She didn't want to move, and she decided that she'd had enough of retail buying, anyway. So she used this resume and cover letter to open numerous doors, and she finally chose a job as a Marketing Manager of a nonprofit organization.

With the enclosed resume, I would like to make you aware of my extensive sales, merchandising, and management skills as well as my interest in exploring the possibility of utilizing my experience to benefit your organization.

After earning a B.S. degree (cum laude) from the University of Idaho at Boise, I was recruited by Lord & Taylor as an Associate Buyer in 1997. I achieved unusually rapid advancement to Buyer after only one year and four months, and since 1999 I have excelled in handling a $10 million volume while buying for 22 stores. The buying function had been handled in New York City for the previous five years, and I instituted a major reorganization which led to increased sales.

My sales and gross margin results have been consistently superior, and I have never received anything less than "above average" on annual performance evaluations of my business, sales, marketing, merchandise planning, and inventory control skills. I am well known for my ability to establish and maintain effective working relationships with people at all levels, from top-level buying and merchandising experts in New York City to store managers and vendors. I pride myself on my ability to react quickly to emerging trends and to respond decisively in averting problems before they happen.

If you can use a dynamic and results-oriented individual with excellent communication skills, I hope you will contact me to suggest a time when we can meet to discuss your goals and needs and how I might help you. I can provide excellent references.

Thank you in advance for your time and professional courtesies.

Yours sincerely,

Lurene Rhoades

LURENE RHOADES

1110½ Hay Street, Fayetteville, NC 28305   •   preppub@aol.com   •   (910) 483-6611

OBJECTIVE
I want to contribute to an organization that can use a dynamic and results-oriented young professional who has enjoyed promotion to increasing responsibilities because of an ability to produce outstanding bottom-line results.

EDUCATION
Bachelor of Science in Criminal Justice, *cum laude,* University of Idaho at Boise, 1996.
- Named to Social Science Honor Society (Pi Gamma Mu), the freshman Honor Society (Phi Eta Sigma), and Who's Who Among College Students.
- Worked as a Writing Lab Tutor; elected Vice President of Criminal Justice Club; was honored by selection as a University Ambassador.
- Excelled in numerous professional development courses related to purchasing, sales, merchandising, and finance sponsored by Lord & Taylor Department Stores.

COMPUTERS
Highly proficient with computers including Lotus 1-2-3 and AmiPro; utilize LAN to provide timely information; also proficient with all merchandise systems including POM, Markdown, IMS, Store SKU Database, MPO/MPT, and SAR.

EXPERIENCE
Have excelled in the following track record of advancement with Lord & Taylor Department Stores, Boise, ID (1997-present).
1999-present. BUYER. Was promoted to Buyer because of my exceptional performance as an Associate Buyer. Am now responsible for a $10 million sales volume while buying for the Juniors departments for 22 stores.
- **Superior sales results**: Increased sales 1.1% in 1999 compared to the previous year; am currently showing an 8.9% sales increase in 2000 compared to 1999; reorganized the Juniors area and increased sales after taking over buying which had been handled in New York City for the previous five years.
- **Gross margin increase:** Increased GM from 36.2 in 1999 to 37.1 in 2000.
- **Sales and marketing management:** Consistently maintain "above average" on annual performance evaluations, and have been verbally commended for my insightful sales and marketing management.
- **Communication:** Maintain outstanding relationships with store management.
- **Business and professional management:** React prudently to changing market trends to maximize sales; work with vendors to build profitable relationships.
- **Merchandise planning and inventory management:** Am skilled in planning and achieving balanced assortments that meet customer demand.

1997-99: ASSOCIATE BUYER. In unusually rapid advancement, was promoted to buyer after only 1 year and four months in this job and was given responsibility for a $10 million sales volume; learned the duties of a buyer while working with Ladies Ready to Wear, Ladies Sportswear, Accessories, Cosmetics, Fragrances, Lingerie, Jewelry, and Hosiery.
- Played a key role in increasing sales in the Misses Suit Department.

Other experience: *Partially financed college education working up to 30 hours a week.*
1994-97: Sales Representative & Sales Support Specialist. Chic Boutique, Boise, ID. In addition to sales, handled additional responsibilities which included maintaining security and adhering to a strict theft reduction system; verified status of incoming and outgoing merchandise and processed price reductions.

PERSONAL
Outstanding decision maker and problem solver who thrives on multiple responsibilities.

Date

Exact Name of Person
Title or Position
Name of Company
Address (number and street)
Address (city, state, and zip)

Dear Exact Name of Person: (or Dear Sir or Madam if answering a blind ad.)

The Objective of the resume is a blend of all-purpose and specific. He mentions his specialized knowledge of the automotive industry as well as his sales and management skills which are transferable to any field.

I would appreciate an opportunity to talk with you soon about how I could benefit your organization through my outstanding abilities gained in a multifunctional business where I oversaw activities including sales, training and supervision, merchandising and promotion, sales and customer service, as well as administrative and fiscal operations.

As the Store Manager of a Southern Auto location which had $2.5 million in sales its last fiscal year, I have become very efficient at managing my time while dealing with three different operational areas — parts, tires and service, and automotive accessories. This store averages from 1,500 to 1,700 transactions a week with average weekly sales in the $40-60,000 range. In my five years as Store Manager I have achieved consistently high levels of productivity, sales, and customer satisfaction.

As you will see from my enclosed resume, before joining Southern Auto I earned rapid advancement with Quality Auto Parts. In my five years with this organization I was promoted to Store Manager after starting as a part-time sales person and then becoming a Merchandiser, a Parts Specialist, and Assistant Manager. As Store Manager I was involved in making decisions concerning merchandising, computer operations and fiscal control, inventory control, and public relations as well as internal employee counseling and supervision.

A dedicated and hard-working professional, I can be counted on to find ways to ensure customer satisfaction and productivity while always impacting favorably on the organization's bottom line.

I hope you will welcome my call soon to arrange a brief meeting at your convenience to discuss your current and future needs and how I might serve them. Thank you in advance for your time.

Sincerely yours,

Eugene Lobato

EUGENE LOBATO

1110½ Hay Street, Fayetteville, NC 28305 • preppub@aol.com • (910) 483-6611

OBJECTIVE   To benefit an organization in need of an experienced manager with a strong background in inventory control/parts ordering, merchandising and sales, public relations, and fiscal operations along with specialized knowledge of the automotive parts business.

EXPERIENCE   **STORE MANAGER.** Southern Auto, Atlanta, GA (1991-present). Direct and oversee all phases of daily operations in an established store with 28 employees and with average weekly sales of from $40,000 to $60,000; motivate employees to achieve high levels of productivity, sales, and customer satisfaction.
- Played an important role in the success of a location with $2.5 million in annual sales and from 1,500 to 1,700 transactions a week.
- Received an Award of Excellence as an Auto Parts Specialist in recognition of my professionalism and knowledge of the inventory control aspect of the business, 2000.
- Received Customer Service Award Pin for my exceptional customer relations.
- Earned certification in tires and parts in recognition of my expertise in providing customer service in these areas, 1999.
- Was chosen to attend a corporate training program for store managers in 1999.
- Participated in setting up and running a job fair booth in order to recruit management trainees for Southern Auto at technical colleges throughout the southeast, 1999.
- Carried out interesting sales merchandising and promotional activities which helped to increase sales of additional services once customers entered the store.
- Became skilled in time management while overseeing the operation of distinctly different areas within one location — parts, tires and service, and automotive accessories.

STORE MANAGER. Quality Auto Parts, Macon, GA (1986-91). Earned rapid promotion with this business and was placed in charge of overseeing all aspects of store operations from personnel, to sales, to inventory control.
- Advanced from a part-time sales position to Merchandiser, then to Parts Specialist and Assistant Manager, and in 1990 was promoted to Store Manager.
- Became familiar with management unique to the automotive parts industry involving public relations, computer operations/fiscal controls, and parts and inventory control.
- Supervised as many as 14 employees in a location which averaged from $15,000 to $18,000 in sales a week.

EDUCATION   Completed one semester of Business Administration, Priory College, Atlanta, GA.
Studied Electronic Engineering and Business Management, Atlanta Technical Community College, GA.

TRAINING   Was selected for corporate-sponsored training including:
"Introduction to Management" — a part of the Southern Auto Management School
"Technical Electronic Ignition Course" — Wells Manufacturing Corp.

CERTIFICATIONS   Received ASE (Automotive Service Excellence) certification as a Parts Specialist and Western Auto certification as a Master Tire Specialist and Parts Specialist.

PERSONAL   Am a well-rounded professional with excellent communication skills in all areas — dealing with the public and with employees. Have a pleasant and friendly personality.

Exact Name of Person
Title or Position
Name of Company
Address (number and street)
Address (city, state, and zip)

**Retail Store
Management, Transitioning
into Outside Sales**

A desire to finish her
degree is what has
prompted this experienced
retail manager to look for
employment outside
retailing.

Dear Exact Name of Person: (or Dear Sir or Madam if answering a blind ad.)

With the enclosed resume, I would like to indicate my interest in your organization and my desire to explore employment opportunities.

As you will see from my enclosed resume, I am an experienced manager of people, assets, and financial resources. In my current position I am managing the store which is the Top Volume Store in sales in the region. Although I am excelling in my current position and am held in high regard by upper management, I am interested in transferring my considerable management skills to another industry.

I hope you will welcome my call soon to arrange a brief meeting at your convenience to discuss your current and future needs and how I might serve them. Thank you in advance for your time.

Sincerely yours.

Gerry Reeves

Alternate last paragraph:
I hope you will call or write me soon to suggest a time convenient for us to meet and discuss your current and future needs and how I might serve them. Thank you in advance for your time.

GERRY REEVES

1110½ Hay Street, Fayetteville, NC 28305 • preppub@aol.com • (910) 483-6611

OBJECTIVE

To benefit an organization that can use a persuasive and dynamic professional who combines outstanding sales and marketing abilities, management experience, and a proven ability to make sound decisions and achieve ambitious bottom-line goals.

EDUCATION

Completing Bachelor's degree in my spare time at night; completed three years (98 credit hours) of course work from Baptist College, Austin, TX, with a concentration in Marketing. Have excelled in numerous management and executive development training programs.

EXPERIENCE

STORE MANAGER. Toys "R" Us, Denton, TX (1996-present). Manage up to 50 employees while controlling a $625,000 inventory level and maintaining tight operational control of a $2 million store.
* Am managing the store which is considered the Top Volume Store in sales in the entire region.
* Have hired, trained, and developed several managers who have gone on to become key management professionals for the Toys "R" Us chain.
* Increased profit margin from 37% to 39.2% in a one-year period while also increasing profit by $15,000 year-to-date through effective cost-cutting measures on store-controlled expenses without jeopardizing overall store productivity.
* Although I am highly regarded in my current position and enjoy the fast pace of this bustling retail environment, I am seeking an equally challenging position which will fully energize my leadership and energy while permitting me to complete, in my spare time, the year of studies remaining for my college degree.

MANAGER. Fashion Coordinators, San Antonio, TX (1996). Was recruited by this company to take over its multiunit operations; raised sales at the Dellwood Park Mall location 80% over the previous year's figures in my first month supervising that location, and then played a key role in closing the Centerfield Mall location.
* At the Centerfield Mall location, inventoried equipment, supplies, and client records and selected team members to be transferred.
* Was successful in raising sales average from $120-130 per client to $190-200 per client consistently per pay period.
* Sought new acquisitions in client base to increase business, and serviced existing clients with a standard of excellence in customer service; was effective in statistical management, including sales average, client survey scores, and payroll management.

SENIOR STORE MANAGER. The Paladium, San Antonio, TX (1992-96). Worked alone with no direct supervision on implementing company guidelines and goals among three stores generating $2.3 million in sales.
* Promoted to Senior Store Manager after consistently exceeding expectations in all aspects of managing overall operations
* Set sales goal and payroll allocations with given budget among the three stores.
* Kept shortage levels consistently under goal, and brought a high-shortage store down from a 3.8% shortage to .96% in a six-month period.
* Was the Liaison between corporate and six stores in Texas through 4th Quarter.

CO-MANAGER. New York Fashions & Accessories, Houston, TX (1990-92). Supervised the daily operations of a store with annual sales exceeding $1.5 million after being promoted from Assistant Manager to Co-Manager in a 10-month period; responsible for productivity of a 13-member sales team, and led by example with personal sales always exceeding given goals.
* Organized and presented merchandise to create a unique fashion image tailored by watching customer trends.
* Utilized available fixtures and equipment for optional usage.

Date

Exact Name of Person
Exact Title
Exact Name of Company
Address
City, State, Zip

Retail Sales and
Management, Relocating to a
New Area

Dear Exact Name of Person: (or Dear Sir or Madam if answering a blind ad):

This professional found
herself in a job hunt when
her husband left military
service and they relocated
geographically. She had
acquired an impressive
background in sales and
retail store management,
and her ability to turn
around troubled operations,
boost sales, train sales
personnel, and manage
accounts interested many
employers.

With the enclosed resume, I would like to make you aware of my extensive management experience and express my interest in exploring employment opportunities with your organization. My husband and I are in the process of relocating, and I can provide outstanding personal and professional references from all previous employers.

As you will see from my enclosed resume, I offer 16 years of experience in customer service, 12 years of experience in personnel management, as well as a 12-year background in payroll, budgeting, and profit margin accountability. In retail management positions, I have been very successful in reducing the loss rate by training staff on detection and prevention of shoplifting as well as internal theft. For example, as the Store Manager of a high-volume women's clothing store with a staff of 12 associates and two assistant managers, I reduced the loss rate by 38%. In another women's apparel store with a staff of 20 associates and three assistant managers, I decreased the loss rate by 68%.

In my most recent experience, I have excelled in management positions in the advertising and direct mail field. In my current job I personally manage large accounts while also overseeing quality assurance for the company as well as the training of staff in quality assurance and other job duties.

I am especially skilled as a troubleshooter, and I offer 10 years of experience in troubleshooting stubborn problems. In one position, I was recruited especially to take over the management of a failing operation which was scheduled to be closed. By retraining and motivating staff to achieve high sales goals, I essentially rescued this store and was able to transform that troubled operation into a multimillion-dollar store in one year.

If you can use an adaptable young professional who can handle pressure and deadlines and who is known for high levels of drive and initiative, I hope you will contact me to suggest a time when we might meet to discuss your needs. I can provide outstanding references at the appropriate time.

Sincerely,

Sun L. Kagawa

SUN L. KAGAWA

1110½ Hay Street, Fayetteville, NC 28305 • preppub@aol.com • (910) 483-6611

OBJECTIVE   I want to contribute to an organization that can use a skilled management professional with extensive experience in customer service, sales, and personnel management.

EXPERIENCE   **ACCOUNT MANAGEMENT SUPERVISOR.** Mendelson Consulting Services, Bethesda, MD (1999-present). Manage large corporate billing accounts while supervising account management staff and all aspects of quality control.

- **Customer service:** Initiate contact with new clients and create billing designs that meet their needs; coordinate production of the final product and communicate the client's point of view.
- **Production:** Work with multiple departments to ensure client deadlines are met; coordinate with plant managers to ensure adequate staffing and supplies.
- **Quality assurance:** Monitor the progress and accuracy of all jobs at every stage of production; maintain constant vigilance at every stage of production and resolve errors which occur.
- **Training:** Train new account managers and receptionists in customer service and other areas.

VICE PRESIDENT OF OPERATIONS. Gerhard Services, Bethesda, MD (1998-99). Oversaw daily operations of a small direct mail advertising company.

- **Sales:** Worked with the owner in creating effective presentations and closing the sale.
- **Design:** Created the layout, format, and overall design of the *Gerhard Services Book*, and worked with clients in designing ads to communicate their product or service. Worked with graphic designers on completion of ads.
- **Distribution:** Used postal software to sort mailers for discounted bulk mail rate, and coordinated packing and delivery to bulk mail center for distribution.

ASSISTANT MANAGER. CVS, Bethesda, MD (1996-97). Managed a staff of 16 associates and two pharmacists while serving a variety of clients and needs.

- **Customer service:** Assisted customers in locating the products needed. Coordinated with pharmacist.
- **Sales:** Managed the customer service function, and supervised add-on sales promotions while promoting staff to meet company goals; tracked and maintained sales daily.
- **Loss prevention:** Worked with the Loss Prevention Supervisor to improve awareness of proven techniques in reducing loss and theft; trained staff in prevention and in handling loss prevention situations, and instilled in staff knowledge about how to prevent/apprehend shoplifters and internal thieves.
- **Staffing & scheduling:** Interviewed, hired, and trained new associates. Acquired knowledge of OSHA regulations and labor laws. Used projected sales and current trends to schedule staff.

STORE MANAGER. Exclusively Ladies, Inc., Bethesda, MD (1995-96). Managed 12 associates and two assistant managers in a high-volume women's clothing store; took on a store with lagging sales and transformed it into a multimillion-dollar store in one year.

- Made changes in all areas of store operations including customer service, sales, staffing and scheduling, merchandising, accounting, and loss prevention.
- Decreased the store's loss ratio by 38%.

EDUCATION   Completed extensive management and sales training sponsored by my employers.

PERSONAL   Outstanding personal and professional references upon request. Strong work ethic.

Date

Exact Name of Person
Exact Title
Exact Name of Company
Address
City, State, Zip

**Retail Sales and
Management, Responding
to an Advertisement**

Although she is held in high
regard and is excelling in
her job, this successful
retailer saw an ad that
caught her eye, and she
is responding to it.

Dear Exact Name of Person: (or Dear Sir or Madam if answering a blind ad):

I am writing to express my strong interest in the position of Area Buyer which your company recently advertised in the *Pittsburgh Times*. With the enclosed resume, I would like to make you aware of my experience in all aspects of purchasing, sales forecasting, events planning and development of promotions, and merchandising, as well as my analytical, planning, and negotiation skills.

As you will see from my resume, I have recently been excelling as a Buyer for Nordstrom Department Stores, where I was handpicked for my most recent position because of my analytical and problem-solving abilities. Assuming control of an area that was consistently overstocked by at least $500,000, I quickly reined in the excesses, and within six months Intimate Apparel was within established inventory guidelines for the Group.

Throughout my career in retail, I have applied my strong aptitude for creative and analytical thinking to problems related to increasing sales while maximizing profitability. An articulate communicator, my strong negotiation skills have resulted in acquiring the best prices and terms for my employers in interactions with national vendors.

If you can use a self-motivated professional whose abilities have been proven in a number of challenging environments, I hope you will write or call me soon to suggest a time when we might meet to discuss your needs and goals and how my background might serve them. I can provide outstanding references at the appropriate time.

Sincerely,

Natalia Sosnkowski

NATALIA SOSNKOWSKI

1110½ Hay Street, Fayetteville, NC 28305 • preppub@aol.com • (910) 483-6611

OBJECTIVE

To benefit an organization that can use a self-motivated, articulate professional with strong analytical, planning, and negotiation skills who offers a background in purchasing, sales forecasting, promotions and events planning, and merchandising.

EXPERIENCE

With Nordstrom Department Stores, excelled in challenging positions as Group Buyer for Accessories and Intimate Apparel:

1997-present: **GROUP BUYER.** Intimate Apparel, Pittsburgh, PA. Was handpicked to assume control of this troubled division which was consistently overstocked by $500,000 to $1 million; brought the group into compliance with inventory guidelines within six months.

- Manage a total sales volume of more than $10.6 million dollars while handling all aspects of merchandise selection for the Intimate Apparel departments in 22 stores.
- Analyze sales figures and budgetary requirements for each department against current year sales trends, generating sales forecasts and projections.
- Using sales projections and my industry experience, make buying commitments for the group; decide on merchandise purchased for all departments for a 4-6 month period.
- Track merchandise sales, analyzing department and group trends to identify items that need to be marked down; determine percentage or amount of the price reduction.
- Monitor shipping and receiving, cross-checking with store personnel to ensure that items shipped by the vendor match the merchandise ordered.
- Interact with store managers and associates, providing direction to store personnel regarding merchandising, upcoming events, new product information, and promotions.
- Generate 4.5% of total store volume for all stores in the group; facilitate an average yearly sales increase of 5%.
- Served on the BSS Core Committees for Foundations and Daywear (2000) and Sleepwear and Robes (1999); received two Silver Achievement Awards (1999 & 2000) and a Pacesetter Award (1998).

1991-1997: **GROUP BUYER.** Accessories, Hosiery, Handbags, & Jewelry, Pittsburgh, PA. Oversaw all buying functions for the accessories departments of 11 stores; held responsibility for a total sales volume of $4.5 million.

- Developed sales projections for the group based on analysis of previous year, year-to-date, and category trends, budgetary requirements, and other marketing data.
- Consistently generated an average annual sales increase of more than 5% while maximizing profit margin through careful management of inventory levels and expenses.
- Negotiated with vendors to acquire the best prices and terms on new product as well as obtaining monetary refunds or merchandise credits for product that was not selling.
- Monitored sales of specific items by department, to ensure a strong in-stock position on fast-moving items and planned promotions to boost sales of slow-moving product.
- Composed and prepared a variety of written materials, including advertising copy, merchandising plans, etc., designed to increase the Group's visibility and profitability.

Highlights of earlier experience:
BUYER. Northland Department Stores, Philadelphia, PA. Performed all buying functions for an 18-store regional chain; held final responsibility for annual sales of up to $1.5 million.
BUYER and **ASSISTANT BUYER.** Vogue Ladies Specialty Stores, Philadelphia, PA. Started with this small chain of premium ladies specialty stores as an Assistant Buyer and advanced to increasing responsibilities. Performed all buying functions in assigned departments for 14 stores; was responsible for total annual sales of more than $3 million.

PERSONAL

Excellent personal and professional references are available upon request.

Exact Name of Person
Title or Position
Name of Company
Address (number and street)
Address (city, state, and zip)

Retail Sales, Seeking Promotion into Area Sales Management

This accomplished retailer has served her employer with distinction, and now she seeks promotion to an Area Sales Management position.

Dear Sir or Madam:

With the enclosed resume, I would like to make you aware of my interest in the position of Area Sales Manager with Nordstrom.

As you will see from my resume, I have served Nordstrom with distinction since 1998, when I started as a Sales Associate. I subsequently advanced to Business Manager of the Chanel line and recently have transitioned to the Estee Lauder line since the corporate decision was made to eliminate Chanel. I am very familiar with the Nordstrom organization, and I am confident that I could make a valuable contribution as an Area Sales Manager. With an aggressive sales orientation, I led the Chanel business to end 4% up for the year even though the product line was being discontinued.

I offer proven retail management ability, and most of my retail management training and experience was as a Co-Manager with Intimate Boutique. I began as a part-time sales associate and was quickly promoted to Co-Manager in charge of up to 12 people regularly and up to 40 people during the holiday season. I became highly respected for my exceptionally strong management and motivational skills as I led both the fragrance department and the bra department to 12% increases. I was able to achieve those increases through my ability to train and motivate employees as well as through my exceptionally strong merchandising skills. I was singled out to receive the company's prestigious "Best of the Best" ("BOB") award which recognized me as an outstanding leader and motivator. On numerous occasions, the company selected me to oversee grand openings of new stores, normally a responsibility reserved for managers rather than co-manager. At stores in Evanston, Springfield, Joliet, and other cities, I oversaw the grand opening and spent a week in each location supervising the staff, training employees, and providing oversight for store operations.

Although I am certain there are management opportunities available at other retailers including Intimate Boutique, I am hopeful that Nordstrom will consider me for the position of Area Sales Manager. I very much enjoy the Nordstrom organization and its philosophy of merchandising, and I want to be an integral member of the management team responsible for achieving ambitious sales goals.

You would find me in person to be a vivacious and highly motivated individual who would be an asset to any area. I hope you will meet with me in person to discuss my desire to become an Area Sales Manager so that I can continue contributing to the bottom line in an aggressive and resourceful way.

Sincerely,

Ellie B. Hatherly

ELLIE B. HATHERLY

1110½ Hay Street, Fayetteville, NC 28305   •   preppub@aol.com   •   (910) 483-6611

OBJECTIVE

To contribute to an organization that can use a dedicated young professional and exceptionally strong merchandiser with extensive experience in retail management and problem solving and with proven public relations, sales and marketing skills.

EDUCATION

Completed nearly three years of college, Springfield College, Springfield, IL; am completing degree in my spare time as my schedule permits.
Extensive retail management training sponsored by Intimate Boutique.

EXPERIENCE

BEAUTY ADVISOR. Estee Lauder, **Nordstrom**, Oak Park, IL (Oct. 1999-present). After corporate decisions were made to remove the Chanel product line from Nordstrom, I transitioned to Beauty Advisor.

BUSINESS MANAGER & ANALYSTE. Chanel, **Nordstrom,** Oak Park, IL (Oct. 1998-Oct. 1999). Supervised one full-time analyste and a full-time makeup artist while working extensively with sales representatives in the process of coordinating special events.
*   Completed sales reports; consistently met or exceeded sales goals.
*   Even though the product line was removed from Nordstrom, ended +4% for the year.
*   Managed a $90,000 inventory and assured optimum inventory turnover.

SALES ASSOCIATE. Nordstrom, Oak Park, IL (April 1998-Sept. 1998). Consistently met SPH goals and learned to expertly handle markdowns and RTVs.
*   Was recognized for superior customer service skills.
*   Was frequently commended for my strong leadership and management abilities.

CO-MANAGER. Intimate Boutique, Oak Park, IL (1990-98). Began as a part-time sales associate and was quickly promoted to Co-Manager in charge of supervising up to 10 people regularly and up to 25 people during the holiday season.
*   **Staff management responsibility:** As the $1.5 million store grew, played a key role in sales increases and advanced in managerial responsibilities to supervise 12 people regularly and 40 people during the holiday season.
*   **Sales leadership:** Always achieved or exceeded my personal sales goals, and led the store to consistently achieve or exceed store sales objectives.
*   **Department management:** Increased **bra sales** by 12% through my ability to more effectively merchandise products and train employees; also increased **fragrance sales** by 12% through my merchandising flair, ability to control stock, and ability to train and motivate employees.
*   **Store opening responsibilities:** Was entrusted with the responsibility of overseeing the grand opening of several new stores (usually a responsibility reserved for a manager instead of a co-manager); supervised the grand opening of stores in Evanston, Springfield, Joliet, and other cities, which was a week-long responsibility in each location.
*   **Management awards:** Received the "Best of the Best" ("BOB") award given to outstanding leaders and motivators who demonstrated a proven ability to motivate staff.
*   **Employee management:** Became skilled in overseeing large numbers of employees which included scheduling employees; prepared payroll; hired new sales professionals, and developed a knack for identifying highly motivated individuals with problem-solving skills and a resourceful nature.

PERSONAL

Can provide outstanding personal and professional references. Strong leader.

Exact Name of Person
Exact Title of Person
Exact Name of Company
Exact Address
City, State zip

**Retail Sales,
Superstore Background**

Dear Exact Name:

The format for Mr.
Hilferty's resume was
chosen especially
because it showcases
his track record of
promotion within the
organizations which
have employed him.
Employers are often
curious about why
people are job
hunting, so Mr.
Hilferty lets
prospective
employers know in
the cover letter that
he is just trying to
find employment a
little closer to home
so that he doesn't
have to commute to
work a long distance.

With the enclosed resume, I would like to make you aware of my strong skills in the area of operations management, sales, and sales management with a view to exploring employment opportunities within your organization. Although I have been working in Coconut Grove, I own a home in Orlando and am seeking to relocate to the Orlando area.

As you will see from my resume, I have excelled in roles as a Sales Manager, Operations Manager, Store Manager, and Project Manager as well as Warehouse Manager. In one job as a Store Manager and Project Manager for Dollar Tree, I completed numerous assignments which involved solving profitability, merchandising, and operations problems in stores throughout Florida.

In 1993 Staples recruited me and I earned rapid promotion because of my strong operations management skills. After managing operations for an $18 million store in Jacksonville, I was promoted to manage operations for a $24 million store in Orlando which grew to $35 million in annual sales volume during my three years as Operations Manager. I have routinely managed between 30 to 80 people while scheduling up to 130 employees for maximum efficiency.

In 1996 Office Max aggressively recruited me, and I have recently excelled in jobs as Sales Manager and Operations Manager in Coconut Grove. I offer proven abilities related to P & L management, and I can provide outstanding personal and professional references at the appropriate time.

If you can use my extensive management skills and operational problem-solving experience, I hope you will contact me to suggest a time when we might meet to discuss your needs and goals and how I might serve them. Thank you in advance for your time.

Yours sincerely,

Donald Hilferty

DONALD HILFERTY

1110½ Hay Street, Fayetteville, NC 28305 • preppub@aol.com • (910) 483-6611

OBJECTIVE

To benefit an organization that can use a seasoned sales professional and experienced sales manager with exceptional communication and customer service skills along with a proven ability to manage operations for maximum profitability.

EDUCATION

Extensive sales and sales management training programs and courses sponsored by Staples, Dollar Tree, Office Max, and Costco Membership Warehouse Corporation.
Through professional training programs, have earned Certificates in the following areas:

Inventory Management Certification   Sales Management Certification
Warehouse Management Certification   Operations Management Certification
Store Management Certification

EXPERIENCE

SALES MANAGER & OPERATIONS MANAGER. Office Max, Coconut Grove, FL. Was recruited away from Staples by Office Max, and excelled in these positions of responsibility with this major retailer of electronics, appliances, music products:
Sales Manager. (1998-present). Train and manage up to 30 people while managing car stereo sales and installation as well as appliance sales and delivery.
- In May 2000, the overall store was ranked highest ever in the region, and in April 1999 car stereo sales ranked #1 in the company and in the region.

Operations Manager. (1996-98). While routinely acting as both Store Manager and Operations Manager, was responsible for managing labor hours based on a percentage of sales while directly supervising between 25-80 individuals and overseeing schedules for a work force of 130.
- Managed overall operations including cash management, personnel, customer service, customer-based scheduling, and control of P & L.

OPERATIONS MANAGER. Staples, Orlando and Jacksonville, FL. Was recruited by Staples and then was promoted from Warehouse Manager to Operations Manager in this progression:
Operations Manager. Orlando, FL (1993-96). Was promoted to manage operations for a $24 million store which increased its sales volume to $35 million in three years.
- Played a key role in helping the store achieve the highest net operations profit for 1994 and 1995 in Staples' Florida region.
- Demonstrated strong P & L management skills while managing labor hours for maximum profitability.

Operations Manager. Jacksonville, FL (1993). Earned rapid promotion to the job above because of my skill in managing operations for an $18 million store.
- Managed the P & L; with the General Manager, provided monthly reports to the district with all variances identified and explained.

STORE MANAGER & PROJECT MANAGER. Dollar Tree, Jacksonville, FL (1991). Excelled in a job as a problem solver and troubleshooter while functioning as the "right arm" for the Florida Regional Manager.

MERCHANDISE MANAGER. Costco Membership Warehouse, Jacksonville, FL (1987-90). Merchandised a complete hardlines area of the store; hired sales and installation employees and worked with buyers to increase stock levels to maximize sales; managed 80 people.

PERSONAL

Outstanding personal and professional references are available upon request.

Exact Name of Person
Exact Title
Exact Name of Company
Address
City, State, Zip

Route Sales,
Seeking Outside Sales

Dear Exact Name of Person (or Dear Sir or Madam if answering a blind ad):

With the enclosed resume, I would like to make you aware of an experienced, motivated professional with excellent communication, time management, and computer skills as well as a background in office administration, accounting and inventory control, printing, and sales.

In my present position with General Foods, I was promoted twice within one year because of my exceptional performance in product distribution, marketing, and inventory control as well as my skill in acting as a direct marketing consultant to the customer on in-store promotional techniques. I supervise one employee, and in my short time with the company I have increased the dollar amount of sales on my route while developing new accounts and servicing existing customers.

Ms. Moritz has learned through the grapevine of a job which would place her in an outside sales position. She made a successful career change previously when she emerged from jobs in office environments and got into route sales. After a taste of sales, she has decided that sales is well suited to her outgoing personality and desire to help customers.

In previous positions with Smith College, I served as Administrative Assistant, supervising 18 work-study students in completing the administrative activities of the admissions office. I updated and maintained an accurate database of nearly 14,000 new, current, and prospective students and provided technical assistance to staff members which smoothed the transition to the new computer system. In an earlier work-study position as an Administrative Aide, I demonstrated my technical proficiency and detail orientation, developing film, designing and setting print pages, and operating a precision paper cutter and binder.

If you can use an experienced professional with a strong background in office administration, accounting and inventory control, and sales, then I look forward to hearing from you soon, to arrange a time when we might meet to discuss your needs. I can assure you in advance that I have an excellent reputation, and would quickly become a valuable addition to your organization.

Sincerely,

Leslie C. Moritz

LESLIE. C. MORITZ

1110½ Hay Street, Fayetteville, NC 28305   •   preppub@aol.com   •   (910) 483-6611

OBJECTIVE

To offer my outstanding communication and management skills to an organization that can use a poised young professional known for exceptional initiative and problem-solving ability.

LANGUAGES

Speak German, Spanish, and English

EDUCATION

B.A., Spanish, Smith College, Dallas, TX, December 1996.
- Was inducted into the Foreign Language Honor Society.
- Received the Yolanda M. Cowley Award in recognition of outstanding achievements in Spanish as well as acknowledgment of overall academic performance.

A.A., General Education, Dallas Technical Community College, Dallas, TX, 1987.
- Completed in-depth computer programming courses, U.S. Army, Ft.Hood, TX.

EXPERIENCE

ROUTE SALES REPRESENTATIVE. General Foods, Dallas, TX (1997-present). Have been promoted twice in one year because of my excellent performance in product distribution, marketing, inventory control, and acting as a consultant on in-store promotional techniques.
- Supervise two individuals.
- While excelling in a track record of promotion with this industry giant, have learned valuable marketing techniques, selling strategies, and merchandising secrets.
- Have increased the dollar volume of sales on my route while also gaining new accounts.

ADMINISTRATIVE ASSISTANT. Smith College, Dallas, TX (1994-1996). Began as an Administrative Assistant and was promoted to Secretary to oversee the administrative duties of a busy admissions office including coordinating tours, greeting prospective students and their families, scheduling appointments, receiving and distributing mail, and answering a multiline telephone.
- Supervised up to 18 work study students.
- Ensured that all student files matriculate through the system from the point of application to enrollment.
- Maintained an accurate database of thousands of prospective students.
- Provided assistance to staff members contributing to the smooth flow of transition to an upgraded computer software system.

ADMINISTRATIVE AIDE. Smith College, Dallas, TX (1993-1994). Provided administrative support during a work study program in the college's print shop; handled a variety of support tasks including answering telephones, running errands, and fulfilling printing requests for various departments throughout the campus.
- Demonstrated technical proficiency while operating a precision paper cutter, developing film, binding notepads, designing and setting print pages, and conducting research.

QUALITY CONTROL SPECIALIST. Reese Printing Co., Dallas, TX (1993).
While working through Adia Temporary Services, developed highly refined attention-to-detail skills while ensuring a quality product through upholding strict company standards; set up paper review machine; checked labels for print faults; and packaged labels.

PERSONAL

Am an outstanding motivator and communicator with exceptional supervisory skills. A hands-on supervisor/manager, firmly believe in leading by example.

Date

Exact Name of Person
Title or Position
Name of Company
Address (number and street)
Address (city, state, and zip)

**Software Sales,
Seeking Position with
International Company**

Dear Sir or Madam:

This aggressive young
professional is on the "fast
track" in his company, but
he is feeling restless and
wants to "see what's out
there." The resume and
cover letter are designed
to interest employers in
numerous fields.

I am writing to express my strong interest in the position of **Country Manager –
Japan**, which was recently posted in the career opportunities section of the Microsoft
web site. With exceptional leadership and personnel management experience along with
an extensive sales and marketing background related to software sales and distribution, I feel I am ideally suited to your needs. I was born in Tokyo, Japan, speak both
English and Japanese fluently, and have previously worked in various overseas locations, including Japan.

As you will see from my resume, I am currently excelling as the President and
Sales Manager of Imperial Technologies, a busy local software reseller with annual
sales of nearly a million dollars. In this position and a previous job as Executive Vice
President of Golden Software, I have interacted closely with vendors, manufacturers,
distributors, and sales representatives within the software industry on a daily basis.
While directing the sales and marketing efforts at each of these businesses, my exceptional leadership and motivational skills have resulted in growth of market share and
strong annual sales increases despite fierce competition. In my current entrepreneurial
role, I have developed all the company's accounts "from scratch."

You will notice that I have also served my country as a junior military officer. I
advanced to the rank of Captain in the U.S. Army after entering military service upon
graduation from college in 1984 with a Bachelor of Arts in International Relations and
minors in Political Science and History. During my military service, I excelled in various leadership positions worldwide, managing organizations that ranged from a 40-
man platoon, to a company of more than 100 employees, to responsibility for human
resource actions in an organization with over 500 personnel. As a military adviser I
provided guidance and assistance in formulating training and operational plans, and I
refined my exceptional communication skills in the process of conducting briefings for
high-level executives.

If you can use an articulate professional who is extremely familiar with Japanese
language and culture and who possesses proven management and entrepreneurial skills
along with practical experience in software distribution, I hope you will write or call me
soon to suggest a time when we might meet to discuss your needs. I can provide outstanding references at the appropriate time.

Sincerely yours,

Tadashi Nomura

TADASHI NOMURA

1110½ Hay Street, Fayetteville, NC 28305   •   preppub@aol.com   •   (910) 483-6611

OBJECTIVE   To contribute to an organization that can use an articulate professional with outstanding communication and sales skills along with a strong bottom-line orientation who has excelled in leadership and personnel management positions in the software industry and in the U.S. Military.

LANGUAGES   Speak, read, write, and translate **Japanese** and **English** fluently (born in Tokyo, Japan).

EDUCATION   **Bachelor of Arts** in **International Relations** with minors in Political Science and History, University of California at Berkeley, Berkeley, CA, 1986.
Completed extensive formal and on-the-job training in **sales** and **marketing.**
Excelled in numerous **leadership** and training courses sponsored by the U.S. Army; graduate of the eight-month Infantry Officer Advanced Course and Ranger School, the military's premiere physical, mental, and leadership "stress test" course; as well as other courses designed to refine **management** and **communication** skills.

SOFTWARE   Proficient with Mail Order Manager (MOM) Program, MS Office, and working knowledge of many of the Adobe products to include PageMaker and Photoshop.

EXPERIENCE   **PRESIDENT** and **SALES MANAGER.** Imperial Technologies, San Jose, CA (1998-present). Manage all operational aspects of this local software reseller with annual sales of $950,000; manage human, fiscal, and material resources; sales and marketing; and performing liaison with vendors, manufacturers, and distributors; have developed all accounts "from scratch."
- Despite strong competition from other software resellers in the area, have led the company to continuously achieve **25% sales increases annually** since the founding of the business.
- Supervise six employees, directing marketing, sales, and customer service efforts.
- Interact with software vendors, manufacturers, distributors, and sales representatives on a daily basis, acquiring vital information concerning new products, pricing, and shipping.
- Track sales of current titles by manufacturer, category, and type of software in order to anticipate potential growth areas and ensure a strong in-stock position on fast-moving titles.
- Interview, hire, and train all personnel, instructing them in company policies and procedures, customer service, inventory control, and product knowledge.

EXECUTIVE VICE PRESIDENT. Golden Software, San Francisco, CA (1994-1998). Was instrumental in the successful growth of this software reseller; managed the operation of this company while quickly mastering all aspects of the software resale industry.
- Formulated and developed long and short-term sales projections, analyzing sales figures from previous years and sales trends for the current fiscal year.
- An articulate communicator and talented motivator, inspired the sales force to excel, producing increases in sales and market share.
- Supervised 12 employees in areas which included sales and customer service, inventory, and shipping; interviewed, hired, and trained all personnel.
- Oversaw all inventory control and ordering functions, coordinating with vendors, manufacturers, sales representatives, and distributors throughout the industry.

PERSONAL   Am an adaptable professional with a reputation for unquestioned loyalty and honesty.

Exact Name of Person
Exact Title
Exact Name of Company
Address
City, State, Zip

**Technical Sales,
Transitioning from Textiles
into Another Industry**

If you notice the first job
on his resume, you will see
that he doesn't go into
much detail. He used this
resume and cover letter to
transition out of textile
sales, so he didn't want to
"talk the talk" of the textile
industry. He wanted his
resume and cover letter to
work in a "generic" way, so
that he could approach
employers in any industry.

Dear Exact Name of Person (or Dear Sir or Madam if answering a blind ad):

With the enclosed resume, I would like to make you aware of my background in sales and management and express my interest in discussing the possibility of employment with your company. Although I am held in high regard in my current job and can provide an excellent reference at the appropriate time, I am writing to you confidentially and would appreciate your not contacting my current employer until after we talk.

I am currently excelling as an Area Sales Manager, and I have developed innovative marketing ideas for new products while establishing and maintaining effective working relationships with my accounts. In my previous experience, I worked as a supervisor for both Hanes and then for Clothes-Knit Industries. While with Clothes-Knit, I was promoted from a supervisory position to Technical Service Representative, a job which required me to resolve problems and issues among customers, sales, manufacturing, quality control, process development, and management. I have earned a reputation as an exceptionally strong problem solver with an ability to think strategically as well as operationally when tackling a complex issue.

While earning my Bachelor of Business Administration degree, I financed my college education by working at a prominent bakery, and upon college graduation I took over the management of this 12-employee operation with wholesale and retail accounts in several cities. I was instrumental in developing accounts with industry and convenience stores, and I developed and implemented innovative marketing strategies.

If you can use a versatile professional who has excelled in both sales and management positions in the textile industry as well as in other environments, I hope you will contact me to suggest a time when we might meet to discuss your needs and how I might serve them. Thank you in advance for your time.

Sincerely,

George Louik

GEORGE LOUIK

1110½ Hay Street, Fayetteville, NC 28305 • preppub@aol.com • (910) 483-6611

OBJECTIVE

To benefit an organization that can use an enthusiastic, highly motivated sales professional and experienced general manager with a proven ability to establish and maintain strong working relationships while utilizing my problem-solving and communication skills.

EDUCATION & TRAINING

Bachelor of Business Administration (BBA), Texas State University, Austin, TX, 1989. majored in Business Administration with a minor in Economics and Management. Excelled in extensive sales and management training and professional development courses.

EXPERIENCE

AREA SALES MANAGER. Lowe & Associates, Birmingham, AL (1999-present). Sell textile replacement and OEM parts to textile mills.

ACCOUNT REPRESENTATIVE. Mader, Inc., Dothan, AL (1998). Developed marketing ideas for new products while developing and maintaining effective working relationships with new and existing accounts; left the company when it went into Chapter 11.
- Refined my ability to deliver the highest possible customer service by learning the function of our products in customers' operations, both fiberfill and nonwoven.
- Became respected for my ability to communicate effectively both orally and in writing.

Was promoted in the following track record because of my exceptional bottom-line results and sales ability, Clothes-Knit Industries:

1995-97: TECHNICAL SERVICE REPRESENTATIVE. Plano, TX. Was promoted to serve as a Technical Service Representative resolving problems and issues among Clothes-Knit customers, sales, manufacturing, quality control, process development, and management personnel.
- Assured customer satisfaction related to quality complaints and technical assistance.
- Developed excellent problem-solving and conflict resolution skills while negotiating claims and disposition of "off quality goods."
- Gained experience in open-end yarn manufacturing, knitting, and weaving, as well as dyeing and finishing through my involvement with 10 yarn manufacturing facilities with combined shipments of 4.5 million pounds per week.
- Conducted numerous courtesy visits in order to market and promote Clothes-Knit.

1995: SUPERVISOR. Connell Textiles, Corpus Christi, TX. Excelled as a Supervisor in open-end yarn production with capacity of more than 1 million pounds per week; motivated and managed 40 employees and led them to achieve and exceed ambitious production goals.
- Continuously ran high efficiencies while emphasizing the highest quality standards, implementing cost reduction goals, and promoting intense safety consciousness.
- Was responsible for the carding and spinning departments; equipment consisted of Trutzschler opening and carding, Rieter 851 drawframes, and Schlafhorst SE 9s.

GENERAL MANAGER. Sweet & Tasty Bakery, Inc., Corpus Christi, TX (1987-94). For this wholesale and retail bakery serving Corpus Christi, Deer Park, Bellaire, and Arlington, developed marketing strategies for a wide range of quality baked goods, and developed large accounts with local industry and convenience stores; supervised 12 employees daily.

PERSONAL

Can provide outstanding personal and professional references.

Date

Exact Name of Person
Title or Position
Name of Company
Address (number and street)
Address (city, state and zip)

**Telephone Services Sales,
Transitioning to Outside
Sales in Another Industry**

Although he enjoyed many
aspects of his outside sales
job in the telephone
industry, he decided the
compensation structure fell
short of his needs. He used
this resume and cover
letter to seek an outside
sales position in another
company, and he sought a
compensation structure
comprised of salary plus
commission that would
reward an ambitious hard
charger.

Dear Sir or Madam:

With the enclosed resume, I would like to make you aware of my background as an experienced sales professional with exceptional communication skills, natural leadership ability, and a strong bottom-line orientation which I could put to work for your company.

As you will see from my resume, I earned a Bachelor of Science in Health and Physical Education from Mount Laurel College in Mount Laurel, NJ.

I have recently excelled in outside sales environments in which I serviced existing accounts and developed new business. I am skilled at building a solid customer base through prospecting as well as through networking with repeat and referral customers. My natural sales ability and strong focus on ensuring customer satisfaction while maintaining bottom-line profitability have led to record-breaking sales for my employers. I have refined my public relations skills and built a strong network of contacts within the medical, legal, and professional communities while representing the company at Chamber of Commerce events as well as at events such as golf tournaments.

Although I am highly regarded by my present employer and can provide excellent personal and professional references at the appropriate time, I am interested in selectively exploring opportunities within the health systems field because that is most related to my undergraduate education. I feel that my natural salesmanship and strong network of personal contacts within the community would make me a valuable asset to the area, and I am extremely knowledgeable of the Fair Lawn community.

If you can use a confident, articulate professional whose abilities have been proven in a variety of challenging sales and management environments, then I look forward to hearing from you soon to suggest a time when we might meet to discuss your needs, and how my background might serve them.

Sincerely,

Robert W. Doyle

ROBERT W. DOYLE

1110½ Hay Street, Fayetteville, NC 2830   •   preppub@aol.com   •   (910) 483-6611

OBJECTIVE

To benefit an organization that can use an articulate, experienced sales professional with strong written and verbal communication skills who offers exceptional natural sales ability as well as a track record of excellence in a variety of challenging sales and management environments.

EDUCATION & TRAINING

Bachelor of Science in **Health & Physical Education**, Mount Laurel College, NJ, 1989. Completed the Stephen Covey **7 Habits of Highly Effective People** course sponsored by Mobile.
Completed Professional Selling Skills course sponsored by Mobile.
Completed Introduction to Computers, Bowden Technical Institute.

EXPERIENCE

ACCOUNT EXECUTIVE. Mobile Communications, Inc., Fair Lawn, NJ (1999-present). Call on new and established commercial accounts throughout Fair Lawn and the surrounding area, presenting the line of products and digital mobile telephone services offered by Mobile Communications, Inc.
* Service and maintain existing accounts, calling on dissatisfied customers to troubleshoot and resolve customer service complaints.
* Quickly developed a solid customer base, partly through utilizing the network of repeat and referral customers I have built in my years of sales experience in the Fair Lawn market.

OUTSIDE SALES REPRESENTATIVE & PUBLIC RELATIONS REPRESENTATIVE. Eastman Glass Co., Fair Lawn, NJ (1995-99). Serving as the only sales representative for three offices in New Jersey, contributed to record-breaking sales figures from 1996-1999.
* Consistently increased and maintained customer base by quickly responding to customer needs and developing innovative and effective marketing strategies designed to enhance sales and increase customer confidence and loyalty.
* Refined public relations skills and built a strong network of contacts within the medical, legal, and professional communities while representing the company at Chamber of Commerce events as well as at events that we sponsored, such as golf tournaments.

ASSISTANT TO THE BRANCH MANAGER and **SALESMAN.** Granby Toys Corp., Fair Lawn, NJ (1989-94). As a key member of a highly successful team for a branch that was consistently one of the two top locations since the corporation's opening, handled a variety of operational activities.
* Assumed the duties and responsibilities of the Branch Manager and Warehouse Manager in their absence, as well as taking on other management tasks, as needed.
* Developed marketing strategies and ensured exceptional customer service, increasing sales and maintaining our existing customer base.
* Recruited, interviewed, hired and trained personnel.
* Earned numerous awards, including the 1989 Most Improved Branch Award and the 1992 President's Award for the best overall branch.

MANAGER. Dodd's Toys, Wholesale Division, Teaneck, NJ (1986-89). Directed and supervised a full-time staff of five employees while managing a $500,000 inventory and achieving a successful operating profit; attained total sales of over $1.3 million in 1988.

PERSONAL

Maintain a positive attitude. Highly motivated by new challenges. Known as a "winner by nature." Possess innovative ideas and the ability to transform concepts into realities.

Date

Exact Name of Person
Title or Position
Name of Company
Address (number and street)
Address (city, state, and zip)

**Television Advertising Sales,
Seeking to Relocate**

This accomplished
advertising professional is
seeking to "go back home"
to a previous employer. You
will see that his cover letter
is very industry oriented,
since he is not interested in
seeking employment
outside his field.

Dear Sir or Madam:

With the enclosed resume, I would like to make you aware of my experience in sales and management and my desire to put my talents to work for you. I began my broadcast career at WXM, as a Yellow Page, back-room, thought-you-read-the-rating-book-down-one-side-and-start-over-on-the-next-page trainee. I left WXM to assume a major list and promotion opportunity at KFTM in Providence.

You will see from my resume that I am currently a Sales Manager at WRCB, TV 40 in Ohio, where I am managing a sales force covering Cleveland, which is the 29th largest market. While managing a sales force of six account executives, I have exceeded all expectations in terms of revenue generation as well as personnel training and development. Although I am highly regarded by this employer and can provide excellent references at the appropriate time, I am interested in relocating to the Northeast and am very interested in the possibility of returning to WXM.

In a prior position with KFTM-TV in Providence, Rhode Island, I excelled in a track record of promotion and was credited with being the driving force behind the station's being recognized as a "Top Performing" station in RICHTER TV's national survey. I began with the station as an Account Executive and achieved the status of Top Biller each year while also winning all the sales incentive contests. Then I was promoted to General Sales Manager, and I took the national revenue share from less than rating share to greater than audience delivery. After my promotion to General Sales Manager, I made numerous contributions to the bottom line while expanding the local staff from four to eight account executives.

I have had significant success with many forms of value-added selling: vendor, Doorknob Delivery, and musical themes (jingles). When our vendor specialist pitched KNVR-TV, the Sales Manager called me to verify our unbelievable sales figures. Our achievements with the Bag Lady promotion were equally spectacular.

I hope you will contact me to suggest a time when we might meet to discuss your needs and how I might serve them. I can provide excellent professional references. Thank you in advance for your time.

Yours sincerely,

Gene M. Dusseau

GENE M. DUSSEAU

1110½ Hay Street, Fayetteville, NC 28305   •   preppub@aol.com   •   (910) 483-6611

OBJECTIVE

I want to serve as the General Sales Manager at WXM-TV.

EXPERIENCE

LOCAL SALES MANAGER. WRCB, TV 40, Cleveland, OH (1998-present). While managing a sales force of six account executives, have exceeded all expectations in terms of revenue generation as well as personnel training and development.
- Have achieved a 45% increase in sales compared to last year.
- Cover a market (Cleveland) which is the 29th largest market.

OWNER & GENERAL MANAGER. East Side Diner, Providence, Rhode Island (1996-97). Increased sales by 25% in one year, reduced food costs by 8%, and lowered labor costs by 4% while restructuring and retraining the staff for a more aggressive customer service orientation.
- Supervised 8 employees including kitchen and wait staff.

GENERAL SALES MANAGER. KFTM Fox 28, Providence, Rhode Island (1992-96). Increased sellout by 22% and raised unit costs by 12% while excelling in all aspects of this sales management role.
- Increased local market share by 3% in one year.
- Increased revenue in 1995 and 1996 by 11% and 19% respectively.
- Increased regional market share by 6% in one year.

Excelled in the following track record of promotion with KFTM-TV, Providence, Rhode Island:

1987-92: GENERAL SALES MANAGER. Through my aggressive bottom-line orientation and strong personal initiative, led the sales department to be recognized as a "Top Performing" station in RICHTER TV's national survey.
- Realized a 19% revenue share difference over audience delivery.
- Initiated a revenue-generating vendor program that generated over $1 million dollars.
- Achieved almost 2 months of local budget in 1st quarter with Bag Lady Promotion.
- Achieved and maintained market leadership in sponsorship selling and new account development.
- Expanded local staff from four to eight account executives.

1983-87: NATIONAL SALES MANAGER. Established a short-term computer forecasting model for pricing and goal orientation that was adopted corporatewide.
Reworked the rep relationship based on spot rate and share.
Took national revenue share from less than rating share to greater than audience delivery.

1980-83: ACCOUNT EXECUTIVE. Began with a small client list, and achieved the status of Top Biller each year; was the winner of every sales incentive contest.

1978-80: WXM-TV, RICHTER Broadcasting, Newton, MA: Began as a trainee and developed a large client list.

EDUCATION

B.A. degree in History, Minor in English, Emerson College, Boston, MA.
Completed TVB General Sales Manager Seminar, Harvard Business School.

Date

April Stanfield
Stephens & Rothchild, Inc.
P.O. Box 3098
Houston, TX 89023

**Territory Manager,
Food Service Industry**

In this resume, you will see
the background of a
professional who is in his
second career. In his first
career, he worked for nearly
20 years as a funeral
director. Then he
transferred his "people"
skills and sales ability into a
sales position. Having
established an excellent
reputation in his second
career, he has prepared this
resume in response to a
food industry company that
is attempting to recruit him
away from his current
employer.

Dear Ms. Stanfield:

With the enclosed resume, I would like to formally indicate my interest in discussing the Food Broker positions available with your company. Although I am excelling in my job with Delby Food Service and can provide excellent references at the appropriate time, I would appreciate your treating my enquiry in confidence at this time.

As you will see from my resume, in 1996 I made a career change and became a Territory Manager with Delby Food Service. I rapidly became successful. In my first assignment I took over an existing territory and, with no prior food service experience, boosted sales 25% in my first month. Since then I have played a key role in helping my district to its #1 ranking among the corporation's 62 districts with sales in our district of $160 million. Although I am now living in Dallas, I have cheerfully adapted to varying territorial assignments as company needs have required, and I have established and maintained relationships with restaurants as well as day care and health care organizations all over Texas. I believe much of my success derives from the fact that I truly feel I am "in partnership" with my accounts.

In my previous experience, I was a funeral director, which is itself a "people business." With a reputation as an outstanding communicator and negotiator, I became skilled at establishing rapport with people from every race and background, and I maintained effective relationships with law enforcement officials, the media, as well as a variety of state, local, and federal officials. I genuinely enjoy working with people.

If my skills and experience interest you, please contact me to suggest a time when we might talk in more detail about your needs. I am single and can relocate as your needs require. Thank you in advance for your time, and I send belated wishes for a Happy New Year.

Yours sincerely,

Gary Rosenko

GARY ROSENKO

1110½ Hay Street, Fayetteville, NC 28305 • preppub@aol.com • (910) 483-6611

OBJECTIVE I want to contribute to the success of an organization that can use a versatile and knowledgeable professional who offers highly refined skills in sales and customer service.

EXPERIENCE **TERRITORY MANAGER.** Delby Food Service, Crowley, TX (1996-present). Was recruited in 1996 for a position with the largest food service company in the U.S., and have rapidly become successful; in my first assignment, took over an existing territory and, with no prior food service experience, boosted sales 25% in my first month.
- Have played a key role in helping my district to its #1 ranking among 62 corporate districts with overall district sales of $160 million.
- Establish and nurture accounts with restaurants, health care, and day care organizations.
- Have cheerfully adapted to varying territorial assignments within the company as corporate needs have required; established and maintained excellent relationships in counties all over Texas.
- Am skilled at all aspects of my job including collecting delinquent accounts, establishing and maintaining rapport, and increasing profitability of existing accounts.
- Believe that success in sales comes from establishing a "partnership" with my accounts.

FUNERAL DIRECTOR. Dallas Funeral Service Crematory, Dallas, TX (1995-96). Used my extensive experience in funeral directing to enhance profitability and efficiency of funerals; introduced several new techniques which simplified funeral arrangements.
- Applied my knowledge of laws related to funeral home administration/licensing.
- Gained a reputation as an outstanding communicator who easily establishes rapport with people from every race and background and became very knowledgeable with regard to discussing and tailoring funeral needs to specific religious beliefs.

FUNERAL DIRECTOR. Jason G. Smith Funeral Home, Dallas, TX (1981-94). Excelled in handling the full range of activities involved in the selling, conducting, and pre-need arranging of funerals.
- Wrote the policy training manual related to OSHA, EPA, and other similar regulations.
- Maintained outstanding relationships with law enforcement officials, the media, and with a wide variety of community, state, and local organizations and officials.
- Was respected for my excellent skills in managing people and resources while routinely coordinating numerous simultaneous projects under tight deadlines.

EDUCATION Associate's **Degree in Business**, Texas Central College, Dallas, TX, 1972.
Received **Diploma in Mortuary Science**, Brazelton, IN, 1975.

LICENSE **Licensed Funeral Director**; became a Texas Funeral Service Licensee in 1975.

AFFILIATIONS Have been active in my community; following are highlights of my involvements and affiliations:
- Former Member. Nursing Home Advisory Board and Parks and Recreation Board
- Past member, Administrative Board, Master of Masonic Lodge, Shriner

PERSONAL Outstanding personal and professional references. Genuinely enjoy working with the public.

Territory Sales Management, Building Supply Background

This sales professional offers a proven ability to succeed in the highly specialized environment of the construction and building supplies industry. When his current employer was purchased by a larger industry firm, he decided to explore other opportunities, primarily within the industry to which he has become accustomed.

Dear Sir or Madam:

With the enclosed resume, I would like to make you aware of my background as a seasoned sales professional and experienced sales manager with exceptional communication and negotiation skills.

In my most recent position with Clark-Davidson Company, I joined the organization as a Sales Representative, and my strong sales ability, hard work, and loyalty were rewarded with continuous promotions to higher levels of responsibility. I produced double-digit sales increases with Clark-Davidson, and I rose to Senior Territory Sales Manager, servicing major building supply, hardware store, and farm supply accounts in a five-state region.

At Heath Supplies, I maximized the profitability of existing accounts and developed new clients in a 33-county area of Oklahoma, substantially increasing territory sales by consistently adding new accounts. In this position and in earlier posts with Oak Ridge, Inc., and Clarendon, I earned a reputation as a skillful negotiator and highly effective communicator.

As you will see from my resume, I have an Associate of Applied Science degree from Tulsa Technical Community College. I further supplemented my degree program with numerous courses sponsored by my employers related to sales and marketing, sales management, customer service, techniques for prospecting and closing the sale, and account management. I feel that my strong combination of education, experience, and proven sales ability will be a valuable asset to your organization.

If you can use a motivated sales professional and experienced sales manager with outstanding communication and negotiation skills and a strong bottom-line orientation, I hope you will contact me to arrange a time when we might meet to discuss your needs. I can assure you in advance that I have an excellent reputation and would quickly become a worthy addition to your company.

Sincerely,

Raymond B. TePaske

RAYMOND B. TEPASKE

1110½ Hay Street, Fayetteville, NC 28305 • preppub@aol.com • (910) 483-6611

OBJECTIVE   To benefit an organization that can use a seasoned sales professional and experienced sales manager with exceptional communication and negotiating skills.

EDUCATION   **Associate of Applied Science degree in Agricultural Business Administration,** Tulsa Technical Community College, Tulsa, OK, 1995.
Completed numerous courses sponsored by my employers related to sales and marketing, sales management, customer service, techniques for prospecting and closing the sale, and account management.

EXPERIENCE   **SENIOR TERRITORY SALES MANAGER.** Clark-Davidson Company, El Reno, OK (1996-2000). Began with this company as a Sales Representative, and was promoted to increasing responsibilities based on my exceptional production; serviced major building supply, hardware store, and farm supply accounts in a five-state territory for this large manufacturer of construction mixes and commercial construction products.
Major responsibilities:
- Attended major trade shows throughout the country, soliciting new business and networking with existing clients and distributors.
- Developed new accounts, and serviced established accounts, selling Sakrete dry mixes; Clark-Davidson construction mixes and coatings; and Surewall exterior wall systems.
- Successfully dealt with buyers in a wide variety of environments, from small hardware stores and major chain stores, as well as architectural firms, construction companies, and building owners.
Accomplishments:
- Sales in the region where I served as Sales Manager grew from $1.4 million to over $4 million during my tenure.
- Produced double-digit sales increases in 10 of 14 years with Clark-Davidson.
- Was named **Salesman of the Year, Midwest Region** for 2000.

SALES REPRESENTATIVE. Heath Supplies, Tulsa, OK (1988-1996). Developed new accounts and maximized profitability of existing accounts while calling on building supply dealers, contractors, and farm supply dealers, covering a 33-county area in Oklahoma.
- Serviced established clients, and solicited new accounts, selling galvanized and painted steel roofing and siding.
- Assisted customers with ordering by figuring building supply costs.
Accomplishments:
- Substantially increased territory sales volume by consistently adding new accounts.
- Earned a reputation as a skillful negotiator and highly effective communicator.

Other experience:
SALES REPRESENTATIVE. Oak Ridge, Inc. For this janitorial supplies business, developed new accounts and achieved top-notch sales results.
TRAFFIC MANAGER. Clarendon, Inc. Issued billing orders for approximately 600 rail movements per month while also handling scheduling, routing, and rating.

PERSONAL   Outstanding personal and professional references are available upon request.

Date

Reference: Job #GA-TSZ
TRAVELSPAN Human Resources
400 Fortune Parkway, NW
Atlanta, GA 30339

Dear Sir or Madam:

With the enclosed resume describing my considerable expertise in the travel industry, I am responding to your recent advertisement for a Sales Manager in your Atlanta office. I am single and willing to relocate, and I find the Atlanta location particularly appealing.

As you will see from my resume, I am currently excelling as Senior Travel Agent with a travel agency in Colorado. I offer advanced computer skills and am my office's "internal expert" on all matters of software and hardware technology, including troubleshooting hardware malfunctions. I have completed Datas II, Worldspan, and Advanced Professional Sabre courses and am very interested in teaching Worldspan software. I am also my agency's expert on advanced ticketing applications including ticket exchanges, coupon redemption, and group airline ticketing.

With a commitment to continuous professional training, I am always seeking ways to improve my knowledge in my spare time. I hold an A.A. degree in Liberal Arts.

Although I am equipped to book travel worldwide, I offer particularly strong knowledge related to most major U.S. cities, the Caribbean, Great Britain, Italy, Greece, and Bermuda. I have traveled extensively myself and am a former resident of St. Croix.

I can provide outstanding references from my current employer as well as from both corporate and leisure clientele. A hard worker who thrives on new challenges and who rapidly masters new concepts, I feel certain I could excel as a Sales Manager in your Atlanta office. I, of course, know of your company's fine reputation, and I would be honored to be associated with a company respected for its industry leadership and commitment to customer service.

I hope I will have the pleasure of meeting with you in person to discuss my strong qualifications for and interest in the position you advertised. I look forward to hearing from you soon to suggest a time when we can talk about your needs and my ability to meet them. Thank you in advance for your time.

Sincerely yours,

Frances Rothstein

FRANCES ROTHSTEIN

1110½ Hay Street, Fayetteville, NC 28305 • preppub@aol.com • (910) 483-6611

OBJECTIVE To offer my experience to an organization that can benefit from my knowledge of domestic and international travel planning related to leisure travel, corporate accounts, and tour packages as well as my expertise related to travel industry computer technology.

LEADERSHIP Am highly respected within the community in which I work, and serve as Chairwoman of the Board of Directors, Scottish Pilot Club of San Angelo.

EXPERIENCE **SENIOR TRAVEL AGENT.** Travelers, Inc., San Angelo, CO (1990-present). Have become the top sales agent while gaining broad exposure in all aspects of the travel industry; have earned a reputation as a knowledgeable professional and serve a large repeat clientele because of my courteous service orientation and attention to detail.
- **Management:** Provide oversight and technical leadership to four other junior travel agents.
- **Advanced Computer Skills:** Am the office's "internal expert" on computer software and hardware and am the individual who teaches software enhancements to office personnel while also troubleshooting hardware malfunctions; have excelled in the following courses:
  Datas II, Atlanta
  Worldspan, Atlanta
  Advanced Professional Sabre, Dallas
- **Areas of Expertise:** Am equipped to book travel worldwide, but offer particularly strong knowledge of most major U.S. cities as well as the Caribbean, Bermuda, Great Britain, Greece, Italy, and most major cruise lines; am a former resident of St. Croix, U.S. Virgin Islands.
- **Commitment to Continuous Professional Training:** In my spare time, am working on the Disney College of Knowledge Diploma; have attended several CLIA workshops, and have also attended two "See the Ships" seminars and Carnival Cruise Lines seminars in Miami; currently enrolled in a Microsoft Office course at Richmond Community College.
- **Advanced Ticketing Applications:** Am in charge of advanced ticketing applications from ticket exchanges, coupon redemption, and group airline ticketing.

Highlights of other experience: Polished public relations and office operations skills in earlier jobs including:
- **OFFICE MANAGER:** For a dentist office with four partners, was in charge of accounts receivable and billing; filed insurance claims and formulated payment plans.
- **DEPARTMENT SECRETARY:** Earned promotion based on my accomplishments and professionalism at a prominent university.
- **ART INSTRUCTOR:** Taught art under ESEA Title I summer school program.
- **VOLUNTEER:** Volunteer within the public school system.

EDUCATION & TRAINING Hold an **A.A., Liberal Arts,** Mount Vernon College, Washington, DC.
Studied computer applications, Titusville Community College, Titusville, CA.
Excelled in a word processing course, Northern Virginia Community College, Manassas, VA.

PERSONAL Enthusiastic quick learner and self starter. Accustomed to producing ongoing reports according to established schedule. Am single and willing to relocate. Excellent references.

Date

Exact Name
Title or Position
Name of Company
Address (number and street)
Address (city, state, and zip)

**Wholesale Food and
Beverage Sales**

Dear Sir or Madam:

When this person
graduated from college, he
couldn't find a job in his
field, even though he had
been educated in furniture
manufacturing and
management! So he took a
variety of "little jobs" which
he wasn't particularly proud
of. That's why you see
those jobs shown on his
resume in a format which
de-emphasizes the dates of
his employment, so that his
resume doesn't stress his
frequent job hopping. Now
he's found employment he
likes in the highly
specialized field of food and
beverage sales, so he used
this cover letter and
resume to apply for an
opening in his
hometown.

With the enclosed resume, I would like to indicate my interest in exploring employment opportunities within your organization. I am responding to your classified ad for a sales position in the Pierce County area. I believe you might find that my experience is ideally suited to your needs. My correspondence with you has grown out of a conversation I recently had with Jim Rushwood about The Highland Company's plans to expand product distribution in the off-premises arena. I feel certain that my in-depth knowledge of beverage sales and distribution could be useful to you in your growth efforts.

Since 1999, I have excelled in handling increasing responsibilities with Rushwood Wholesale Company, Inc. I joined Rushwood as a Route Driver delivering wholesale beverages, and I advanced into a pre-sale position serving on- and off-premises accounts. I have merchandised both food and beverage products to all types of retailers, ranging from "mom and pop" stores to large chain stores in 26 counties. I am currently servicing and selling on- and off-premises accounts in the Seattle area with an emphasis on the retail wine trade.

As you will see from my resume, I hold a B.S. degree from Washington State University in Bellevue. After college graduation and prior to entering the wholesale beverage industry, I worked in jobs which helped me refine my skills in production and inventory control, personnel supervision, inspection and quality control, warehouse management, and retail sales.

You might be interested to learn that Pierce County is my home turf; I grew up and was raised there, and I would have some contacts in the county since my extended family still lives in the area. I am mobile and would cheerfully relocate as your needs require.

If you can use a hard-working self-starter known for initiative and persistence, I hope you will contact me to suggest a time when we might meet to discuss your needs and how I might help you. I can provide outstanding references, including the ones shown on my resume, but I would appreciate your not contacting them until after we speak about the job you advertised. Thank you in advance for your time.

Sincerely,

Bruce M. Piper

BRUCE M. PIPER

1110½ Hay Street, Fayetteville, NC 28305 • preppub@aol.com • (910) 483-6611

OBJECTIVE
I want to contribute to an organization that can use an experienced professional who has advanced in the wholesale beverage industry through applying my strong sales, customer service, merchandising, and management skills.

EDUCATION
Hold **B.S. degree in Furniture Manufacturing and Management**, School of Engineering, Washington State University, Bellevue, WA, 1991.
Have completed numerous training programs and professional development programs specific to the wholesale beverage industry.

EXPERIENCE
PRE-SALE ACCOUNTS MANAGER. Rushwood Wholesale Company, Inc. Seattle, WA (1999-present). Joined Rushwood Wholesale Company as a Route Driver delivering wholesale beverages, and advanced into a pre-sale position servicing on- and off-premises accounts.
- Have merchandised both food and beverage products to all types of retailers, ranging from "mom and pop" stores to large chain stores in 26 counties.
- Am currently servicing and selling on- and off-premises accounts in the Seattle area with an emphasis on the retail wine trade.

After graduating from college and prior to joining Rushwood Wholesale Company, Inc., worked in the furniture manufacturing industry in these functional areas:
- **Production and inventory control:** Assisted in production and inventory control while working for Olympia Fabco, Inc., in Olympia, WA (1998-99); was involved in the manufacturing of foam block products and recombined foam for the furniture upholstery and transportation industries.
- **Supervision:** Supervised the Rough-End Department as a detail draftsman working with furniture blueprints and creating production documents for Star Wood Products, Inc., in Spokane, WA (1996-97).
- **Inspection and production control:** For the upholstery manufacturer Madison, Inc., in Olympia, WA (1994), was involved in inspection and production control of frames and covers for upholstery.
- **Retail sales:** Performed retail sales work involving customer orders for building supplies while working for Andrews Builders Supply, Tacoma, WA (1993-94).
- **Warehouse management:** Managed a warehouse along with all inventory records for imported chair frames while working for MJR International, Olympia, WA (1993).
- **General assembly:** Advanced into a position which involved training new personnel while working for Phillips Ltd., Tacoma, WA (1991-93), a producer of high-quality grandfather clocks; ran pneumatic clamps, sanders, and saws, while also keeping in-process inventory in the assembly department.
- **Retail sales:** Assisted in retail sales work at the seconds outlet of P. Kingsbury Fabrics in Bellevue, WA (1991).

AFFILIATIONS
Served on Tacoma Youth Council and Rotary Club.
Served as Engineer Council Representative for WSU Furniture Club.
Active member of Highland Presbyterian Church, Seattle, WA.
Volunteer with Seattle Regional Theater, The Arts Center, Urban Ministry.

INTERESTS
Avid runner and golfer.

ABOUT THE EDITOR

Anne McKinney holds an MBA from the Harvard Business School and a BA in English from the University of North Carolina at Chapel Hill. A noted public speaker, writer, and teacher, she is the senior editor for PREP's business and career imprint, which bears her name. Early titles in the Anne McKinney Career Series (now called the Real-Resumes Series) published by PREP include: *Resumes and Cover Letters That Have Worked, Resumes and Cover Letters That Have Worked for Military Professionals, Government Job Applications and Federal Resumes, Cover Letters That Blow Doors Open,* and *Letters for Special Situations.* Her career titles and how-to resume-and-cover-letter books are based on the expertise she has acquired in 20 years of working with job hunters. Her valuable career insights have appeared in publications of the "Wall Street Journal" and other prominent newspapers and magazines.

Judeo-Christian Ethics Series

BIBLE STORIES FROM THE OLD TESTAMENT
Katherine Whaley
Familiar and not-so-familiar Bible stories told by an engaging storyteller in a style guaranteed to delight and inform. Includes stories about Abraham, Cain and Abel, Jacob and David, Moses and the Exodus, Judges, Saul, David, and Solomon.
(272 pages)
"Whaley tells these tales in such a way that they will appeal to the young adult as well as the senior citizen."
– *Independent Publisher*
Trade paperback 1-885288-12-3—$18.00

BACK IN TIME
Patty Sleem
Published in large print hardcover by Simon & Schuster's Thorndike Press as a Thorndike Christian Mystery in November 1998.
(306 pages)
"An engrossing look at the discrimination faced by female ministers." – *Library Journal*
Trade paperback 1-885288-03-4—$16.00

A GENTLE BREEZE FROM GOSSAMER WINGS
Gordon Beld
Pol Pot was the Khmer Rouge leader whose reign of terror caused the deaths of up to 2 million Cambodians in the mid-1970s. He masterminded an extreme, Maoist-inspired revolution in which those Cambodians died in mass executions, and from starvation and disease. This book of historical fiction shows the life of one refugee from this reign of genocide.
(320 pages)
"I'm pleased to recommend *A Gentle Breeze From Gossamer Wings*. Every Christian in America should read it. It's a story you won't want to miss – and it could change your life."
— Robert H. Schuller, Pastor, Crystal Cathedral
Trade paperback 1-885288-07-7—$18.00

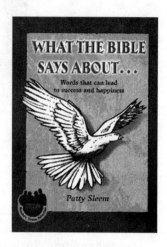

SECOND TIME AROUND
Patty Sleem
"Sleem explores the ugliness of suicide and murder, obsession and abuse, as well as Christian faith and values. An emotional and suspenseful read reflecting modern issues and concerns." – *Southern Book Trade*
(336 pages)
Foreign rights sold in Chinese.
Hardcover 1-885288-00-X—$25.00
Trade paperback 1-885288-05-0—$17.00

WHAT THE BIBLE SAYS ABOUT… Words that can lead to success and happiness
Patty Sleem
A daily inspirational guide as well as a valuable reference when you want to see what the Bible says about Life and Living, Toil and Working, Problems and Suffering, Anger and Arguing, Self-Reliance and Peace of Mind, Justice and Wrong-Doing, Discipline and Self-Control, Wealth and Power, Knowledge and Wisdom, Pride and Honor, Gifts and Giving, Husbands and Wives, Friends and Neighbors, Children, Sinning and Repenting, Judgment and Mercy, Faith and Religion, and Love.
(192 pages)
Hardcover 1-885288-02-6—$20.00

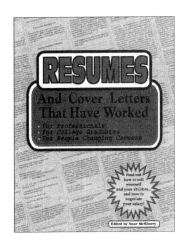

RESUMES AND COVER LETTERS THAT HAVE WORKED

Anne McKinney, Editor

More than 100 resumes and cover letters written by the world's oldest resume-writing company. Resumes shown helped real people not only change jobs but also transfer their skills and experience to other industries and fields. An indispensable tool in an era of downsizing when research shows that most of us have not one but three distinctly different careers in our working lifetime. (272 pages)
"Distinguished by its highly readable samples...essential for library collections."
– *Library Journal*
Trade paperback 1-885288-04-2—$25.00

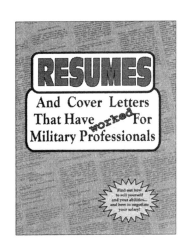

RESUMES AND COVER LETTERS THAT HAVE WORKED FOR MILITARY PROFESSIONALS

Anne McKinney, Editor

Military professionals from all branches of the service gain valuable experience while serving their country, but they need resumes and cover letters that translate their skills and background into "civilian language." This is a book showing more than 100 resumes and cover letters written by a resume-writing service in business for nearly 20 years which specializes in "military translation." (256 pages)
"A guide that significantly translates veterans' experience into viable repertoires of achievement." – *Booklist*
Trade paperback 1-885288-06-9—$25.00

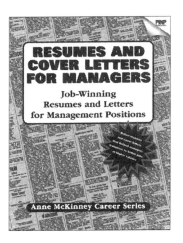

RESUMES AND COVER LETTERS FOR MANAGERS

Anne McKinney, Editor

Destined to become the bible for managers who want to make sure their resumes and cover letters open the maximum number of doors while helping them maximize in the salary negotiation process. From office manager to CEO, managers trying to relocate to or from these and other industries and fields will find helpful examples: Banking, Agriculture, School Systems, Human Resources, Restaurants, Manufacturing, Hospitality Industry, Automotive, Retail, Telecommunications, Police Force, Dentistry, Social Work, Academic Affairs, Non-Profit Organizations, Childcare, Sales, Sports, Municipalities, Rest Homes, Medicine and Healthcare, Business Operations, Landscaping, Customer Service, MIS, Quality Control, Teaching, the Arts, and Self-Employed. (288 pages)
Trade paperback 1-885288-10-7—$25.00

GOVERNMENT JOB APPLICATIONS AND FEDERAL RESUMES:
Federal Resumes, KSAs, Forms 171 and 612, and Postal Applications

Anne McKinney, Editor

Getting a government job can lead to job security and peace of mind. The problem is that getting a government job requires extensive and complex paperwork. Now, for the first time, this book reveals the secrets and shortcuts of professional writers in preparing job-winning government applications such as these:
The Standard Form 171 (SF 171) – several complete samples
The Optional Form 612 (OF 612) – several complete samples
KSAs – samples of KSAs tailored to jobs ranging from the GS-5 to GS-12
Ranking Factors – how-to samples
Postal Applications
Wage Grade paperwork
Federal Resumes – see the different formats required by various government agencies. (272 pages)
Trade paperback 1-885288-11-5—$25.00

COVER LETTERS THAT BLOW DOORS OPEN

Anne McKinney, Editor

Although a resume is important, the cover letter is the first impression. This book is a compilation of great cover letters that helped real people get in the door for job interviews against stiff competition. Included are letters that show how to approach employers when you're moving to a new area, how to write a cover letter when you're changing fields or industries, and how to arouse the employer's interest in dialing your number first from a stack of resumes. (272 pages)

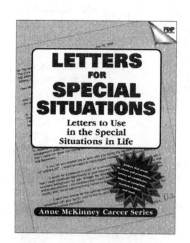

Trade paperback 1-885288-13-1—$25.00

LETTERS FOR SPECIAL SITUATIONS

Anne McKinney, Editor

Sometimes it is necessary to write a special letter for a special situation in life. You will find great letters to use as models for business and personal reasons including:

letters asking for a raise, letters of resignation, letters of reference, letters notifying a vendor of a breach of contract, letter to a Congressman, letters of complaint, letters requesting reinstatement to an academic program, follow-up letters after an interview, letters requesting bill consolidation, letters of reprimand to marginal employees, letters requesting financial assistance or a grant, letters to professionals disputing their charges, collections letters, thank-you letters, and letters to accompany resumes in job-hunting. (256 pages)
Trade paperback 1-885288-09-3—$25.00

PREP Publishing Order Form

You may purchase any of our titles from your favorite bookseller! Or send a check or money order or your credit card number for the total amount*, plus $3.20 postage and handling, to PREP, Box 66, Fayetteville, NC 28302. If you have a question about any of our titles, feel free to e-mail us at preppub@aol.com and visit our website at http://www.prep-pub.com

Name: _____

Phone #: _____

Address: _____

_____

E-mail address: _____

Payment Type: ☐ Check/Money Order ☐ Visa ☐ MasterCard

Credit Card Number: _____ Expiration Date: _____

Check items you are ordering:

☐ $25.00—RESUMES AND COVER LETTERS THAT HAVE WORKED.

☐ $25.00—RESUMES AND COVER LETTERS THAT HAVE WORKED FOR MILITARY PROFESSIONALS.

☐ $25.00—RESUMES AND COVER LETTERS FOR MANAGERS.

☐ $25.00—GOVERNMENT JOB APPLICATIONS AND FEDERAL RESUMES: Federal Resumes, KSAs, Forms 171 and 612, and Postal Applications.

☐ $25.00—COVER LETTERS THAT BLOW DOORS OPEN.

☐ $25.00—LETTERS FOR SPECIAL SITUATIONS.

☐ $16.00—BACK IN TIME. Patty Sleem

☐ $17.00—(trade paperback) SECOND TIME AROUND. Patty Sleem

☐ $25.00—(hardcover) SECOND TIME AROUND. Patty Sleem

☐ $18.00—A GENTLE BREEZE FROM GOSSAMER WINGS. Gordon Beld

☐ $18.00—BIBLE STORIES FROM THE OLD TESTAMENT. Katherine Whaley

☐ $20.00—WHAT THE BIBLE SAYS ABOUT... *Words that can lead to success and happiness.* Patty Sleem

New titles!

☐ $16.95—REAL-RESUMES FOR SALES. Anne McKinney, Editor

☐ $16.95—REAL-RESUMES FOR TEACHERS. Anne McKinney, Editor

☐ $16.95—REAL-RESUMES FOR CAREER CHANGERS. Anne McKinney, Editor

☐ $16.95—REAL-RESUMES FOR STUDENTS. Anne McKinney, Editor

☐ $16.95—REAL ESSAYS FOR COLLEGE AND GRAD SCHOOL. Anne McKinney, Editor

☐ $10.95—KIJABE An African Historical Saga. Pally Dhillon

_____ **TOTAL ORDERED (add $3.20 for postage and handling)**

PREP offers volume discounts on large orders. Call us at (910) 483-6611 for more information.

THE MISSION OF PREP PUBLISHING IS TO PUBLISH BOOKS AND OTHER PRODUCTS WHICH ENRICH PEOPLE'S LIVES AND HELP THEM OPTIMIZE THE HUMAN EXPERIENCE. OUR STRONGEST LINES ARE OUR JUDEO-CHRISTIAN ETHICS SERIES AND OUR BUSINESS & CAREER SERIES.

Would you like to explore the possibility of having PREP's writing team create a resume for you similar to the ones in this book?

For a brief free consultation, call 910-483-6611
or send $4.00 to receive our Job Change Packet to
PREP, Department SALES, Box 66, Fayetteville, NC 28302.

QUESTIONS OR COMMENTS? E-MAIL US AT PREPPUB@AOL.COM